Frommer's®

P9-DFL-048

IRREVERENT

guide to

San Francisco

Frommer's®

IRREVERENT

guide to

San
Francisco

6th Edition

By
Matthew Richard Poole

WILEY
Wiley Publishing, Inc.

other titles in the

IRREVERENT GUIDE

series

About the Author

Matthew Richard Poole, a native Californian, has authored more than two dozen travel guides to California, Hawaii, and abroad, and is a regular contributor to radio and television travel programs, including numerous guest appearances on the award-winning *Bay Area Backroads* television show. Before becoming a full-time travel writer and photographer, he worked as an English tutor in Prague, ski instructor in the Swiss Alps, and scuba instructor in Maui and Thailand. Highly allergic to office buildings and mortgage payments, he spends most of his time traveling the globe and searching for new adventures. His other Frommer's titles include *California, California from $70 a Day, San Francisco from $70 a Day,* and *Portable Disneyland.*

Published by:
Wiley Publishing, Inc.

111 River St.
Hoboken, NJ 07030-5774

ISBN-13: 978-0-471-77335-1
ISBN-10: 0-471-77335-2

Interior design contributed to by Marie Kristine Parial-Leonardo

Editor: Myka Carroll Del Barrio
Production Editor: Ian Skinnari
Cartographer: Elizabeth Puhl
Photo Editor: Richard Fox
Production by Wiley Indianapolis Composition Services

For information on our other products and services or to obtain technical support, please contact our Customer Care Department within the U.S. at 800/762-2974, outside the U.S. at 317/572-3993 or fax 317/572-4002.

Wiley also publishes its books in a variety of electronic formats. Some content that appears in print may not be available in electronic formats.

Manufactured in the United States of America

5 4 3 2 1

A Disclaimer

Prices fluctuate in the course of time, and travel information changes under the impact of the varied and volatile factors that influence the travel industry. We therefore suggest that you write or call ahead for confirmation when making your travel plans. Every effort has been made to ensure the accuracy of information throughout this book and the contents of this publication are believed correct at the time of printing. Nevertheless, the publishers cannot accept responsibility for errors or omissions or for changes in details given in this guide or for the consequences of any reliance on the information provided by the same. Assessments of attractions and so forth are based upon the author's own experience and therefore, descriptions given in this guide necessarily contain an element of opinion, which may not reflect the publisher's opinion or dictate a reader's own experience on another occasion. Readers are invited to write to the publisher with ideas, comments, and suggestions for future editions.

Your safety is important to us, however, so we encourage you to stay alert and be aware of your surroundings. Keep a close eye on cameras, purses, and wallets, all favorite targets of thieves and pickpockets.

CONTENTS

Eating with insomniacs *(71)* • The morning after *(71)* • Wake-up call *(72)* • How about a little fresh air? *(73)* • Bayside Basking *(73)* • All-day hangouts *(74)* • Live music *(74)* • Jack Kerouac woke up here *(74)* • Hippie holdouts *(74)*

Maps

3 DIVERSIONS   92

Basic Stuff   96

Getting Your Bearings   96

The Lowdown   97

Must-sees for first-time visitors (97) • Only in San Francisco *(99)* • A billion Chinese can't be wong *(100)* • Man with Hand in Pocket Feel Cocky *(100)* • Soaking up the sunset *(102)* • Morbid landmarks *(103)* • Soulful Sundays *(103)* • The roar of the fish stalls, the smell of the crowd *(104)* • Urban ferry tales *(104)* • A Desire for Streetcars *(105)* • Cruising Golden Gate Park *(105)* • Museum meccas outside Golden Gate Park *(106)* • If It's Free, It's For Me *(107)* • Museums for special interests *(108)* • Museums for really special interests *(108)* • Outlandish out-of-town archives *(109)* • The bongo-rama beatnik tour *(109)* • Tune in, turn on, drop out *(110)* • The last-call saloon crawl *(112)* • Painted ladies *(112)* • Mural, mural on the wall *(113)* • Are we there yet? *(114)* • Bay Area BART Tour *(114)* • Fabulous footsteps *(115)*

Maps

4 GETTING OUTSIDE   126

The Lowdown   128

Parks (128) • Stretching your legs *(129)* • Bicycles, Bridges, Beers, and Bay Cruises *(131)* • Pedal pushing *(131)* • Working up a sweat *(133)* • Hitting the beach *(133)* GoCar Tours of San Francisco *(134)* • Bathing in the buff beyond Baker Beach *(135)* • Poolside plunges *(135)* • Watersports *(136)* • Reeling them in *(137)* • Par for the course *(137)* • Lawn bowling *(138)* • Islands with a past *(138)* • Skates at the Haight *(140)* • San Francisco Segway Tours *(140)* • The wine country *(140)* • Soothing spas and marvelous massages *(142)*

INTRODUCTION

If Bill O'Reilly and his liberal-bashing ilk are getting you down, come to San Francisco. In a city where parade themes include "Weapons of Ass Destruction" and "Butt Plug Bingo" is a legitimate fundraiser, conservative blowhards are as rare as flying pigs. In fact, it's kind of hard *not* to enjoy a cheeky, irreverent vacation in San Francisco. Where else in the world (except, of course, for New York) will you find a restaurant whose servers are all gorgeous transvestites? Or a big-city mayor who's willing to sacrifice his political career to support gay marriage rights? Or where locals don't even pause for earthquakes under 5.0 on the Richter scale? But to understand why San Francisco's inhabitants are typically instilled with such a casual attitude towards life, you first need to observe our city's oh-so-unconventional upbringing.

From Beatniks to Brotherly Love

San Francisco's reputation as a rollicking city where anything goes dates from the Barbary Coast days when gang warfare, prostitution, gambling, and drinking were major pursuits, and citizens took law and order into their own hands. The city's more modern role as a catalyst for social change and the avant-garde began in the 1950s when a group of young writers and philosophers—including Allen Ginsberg and Jack Kerouac—challenged the materialism and conformity of American society by embracing anarchy and Eastern philosophy, expressing their notions in poetry. They adopted a uniform of jeans, sweaters, sandals, and berets, called themselves "Beats," and hung out in North Beach bars such as Vesuvio, Caffe Trieste, Tosca, and Enrico's Sidewalk Cafe (all of which are still in business).

In the 1960s the torch of freedom passed from the Beats and North Beach to the hippies and Haight-Ashbury, but it was a radically different torch. The hippies replaced the Beats' angst, jazz, and poetry with love, communalism, rock music, and a back-to-nature philosophy. Timothy Leary (and many others) experimented with LSD and exhorted youth to "turn on, tune in, and drop out." In 1967, during the Summer of Love, thousands of young people streamed into the city in search of drugs, sex, and the sounds of the Grateful Dead, Jefferson Airplane, and Big Brother and the Holding Company.

Queers and Quakes

There has been a visible gay community in San Francisco since the mid–19th century, but it wasn't until the 1970s that the gay political-protest movement became a national debate, with San Francisco as the epicenter. The rage against intolerance peaked when Harvey Milk, the first openly gay person to hold a major public office, was shot and killed by a former supervisor who was consistently opposed to Milk's liberal policies (remember the "Twinkie defense"?). Milk's martyrdom was both a political and a practical inspiration for gay rights advocates across the country.

Although severely shaken by the Loma Prieta earthquake in 1989, San Francisco witnessed a spectacular rebound during the 1990s. But the most seismic event to occur in recent history was the modern gold rush of the Internet industry, which changed the face and fortunes of the city faster and more dramatically than anyone anticipated. While investors and pimply-faced programmers were reaping fortunes, the city's locals were far less enamored with the dot-com boom. Sky-rocketing rents pushed out most of the artists and colorful characters that gave San Francisco its bohemian flavor, only to be replaced by out-of-towners more interested in stock options than sedition.

Weird and Wonderful

But the wheel always turns, and now that most of the ex-dot-commers have left for cheaper pastures, kids no longer talk of buying vacation homes, rents and hotel rates have come down a bit, and we're starting to see our weirdoes resurface (the Jesus look-alike with the colorful ribbon streamers in his hair is my favorite). There couldn't be a better time to visit San Francisco, so just come. Enjoy the cool blast of salty air as you stroll across the Golden Gate. Stuff yourself with cheap dim sum in China-town. Browse the vintage clothing shops along Haight Street. Walk along the beach, pierce your nose, skate through Golden Gate Park, ride the cable cars: It's all happening every day in San Francisco, and everyone, whether compassionate conserva-tives or Green Party loyalists, is invited. All you have to do is arrive with an open mind and a sense of adventure—the rest is waiting for you.

YOU PROBABLY DIDN'T KNOW

Why can't I refer to San Francisco as "Frisco"?... Most locals would sooner hear fingernails scratching across a chalkboard. "Frisco" sounds too much like "Vegas" or some other cheeseball city. It's best to skip this ignoble nickname unless you're willing to accept short pours, slow service, and tables by the bathroom.

And why can't I call those cable cars a "trolley"?... That's the other common misnomer that annoys locals and pegs you as a tourist. Trolleys aren't pulled by cables—cable cars are pulled by cables.

What's the steepest street in the city?... The steepest street in San Francisco is **Filbert Street** between Leavenworth and Hyde streets. I once witnessed a big truck lose its brakes on this block as it flew past the TRUCKS PROHIBITED sign and slammed into a parked car. Cool.

Where are the best "vertigo views" of the city?...

Like Jimmy Stewart in the Hitchcock film *Vertigo*, you might upgrade your sphincter factor as you race skyward at 1,000 feet per minute on a Willy Wonka–style tour of San Francisco. Glass-elevator rides are available free at several of San Francisco's skyscraper hotels. The **Westin Saint Francis** (Union Sq.) has the fastest elevator, ascending at 1,000 feet per minute. If you can keep your head up and your lunch down, you'll catch panoramic views of downtown, Coit Tower, and the Bay Area. Around the corner from the Saint Francis, the **Pan-Pacific Hotel** has a 17-story ride, but the glass cars face the *inside* of the building, looking onto a massive atrium. Five blocks away, at the **Fairmont Hotel,** take the skylift, which zips up a pokey 100 feet per minute to the Fairmont Crown, 24 floors up, for a view of Chinatown, Nob Hill, the Financial District, Coit Tower, and the South Bay Peninsula. Beware of wedding parties in the elevators—they can seriously cramp your view. At the Embarcadero Center, the **Hyatt Regency's** glass lifts take you to a revolving restaurant/cocktail lounge that offers a great 360-degree view and overpriced drinks (Mel Brooks panicked on the way up here in *High Anxiety*). And it takes a few stiff sodas to get the nerve to peer 40 stories straight down from the **San Francisco Marriott's Atrium Lounge,** where the only thing between you and pavement is a single pane of glass.

What's the secret to navigating the city?...

First, buy a map—locals always keep one in their car, because parts of San Francisco seem as though someone on an acid trip laid them out. When asking for directions, find out the nearest cross street and the neighborhood where your destination is, but be careful not to confuse numerical avenues with numerical streets. Numerical avenues (Third *Avenue* and so on) are in the Richmond and Sunset districts in the western part of the city. Numerical streets (Third *Street* and so on) are south of Market Street, in the eastern and southern parts of the city. Get this wrong and you'll be an hour late for dinner. Also, since most of the city's streets are laid out in a grid pattern, finding a restaurant or hotel is easier if you know the street number. Street numbers start with 1 at the beginning of the street and proceed at the rate of 100 per block.

Where's the best place to hop on a cable car?...

Here's the secret to catching a ride on a cable car: Don't wait in line with all the tourists at the turnaround stops at the beginning and end of the lines. Walk a few blocks up the line (follow the tracks) and do as the locals do: Hop on when the car stops, hang on to a pole, and have your $5 ready to hand to the brakeman (hoping, of course, that he'll never ask). Yes, they make change. And don't sit like a sissy—stand on the edge and grab that brass rail but good. On a really busy weekend, the cable cars often don't stop to pick up passengers en route because they're full. You might have to stand in line at the turnarounds with the rest of the peasants.

What's the most challenging staircase in the city?...

San Francisco is a city of stairs, and the crème de la crème of steps is on Filbert Street between Sansome Street and the east side of Telegraph Hill. The terrain is so steep here that Filbert Street becomes **Filbert Steps,** a 377-step descent that wends its way through verdant flower gardens and some of the city's oldest and most varied housing. It's a beautiful walk down and great exercise going up.

Where does Jerry Garcia live?...

Jerry's dead, Phish sucks, get a job.

Is Lombard the most crooked street in the city?...

No, the "most crooked" honor goes to **Vermont Street,** between 20th and 22nd streets in Potrero Hill. It's more crooked than Lombard but not nearly as picturesque.

How does one dress for the weather?...

From June to August—summer in the rest of the Western world—fog tends to engulf San Francisco from late afternoon until noon the next day. If you're a baseball fan, you'll soon discover one of the main reasons the Giants built a new ballpark: The old Candlestick Park was so foggy and chilly at night that it was equipped with one of the bay's 26 foghorns. Locals don't mind the mist. They dress in layers and immerse themselves in it. To make the most of a foggy morning, sip a cappuccino in a cozy neighborhood cafe until around noon, when the fog burns off and you can tie your sweater around your waist, roll up your shirtsleeves, and soak up the sun. And no matter what the weather seems like during the day, always bring a sweater or jacket along.

Why do San Franciscans sneer at Seattle?...

Because San Francisco's immigrant Italians were frothing cappuccinos before Seattle even existed. All Seattle did was saturate the planet with cookie-cutter coffeehouse franchises. Do yourself a flavor: Wake up at 6am and head to North Beach because one of the most pleasurable smells of San Francisco is the aroma of freshly roasted coffee beans wafting down Columbus Avenue. Get your fix with a cup of Viennese at the original, unique **Caffe Trieste**—a haven for true San Francisco characters.

What's the city's best tourist attraction for someone who hates tourist attractions?...

Even if you loathe being part of a crowd of out-of-towners, you'll enjoy a tour of **Alcatraz Island.** The rangers have done a fantastic job of preserving The Rock—enough to give you the heebie-jeebies just looking at it—and the self-guided audio tour is eerily superb. Even the boat ride across the bay is worth the price. You shouldn't miss this one, so reserve tickets far in advance.

What am I supposed to do during an earthquake?...

Panic. Earthquakes are fairly common in California, and you won't notice most of them. However, in case of a significant shaker, there are a few basic precautionary measures you should know: When you are inside a building, seek cover; do not run outside into falling debris. Stand under a doorway or against a wall, and stay away from windows. If you exit a building after a substantial quake, use stairwells, not elevators. If you are in your car, pull over to the side of the road and stop—but not until you are away from bridges, overpasses, telephone poles, and power lines. Stay in your car. If you're out walking, stay outside and away from trees, power lines, and the sides of buildings. If you're in an area with tall buildings, find a doorway in which to stand. If you're having cocktails, find a straw.

What are those weird oval-shaped, olive-green kiosks on the sidewalk?... High-tech self-cleaning public toilets, owned and maintained by a mysterious French corporation. They've been placed on high-volume streets to provide relief for pedestrians. They gave them to the city for free—advertising covers the cost. It costs 25¢ to enter, with no time limit, but we don't recommend using the ones in the sketchier neighborhoods such as the Mission because they're mostly used by crackheads and prostitutes.

Dude, where's my car?... You didn't check all the signs on the block you parked on, did you? Chances are you missed the TOW ZONE: NO PARKING FROM 4–6PM MON–FRI sign. Every car-owning local gets his or her car towed in this zone at least once. The golden rules of parking are: 1) read ALL the signs on your side of the block; 2) curb your wheels on hills or risk a ticket; and 3) carry plenty of quarters.

Where is the best place to park?... Parking in the city is based on the lottery system. A quick survey of the neighborhoods will reveal cars parked on sidewalks, in front of fire hydrants, in tow-away zones, on corners, in crosswalks and, in the Mission District, right down the middle of the street. It's a numbers game: There are around 800,000 cars in the city any given day, and fewer than 600,000 parking spaces. That adds up to 2.3 million parking tickets a year and unknown numbers of drivers perpetually circling the city. There are a number of downtown, city-run garages that won't require you to mortgage your house in order to park for a few hours, but in most private garages you can pay up to $30 for a Friday night in popular areas like North Beach. Avoid the whole mess by using public transportation or cabs.

What's the best way to avoid getting mugged?... First, don't look like a potential victim (read: tourist). Muggers aren't a huge problem in San Francisco, but the city does have its share of pickpockets and other scam artists who tend to prey on tourists. Standard rules of urban conduct apply: Don't keep your wallet in your rear pants pocket, and leave your purse at home or keep your hand on it all the time, especially when you're riding a bus (a favorite haunt of pickpockets). The preferred crime in

San Francisco, actually, is car break-ins, especially in the Mission District, where a car parked on the street for more than an hour has at least a 50/50 chance of getting a window smashed. Solution: Don't leave anything in your car except a John Tesh CD.

What should I not ask San Francisco cabbies?...

The most-often-asked cabbie question in San Francisco is: "How often do you have to change your brakes?" Believe us, you don't want to know. One driver estimates that the hills are so treacherous he has to change his brakes once a week, while another casually replies, "Oh, a couple times a year." Either way, most drivers would rather avoid the topic, especially if you're headed down a grade that would rival K2.

What's the best-kept secret about the symphony?...

If you're a morning person who loves classical music, the San Francisco Symphony's **open rehearsals** have a seat with your name on it. Before most concerts, the symphony allows the public to attend open rehearsals at Davies Hall ($19 for general admission, including free Krispy Kreme doughnuts). Aside from the bargain-basement price, many aficionados prefer these rehearsals because the music is equally exquisite and you get to see and hear the performers and conductors in a relaxed, intimate circumstance. Most open rehearsals take place Wednesday mornings, 10am to noon. They sell out quickly for popular international performers, so call the Symphony box office (Tel 415/864-6000) for a schedule while you're still planning your trip, and order tickets in advance if possible. The symphony season starts in September, takes a break for a few months, and then picks up again in June and July.

How long has San Francisco been a gay capital?...

During the gold rush, "real" women were so scarce that desperate prospectors paid them 3 ounces of gold for a kiss. No one knows how many enterprising impostors painted their lips to pick up a few extra nuggets back then, but mascara and falsies have rarely seen a sales slump since. According to Trevor Hailey, the city's premier gay historian, the city became an established haven for the gay lifestyle with the gold rush (the late 1840s). Then, the opening of the Panama Canal (at the turn of the 20th century) led countless gay sailors to this port, followed by an influx of gay artists and entertainers during the bohemian era of the twenties and thirties. World War II brought thousands of Pacific-bound military men—yes, queers in the armed forces, whether General Eisenhower knew it or not—many of whom returned after the war to live where their forbidden lifestyle was more accepted. By the time the Beat movement bongoed to the cultural forefront in the fifties, there was no question that North Beach was the place for gay "angry young men" to proclaim their sexuality to the world. Every major city has a gay subculture, but there's nothing "sub" about San Francisco's gay culture—it is definitely a predominant and celebrated part of life here. In fact, if you stroll along Castro Street between Market and 19th streets, you'll notice that it's the straight people who feel queer.

Which hotel actually launders money?... For years, every coin at the **Westin Saint Francis Hotel** was put through a tumbler that sterilized all those copper pennies and buffalo nickels so that no customer ever received a coin in change unless it could pass the white-glove test. The famous money-laundering service was suspended in 1994 when the career coin washer retired, but the hotel's human resources department was finally able to find a suitable replacement.

What's with the funny-dressed guy in front of the Sir Francis Drake Hotel at Union Square?... That's **Tom Sweeny,** the head doorman at the Sir Francis Drake. The guy's a San Francisco living historical monument. For the past 30 years he's donned his traditional Beefeater attire (you can't miss those $1,400 duds) and posed for countless snapshots—an average of 200 per day. He's shaken hands with every president since Gerry Ford, has run 15 marathons, and put two kids through college.

ACCOMM

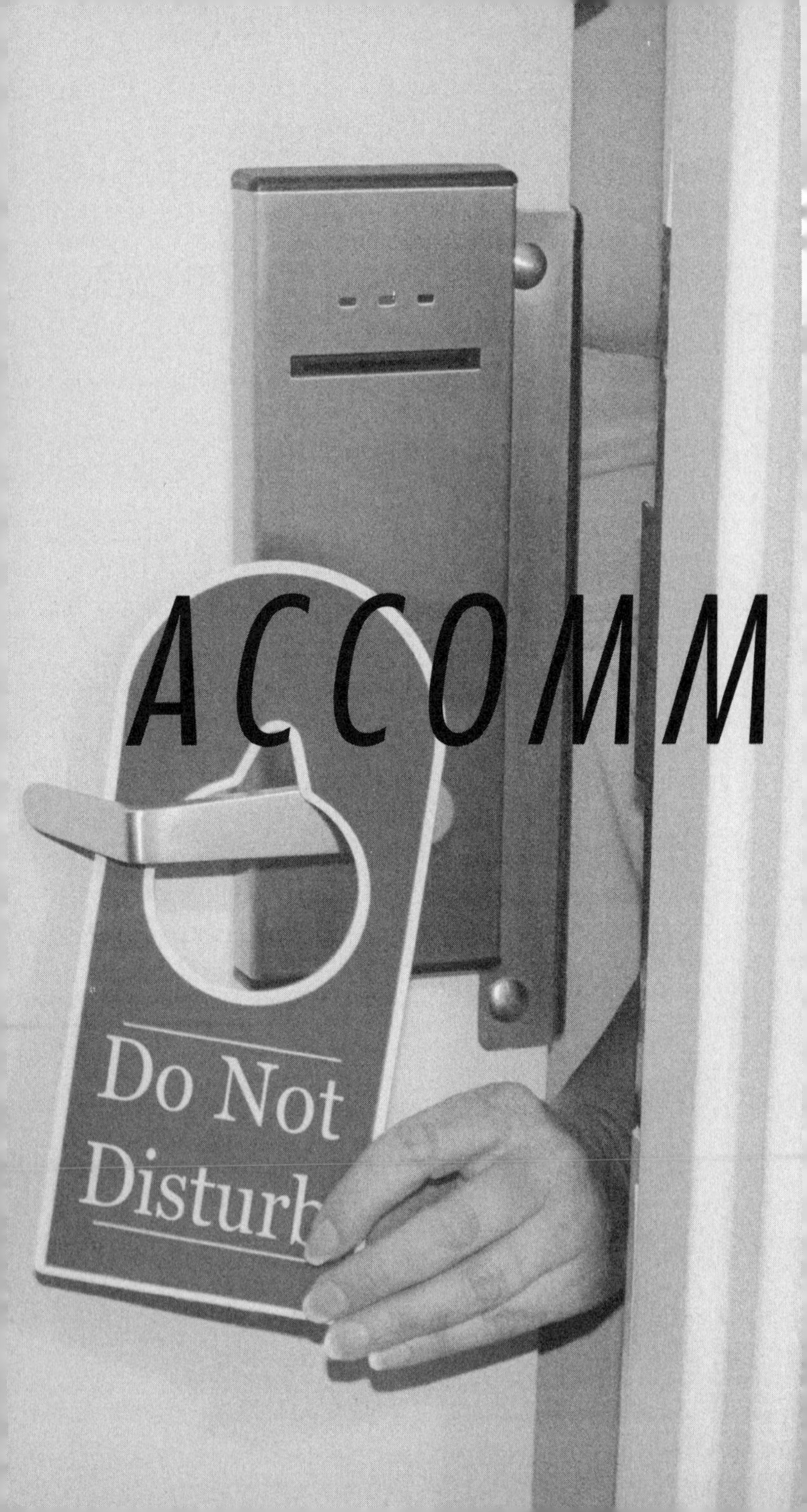

ODATIONS

Map 1: San Francisco Accommodations

Archbishop's Mansion **8**

Central YMCA **14**

The Edwardian
San Francisco Hotel **10**

Elements Hotel **12**

Green Tortoise
Guest House **18**

Hostelling International
San Francisco–
Fisherman's Wharf **1**

Hotel Bohème **19**

Hotel Drisco **2**

Inn at the Opera **9**

Jackson Court **3**

Laurel Inn **4**

The Mandarin Oriental **17**

The Mosser **16**

The Phoenix Hotel **15**

The Queen Anne Hotel **5**

Radisson Miyako Hotel **7**

Red Victorian
Bed, Breakfast & Art **13**

San Remo Hotel **20**

Seal Rock Inn **6**

24 Henry Guesthouse **11**

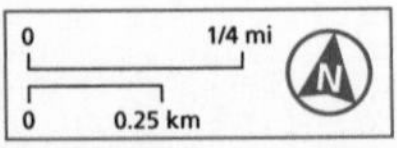

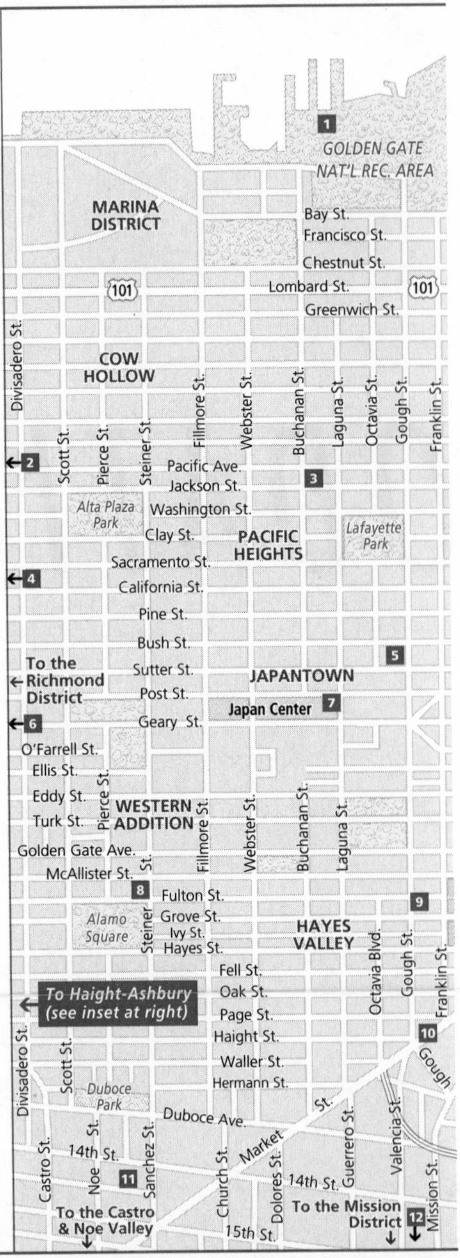

GOLDEN GATE
NAT'L REC. AREA

1

**MARINA
DISTRICT**

Bay St.
Francisco St.
Chestnut St.
Lombard St.
Greenwich St.

{101}

{101}

Divisadero St.

**COW
HOLLOW**

Scott St.
Pierce St.
Steiner St.
Fillmore St.
Webster St.
Buchanan St.
Laguna St.
Octavia St.
Gough St.
Franklin St.

←**2**

Pacific Ave.
Jackson St.

3

Alta Plaza
Park

Washington St.

Clay St.

**PACIFIC
HEIGHTS**

Lafayette
Park

Sacramento St.

←**4**

California St.

Pine St.

Bush St.

5

To the
←Richmond
District

Sutter St.

JAPANTOWN

Post St.

Japan Center **7**

←**6**

Geary St.

O'Farrell St.
Ellis St.

Eddy St.

Pierce St.

**WESTERN
ADDITION**

Turk St.

Fillmore St.
Webster St.
Buchanan St.
Laguna St.

Golden Gate Ave.
McAllister St.

8

Fulton St.

Steiner St.

9

Alamo
Square

Grove St.
Ivy St.
Hayes St.

**HAYES
VALLEY**

Octavia Blvd.
Gough St.
Franklin St.

Fell St.

←To Haight-Ashbury
(see inset at right)

Oak St.
Page St.
Haight St.

10

Waller St.
Hermann St.

Divisadero St.
Scott St.

Duboce
Park

Duboce Ave.

Gough

Castro St.
14th St.
Noe St.
Sanchez St.

11

Church St.
Market St.
Dolores St.

Guerrero St.
Valencia St.
Mission St.

To the Castro
& Noe Valley

15th St.

14th St.

To the Mission
District

12

0   1/4 mi

0   0.25 km

N

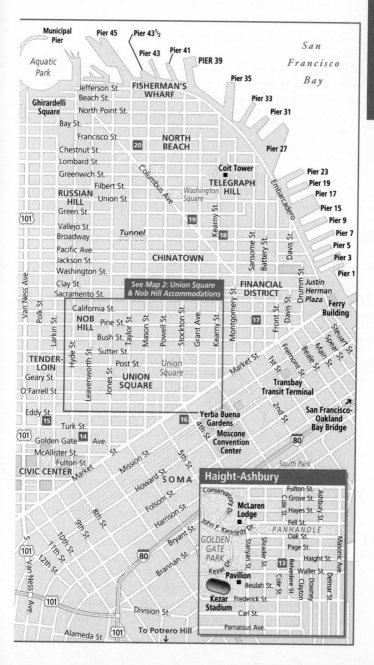

Municipal Pier

Pier 45

Pier 43½

Pier 43 Pier 41

PIER 39

Aquatic Park

San

Francisco

Bay

Jefferson St.

Pier 35

FISHERMAN'S WHARF

Beach St.

Pier 33

Ghirardelli Square

North Point St.

Pier 31

Bay St.

Francisco St.

NORTH BEACH

Pier 27

20

Chestnut St.

Lombard St.

Coit Tower

Pier 23

Greenwich St.

TELEGRAPH HILL

Pier 19

RUSSIAN HILL

Filbert St.

Washington Square

Pier 17

Union St.

19

Pier 15

Green St.

18

Pier 9

101

Vallejo St.

Tunnel

Pier 7

Broadway

Pier 5

Pacific Ave.

Pier 3

Jackson St.

CHINATOWN

Pier 1

Washington St.

Clay St.

FINANCIAL DISTRICT

Justin Herman Plaza

Sacramento St.

See Map 2: Union Square & Nob Hill Accommodations

Ferry Building

California St.

NOB HILL

Pine St.

17

Van Ness Ave.

Polk St.

Larkin St.

Bush St.

Sutter St.

Hyde St.

Leavenworth St.

Jones St.

Taylor St.

Mason St.

Powell St.

Stockton St.

Grant Ave.

Kearny St.

Montgomery St.

Front St.

Davis St.

Steuart St.

Spear St.

Main St.

Beale St.

Fremont St.

1st St.

TENDER-LOIN

Post St.

Union Square

Geary St.

UNION SQUARE

Market St.

Transbay Transit Terminal

O'Farrell St.

Eddy St.

15

16

Yerba Buena Gardens

2nd St.

San Francisco-Oakland Bay Bridge

Turk St.

Moscone Convention Center

101

Golden Gate

14

Ave.

4th St.

80

McAllister St.

St.

5th St.

South Park

Fulton St.

CIVIC CENTER

Market

Mission St.

SOMA

Howard St.

8th St.

Folsom St.

9th St.

Harrison St.

101

10th St.

11th St.

Bryant St.

80

12th St.

Brannan St.

S. Van Ness Ave.

101

Division St.

101

Alameda St.

To Potrero Hill

Columbus Ave.

Kearny St.

Sansome St.

Battery St.

Davis St.

Embarcadero

Drumm St.

Haight-Ashbury

Conservatory Dr.

McLaren Lodge

Fulton St.

Grove St.

Ashbury St.

Cole St.

Hayes St.

Fell St.

PANHANDLE

John F. Kennedy Dr.

Stanyan St.

Shrader St.

Oak St.

Page St.

Masonic Ave.

GOLDEN GATE PARK

Haight St.

13

Belvedere St.

Cole St.

Clayton

Downey

Delmar St.

Waller St.

Kezar Dr.

Pavilion

Beulah

Kezar Stadium

Frederick St.

Carl St.

Parnassus Ave.

Basic Stuff

San Francisco's famous palace hotels—which are as extravagantly grand as grande dames get—are finally getting a run for their money. Sure, the conventional rich may still lust after a night in the **Fairmont Hotel**'s $12,500-a-night penthouse suite: a three-bedroom, four-bath minimansion with a grand piano, two-story circular library with 4,000 volumes, dining room that seats 50, 24-karat gold fixtures, lapis lazuli fireplace, secret passages, and its own vault. If that price tag's too high, the Fairmont's standard rooms, at $289 and up, are still less expensive than equivalent accommodations in New York, London, Paris, or Tokyo. But these days, stylish celebrities—who can afford any room in the city—are shying away from the huge luxury hotels in favor of more chic, intimate boutique hotels that cater to a younger, hipper crowd.

San Francisco's thriving boutique hotel scene is no longer dominated by one or two hospitality czars—dozens of lavish, quirky, extravagant, cozy, and eccentric little hotels dot the entire city—but always near the center of that universe is Chip Conley, whose Joie de Vivre hotels set the "fun" standard in the city. Conley, an anarchistic entrepreneur who is a cross between Conrad Hilton and the Mad Hatter, got his start by following the example of Bill Kimpton, a reclamation genius who started the trend of buying fading older properties and transforming them into chic, contemporary cash cows. The Kimpton Group includes the **Hotel Triton,** an abstract expressionist's dream come true; the **Hotel Monaco,** a renovated 1910 Beaux Arts jewel; the four-star **Prescott Hotel,** where guests get preferred seating at Wolfgang Puck's famous Postrio restaurant; and more than a dozen others. Kimpton hotels tend to be a bit more traditional (and occasionally more expensive) than Joie de Vivre's lodgings, but both focus on creature comforts and meticulously designed interiors. Conley's lodgings usually focus on a theme, from the film-freak **Hotel Bijou** and the literary **Hotel Rex** to **The Phoenix,** a psychedelic-tropical inner-city motel full of urban artistes, and the understated but ultraluxurious **Nob Hill Lambourne,** a spa for health-conscious business travelers. One of the newer groups is Personality Hotels on Union Square, a quintet of downtown boutique hotels that includes the **Hotel Metropolis,** a modernistic beauty that invites guests to "indulge yourself in the wilder side of the color wheel," and **Hotel Diva,** a high-style tribute to stainless steel.

Do you see a pattern here? Cutting-edge interiors and A-list celebrities? Maybe. But there's a difference between a celebrity and a legend, and many of the latter prefer the city's more traditional charms: quiet Victorian elegance and the assurance of privacy, if not anonymity. When Luciano Pavarotti is in town, he stays at the elegant **Inn at the Opera,** a tiny, 25-foot-wide Victorian hotel where services include complimentary clothes-pressing upon arrival. Before his death in 1996, legendary poet Allen Ginsberg chose North Beach's **Hotel Bohème,** a hip, cozy, and surprisingly quiet haven on Columbus Avenue, just footsteps away from Lawrence Ferlinghetti's City Lights Bookstore.

If you're not particularly impressed with the notion of sleeping in the same digs as the rich and famous—or the in-debt and infamous—try one of the city's scores of neighborhood inns. Europeans love the **San Remo Hotel,** a three-story Italianate Victorian on a quiet residential block of North Beach; rooms start at $55, and the funky little rooftop cottage/penthouse with its own sundeck and panoramic view is one of the best deals in San Francisco at $155 a night.

If your budget is tighter than Dwight Yoakam's jeans, you'll be happy to know that for $44 a night, you can stay in a private single room at the fully-staffed **Central YMCA,** where you'll get free continental breakfast in the morning along with the use of the health club and pool. Or go super-cheap ($25 a night) and dorm up at the **Hostelling International San Francisco—Fisherman's Wharf** in Fort Mason, at the edge of the posh bayfront Marina District with close-up views of the Golden Gate Bridge.

Winning the Reservations Game

First of all, forget the major hotels if you're planning to visit in October. Some of them are almost fully booked years in advance during the best-of-all-possible months in San Francisco. Don't let that discourage you, though; the most interesting places to stay, and the best deals, are rarely on the standard list of hotels that appears on travel agents' computer screens, so they don't get booked up as fast. San Francisco's tourist season is year-round, and hotel prices tend to remain fairly fixed throughout the year (a few increase April–Oct). You're not likely to find an off-season bargain rate around Union Square and the Moscone Convention Center, but many hotels, especially in tourist areas, offer special rates for multiple-night stays, including meals or discounts on tours and attractions. The deals range from downright pathetic—a free fancy bottle of water and a Gray Line tour through Fisherman's Wharf—to the sumptuous, whimsical "romance packages" offered by the Joie de Vivre hotels. Not all packages are advertised, so always ask the hotel or reservation agent if any are available. If you want to stick to the tourist-and-conventioneer circuit, last-minute vacancies and special discounts may be available through reservation services, most of which are computerized so they know exactly which rooms are available. Many of these services offer 50% to 75% discounts.

The **San Francisco Convention and Visitors Bureau** offers booking services to the general public by phone (Tel 888/782-9673) or online, where you can look at maps of the city and choose your hotel by neighborhood, style, and price (www.sf visitor.org). Or try **HotelLocators.com** (Tel 800/423-7846; www.hotellocators.com), or **San Francisco Reservations** (Tel 800/737-2060; www.hotelres.com). Hotel specialist sites such as **hotels.com** and **hoteldiscounts.com** are also a good source for bargains. An excellent free program, **TravelAxe** (www.travelaxe.net), can help you search multiple hotel sites at once, even ones you may never have heard of (really, it's a great program). Those opaque fare services such as **Priceline** (www.priceline.com) and **Hotwire** (www.hotwire.com) are better for booking hotels than for airfares; with both, you're allowed to pick the neighborhood and quality level of your hotel before offering up your money, and the savings can be substantial.

Is There a Right Address?

Most of San Francisco's major hotels are located near the **Financial District, Union Square, South of Market** (SoMa), and **Fisherman's Wharf.** The prime spots for world-class luxury hotels are Union Square, **Nob Hill,** and more recently along **Market Street** near the convention center. Many small boutique hotels and inns are mixed among the giant towers and palaces, so don't let the touristy neighborhoods scare you off completely—the location is convenient for walking and for access to public transportation. But—and it's a big "but"—you can easily be sucked into paying much more money than is necessary for a room with about as much personality as a chain hotel in Anywhere, USA. The thing is, you can't tell from the outside of the building or from the lobby what the rooms will be like. Take the Westin Saint Francis, for instance. It's an absolute architectural gem—one of the loveliest hotel exteriors in the Western world—but the rooms in the tower are, well, ordinary. Sure, they're spacious and full of expensive furniture, but they still look like they were punched out of the Universal School of Semi-Fancy Hotel Room Design. The whole thing is just too pastel. The views are spectacular, but you can see those from the glass elevator, and that's free.

Neither **Chinatown** nor **Japantown** is loaded with hotels, but each is worth considering. Japantown isn't as interesting as it sounds—mostly a bunch of import shops and food stands in a bland mall—but it does have the most authentic Japanese hotel in the city, the Radisson Miyako Hotel, with Zen gardens, futon beds, and in-room shiatsu massage. Chinatown is crammed with everything—crammed with people; crammed with fish; crammed with aromas, exotic vegetables, cheap souvenirs, great little food joints—but it's not crammed with good places to spend the night. You can, however, find a bed in Chinatown for as little as $60 if you don't mind sharing a bath. You can't beat the location—near downtown, Union Square, North Beach, and (perish the thought) Fisherman's Wharf.

The **Tenderloin**—usually called by other names to divert attention from its reputation as a seedy, whore- and drug-infested pit—is a block-by-block situation. One minute you can be strolling past a series of charming shops and neighborhood taverns, and the next you're being accosted by panhandlers in front of a homeless shelter or a shop that sells pornography. On the outer edges of the neighborhood are some of the trendiest and most fun lodgings and restaurants in town, but as a rule, the hotels there are either faded old beauties or transient houses best left to guests who rent them by the hour for "professional" purposes.

Van Ness Avenue is a long stretch of wide road that cuts through the city from the Mission District to the Marina. Inch for inch, it has more chain hotels and motels in its immediate vicinity than any other street in the city. The **Civic Center area** houses the ballet, the opera, the symphony, the main library, and City Hall, along with a number of wonderful boutique hotels such as the Inn at the Opera, and restaurants that are virtually empty after 8:30pm (San Franciscans tend to eat before performances). Right in the middle of it all is a plaza that has been a constant battle site for San Francisco's intractable homeless problem. Some find the scene repugnant; others chalk it up as an integral part of urban life. Public transportation is a breeze in this centrally located neighborhood, and parking is very reasonable at the Civic Center garage. (Don't go to any of the private garages near the Opera House or you may have to call home for extra cash.) Lombard Street, in **Cow Hollow,** is Motel Row, dotted with low-profile, inexpensive places to stay. The area stretches from the Marina to the Presidio, and there are plenty of scenic vistas and worthwhile restaurants that are local favorites. Be warned, though: Some motels are a bit marginal, and the neighborhood is far from the thick of the city's most interesting activities. The more residential neighborhoods—the **Mission District,** the **Haight,** the **Castro, Noe Valley,** the **Sunset,** and **Pacific Heights**—have very few hotels, but many boast wonderful inns and bed-and-breakfast houses. The Mission District is a lot of fun but has few places to stay; the Castro, the Haight, and Pacific Heights have several beautiful Victorian bed-and-breakfast options; Noe Valley is charming but primarily residential. Some of the inns in the outer reaches of the Sunset District offer the city's best views of the Pacific Ocean (or, more likely, fog).

The Lowdown

Irresistible deals... Europeans and seasoned travelers love the **San Remo Hotel,** an Italianate Victorian jewel hidden in a residential area of North Beach. The owners haven't raised their rates for so long that single rooms start at $55 (not a misprint), but the San Remo would be a delight at twice that price. Rooms are small but cozy, with antique beds and armoires, ceiling fans, and lace-curtained windows that open wide to let in the cool bay breeze and the sounds of San Francisco's lively Italian neighborhood. The atmosphere is friendly, casual, and international; immaculate bathrooms are shared, and even the water faucets are European—cold on the left, hot on the right. **The Phoenix Hotel** is the exact opposite of the San Remo. It's a retro 1950s-style hotel all the way, as American as Velveeta and Andy Warhol. Of all the city's trendy lodgings, the Phoenix is still the favorite place for visiting rock musicians, writers, and filmmakers to meet. Adjoining this Palm Springs–style hotel is the groovy Bambuddha

Lounge (Tel 415/885-5088; see the Nightlife chapter), a hip restaurant, nightclub, and cocktail lounge serving Southeast Asian cuisine.

Grande dames worth considering... The **Fairmont Hotel** is synonymous with elegant San Francisco since it sits on top of Nob Hill as though it were holding court over the city. The granddaddy of Nob Hill's elite cadre of ritzy hotels, the Fairmont wins high honors for an incredible jaw-dropping lobby. Even if you're not a guest, it's worth a side trip to gape at its massive marble Corinthian columns, vaulted ceilings, velvet chairs, gilded mirrors, and spectacular wraparound staircase.

The **InterContinental Mark Hopkins** is a traditional favorite of San Franciscans who appreciate a more understated elegance. It shares the top of the hill with the Fairmont but is notably less glitzy. It's a few dollars more expensive than its Nob Hill neighbor, too, but by the time you're paying that much, who's counting? The rooms are plush but not extraordinary, unless you want to spring for a large suite with a Jacuzzi and a view. The best part about the hotel is the famous Top of the Mark cocktail lounge, still one of the most romantic spots in the city and worth a visit even if you're not a hotel guest. It has been the traditional spot to kiss a lover goodbye since World War II.

The charm of the **Westin Saint Francis** in Union Square decreased considerably when the huge tower was added on, but it still has some merit. The front entrance, used for the television series *Hotel*, remains magnificent; stroll through the vast, ornate lobby, and you can feel 100 years of history oozing from its hand-carved redwood paneling. Emperor Hirohito, Queen Elizabeth II, Mother Teresa, King Juan Carlos of Spain, and all the U.S. presidents since Taft have graced this lobby. If you're intent on staying at the Saint Francis, get a room in the older part of the hotel—the tower rooms are big and boring, except for their views, and they cost more.

Petite dames worth more than they charge... For the elegance of a grand luxe hotel at as little as half the price, try **The Donatello** in Union Square or the **Hotel Monaco** at the edge of the Theater District. The lavish,

French-inspired Donatello is worth a visit just to see the massive stained-glass dome above the valet parking area in front of the hotel. Inside, the rooms are all oversize, with tall ceilings and huge windows; many of the successful young corporate types who frequent the Donatello happily shell out an extra $100 for rooms that open onto private, landscaped terraces. The guests at the Monaco are less buttoned-down than at the Donatello, but they definitely have a few dollars to throw around. Inside this majestic Beaux Arts landmark, the interior design is more sensual than stately—perfect for the theater crowd. A huge staircase sweeps from the lobby to the living room, and the grand chimneypiece in the "pre-function" room rises to a mural of floating hot-air balloons that recalls *The Wizard of Oz.*

The bellmen in full wooden-soldier regalia outside the four-star **Prescott Hotel** in Union Square are your first clue that this is a scaled-down version of the Fairmont. Your second clue is that the room rates are about the same, give or take a few dollars. But at the Prescott, you get more personalized service, and the penthouse suite only costs $1,200 a night (a fraction of the cost of the Fairmont's penthouse).

In search of painted ladies... San Francisco has no shortage of painted ladies, be they the brazen drag queen variety or the architectural type (Victorian mansions with elaborate paint jobs). Both are found all over town, but the most famous Victorian painted ladies—the ones featured in tourism posters—are on Alamo Square, across the street from the **Archbishop's Mansion,** built in 1904 and now a bed-and-breakfast inn. The huge rooms and ornate decor almost make you dizzy, but "Texans love it," says the owner. "It makes them feel like they're in their own castle for a few nights." Most of the rooms have massive canopy beds, working fireplaces, and deep, old-fashioned bathtubs, and all guests are served breakfast in bed.

The **Red Victorian Bed, Breakfast & Art** in Haight-Ashbury, known affectionately as the Red Vic, is much more eccentric and less expensive than the Archbishop's Mansion. It's right on Haight Street and fits in perfectly, if that gives you a clue. Group meditation is offered every morning in the back of the lobby, and owner Sami Sunchild has left her artistic thumbprint all over the inn with poem-paintings that make you want to run right out and stick a flower in your hair. Each room has its own theme, from a Persian-esque suite that looks like a good home for a hookah-smoking caterpillar to a quasi-psychedelic "LOVE" wall that certainly does not appear to be conducive to sleep. Most rooms have shared baths; be ready for aquariums and other surprises when you go to wash your face. The Red Vic is fun, spiritually uplifting, and it's definitely only in San Francisco.

The queen of San Francisco's Victorian inns is **The Queen Anne Hotel** in Pacific Heights. This majestic 1890 Victorian building, which was once a finishing school for upper-class women, recalls San Francisco's golden days. Walk under rich, red draperies to the lavish "grand salon" lobby, complete with English oak paneling and period antiques. Rooms also contain antiques—armoires, marble-top dressers, and other Victorian pieces. Some have corner turret bay windows that look out on tree-lined streets, as well as separate parlor areas and wet bars; others have cozy reading nooks and fireplaces. Guests can relax in the parlor, with an impressive floor-to-ceiling fireplace, or in the hotel library. It's a classic San Francisco experience.

A room with a view... No hotel boasts better ultraluxury digs with incredible views than **The Mandarin Oriental.** Heaven begins after a rocketing ride on the elevators to the rooms, all of which are located between the 38th and 48th floors of a high-rise. Each of the very roomy accommodations offers extraordinary panoramic views of the bay and city. Most rooms have tub-side views and opulent Asian-influenced decor, handsome furnishings, and all-around comfort and accouterments that make it difficult to find reason to leave your room.

When money's quite tight... There are lots of safe and comfortable, sometimes even scenic, cheap lodgings in San Francisco, starting as low as $25 a day per person. The best bets for quality and location are the YMCA, hostels, budget Chinatown hotels, and Lombard Street motels. The **Central YMCA** offers private rooms with shared baths from $44 a night, including free coffee and muffins in the morning and use of the health-club facilities and pool. There are also rooms with private baths and a dormitory.

The hotel is staffed 24 hours a day, and there are no curfews; both men and women are welcome.

Chinatown's bargains include the **Grant Plaza,** a clean, comfortable hotel that many locals recommend to budget-minded visitors. All rooms have a private bath and start at $59. Another Chinatown cheap sleep is the **Hotel Astoria,** where rooms with shared bath start at $56 (some rooms also have a private bath). Hostels include the **Hostelling International San Francisco—Downtown,** from $25 per night; the **Green Tortoise Guest House,** a North Beach spot that offers a choice of a hostel with dorm facilities ($20–$24) or private rooms with shared bath ($52–$60); and **Hostelling International San Francisco—Fisherman's Wharf** in Fort Mason, a dormitory with a view of the Golden Gate Bridge, from $25.

Lavender lodgings... Gay tourists are to San Francisco what Disney World pilgrims are to Orlando: big business. If the idea of seeing men holding hands is a problem for you, you're in the wrong town, especially during Gay Pride festivities in June. Basically, all San Francisco hotels are gay-friendly; many mainstream hotels offer Gay Pride discounts (ask when you call for reservations), and some lodgings cater almost entirely to a gay clientele. Many others that are not gay per se are staffed by a predominantly gay workforce, which can turn an otherwise ordinary little spot into a really fun place for gay travelers to stay. For the inside word, one of the best and funniest sources is *Betty & Pansy's Severe Queer*

Hip Hostel

*Good news for hip hostellers: There's finally a budget option in the heart of the Mission District's trendy shopping and hopping nightlife. The **Elements Hotel** is a brightly painted crash pad that announces itself from the outside with orange and yellow squares. Inside, options include private rooms, shared dorms, and double-bed and twin-bunk rooms, all with private bathrooms. Add to that Wi-Fi Internet access throughout the hotel, a free high-speed Internet lounge, rooftop parties, lockers, luggage storage, laundry facilities, free linens, TVs (in private rooms), and all the neighboring restaurants and bars, and you've got it made, provided you don't mind the Mission's grit and are up for hunkering down with traveling party people. The hostel is at 2524 Mission St., between 21st and 22nd streets (Tel 866/327-8407 or 415/647-4100; www.elementssf.com). Rates per person are between $25 and $30; expect higher rates and minimum stays during holidays.*

Review, available from A Different Light Bookstore (Tel 415/431-0891 or 800/343-4002). Recommended gay-oriented lodgings include all the Joie de Vivre hotels (see "Basic Stuff," above); the European-style **Edwardian San Francisco Hotel** (Market and Gough sts.); and the Victorian **24 Henry Guesthouse** in the Castro District.

Turning Japanese... Despite its corporate ownership, the **Radisson Miyako Hotel** is an authentic Japanese hotel, even when that means bowing to American preferences by including Western-style beds and bathrooms in many rooms. It's so much like an elegant Tokyo hotel, in fact, that most Japanese tourists opt for other, more "American" hotels for their vacations in San Francisco. Here's what's best about the Miyako: the rates (much lower than Hotel Nikko in Union Sq.), the in-room shiatsu massages, the deep Japanese soak tubs, the *tokonama* (alcoves for displaying Japanese art), the down comforters on the futon beds, the Zen gardens inside the traditional rooms, and the sunlight filtered through shoji (rice paper) screens on every window. Don't confuse this hotel with the Best Western Miyako Inn nearby. The latter is just another cheesy chain motel that happens to be on the border of Japantown—don't waste your time or money there. One of the most Japanese things about **Hotel Nikko** (Union Sq.) is the astronomical fee it charges for a Japanese suite—about $1,500 per night. If that doesn't make you feel like you're in Tokyo, nothing will. These suites are not that much better than the Miyako's, but they do feature a better view of the city and an in-room well for performing the traditional tea ceremony. For those seeking the Asian experience on a budget, the hotel has a few packages starting at $200 (reserve well in advance).

For writers in search of a muse... New York has the Algonquin, and San Francisco has Union Square's **Hotel Rex.** Hang around the lobby or browse in the antiquarian bookstore and you're likely to rub shoulders with celebrated writers and artists gathered for roundtables, book signings, readings, or just socializing. Playwright Wallace Shawn is among the many regular guests here. The walls of the lobby and guest rooms are a gallery of local artists' work, which owner Chip Conley bought to infuse cash into the art community after the 1989 quake. Be sure to look at the ceramic lamps: Each one was individually thrown by a local potter, and each shade is hand-painted.

Even the most ardent literary historians haven't been able to establish with certainty the exact number or locations of all the places Allen Ginsberg is rumored to have slept in his beatnik heyday; in his last years, however, he is known to have stayed at **Hotel Bohème,** a sexy little North Beach hotel just a short walk from Lawrence Ferlinghetti's City Lights Bookstore. A small black awning on Columbus Avenue is the only clue to the hotel's whereabouts (next to Stella Bakery & Cafe); you have to push the doorbell to get buzzed in to the narrow staircase that leads up to the foyer and reception desk. Do it, even if you don't stay there, just to see the foyer's dozens of museum-quality photographs of North Beach in the 1940s and '50s, including many shots of legendary poets and musicians holding forth in local joints.

It'll take a lot more money to spend a night at **The Palace Hotel,** where only writers who had already become rich and famous could afford to stay. Oscar Wilde was here when he was 27 years old and apparently drank the entire town under the table; Rudyard Kipling arrived a few years later but was rejected by both the *Chronicle* and Ambrose Bierce's *San Francisco Illustrated Wasp.* The hotel's most spectacular attributes remain the regal lobby and the Garden Court, a San Francisco landmark that has been restored to its original 1909 grandeur. A double row of massive Italian-marble Ionic columns flank the court, and 10 huge chandeliers dangle above. The real heart-stopper, however, is the 80,000-pane stained-glass ceiling (good special effects made Mike Douglas look like he fell through it in the movie *The Game*).

Meanwhile, as long as you're spending some money, consider the **Huntington Hotel** on Nob Hill, where Eugene and Carlotta O'Neill moved from the Fairmont after they left Tao House in Danville, some 30 miles away. Today the hotel is still a discreet lodging for the "old money" crowd that wants to be left alone, as far as possible from anything resembling flash or celebrity.

The **York Hotel** is neither a fancy landmark nor a charming North Beach haven, but it was home for a while to Ron Kovic, who wrote *Born on the Fourth of July* and *Around the World in Eight Days.* While staying at the York, Kovic wrote eight novels in 38 days, according to Don Herron's *The Literary World of San Francisco* (City Lights

Books). It's also home to the Plush Room, the city's best jazz and cabaret club (see the Nightlife chapter).

For movie hounds... San Francisco is a favorite site of film-makers, and hotels make perfect backdrops. The **Fairmont Hotel** played center stage in the movie *Bullitt,* Steve McQueen's classic thriller that has one of the all-time best movie chase scenes. The **York Hotel** is a must-see for Alfred Hitchcock fans: The stairway scene in *Vertigo* was shot here. Many San Francisco hotels have been featured in movies, but only one was designed as a shrine to them. In the heart of the theater district, **Hotel Bijou** looks like a movie palace from the 1930s, with Hollywood portraits on the walls and each guest room based on the theme of a movie shot in the Bay Area. (Those 65 movies are all available for viewing from the hotel's video library.) Best of all, there is an ornate minitheater that shows San Francisco movies daily.

Taking care of business... To the business traveler, voice mail and a reliable dataport are musts, but sometimes e-mail isn't enough. You've got to have 24-hour access to a fax machine, and if you stay at **The Ritz-Carlton San Francisco,** you'll have one right in your room. The luxurious hotel also offers a full business center, complimentary transportation, and every other amenity a generous expense account can buy. The **Nob Hill Lambourne** is a model hotel for health-conscious business execs. Not only does it feature a full-service spa on the premises, every room has its own exercise equipment as well as personal computer, fax set-up, and compact stereo unit. All this special treatment costs the same or less than a nondescript room at some of the major hotels in the area. A bit farther from the Financial District, in Japantown, the **Radisson Miyako Hotel** caters to a clientele of lots of Japanese business travelers, with fax machines and voice mail in the rooms, as well as translation services. Business travelers seeking offbeat accommodations could try the **Inn at the Opera** or the **Hotel Bohème,** both of which are equipped with in-room voice mail and fax/modem hook-ups, yet offer a European-style ambience quite different from the standard business-travel hotel.

Family values... Oh, to be a kid again. They get all the good stuff and don't ever even think of offering to pay. Even some high-end hotels make a point of catering to youngsters, possibly on the theory that rich children grow up to be rich adults. The **Westin Saint Francis**'s Family Package is geared toward pleasing parents by offering free meals for kids and a free movie each night. The glass-enclosed elevators add an amusement-park thrill to the experience. The **Hotel Metropolis** is just a block from the Powell Street cable-car line, and if that gets boring, the hotel's "rooms just for kids" are perfect for goofing off, with bunk beds, scaled-down furniture, and—the best part—Nintendo.

The best bang for your tourist buck... You wouldn't believe how many crummy "European-style" hotels I've had to slog through to find the gems, but the five-story **Hotel des Arts** is one of the gems. While it has the same floor plan as San Francisco's numerous other Euro-style hotels—small lobby, narrow hallways, cramped rooms—the owners of the des Arts have made an obvious effort to distance themselves from the competition by including a visually stimulating dose of artistic license throughout the hotel. The lobby, for example, hosts a rotating art gallery featuring contemporary works by emerging local artists and is outfitted with groovy furnishings, while the guest rooms are soothingly situated with quality furnishings and tasteful accoutrements. You'll love the lively location as well: right across the street from the entrance to Chinatown and two blocks from Union Square. Considering the price (rooms with a shared bathroom start at $59), quality, and location, it's quite possibly the best budget hotel in the city.

My other favorite "hip on the cheap" hotel is **The Mosser,** a highly atypical budget hotel that incorporates a fusion of Victorian architecture with modern interior design. It originally opened in 1913 as a luxury hotel only to be dwarfed by more modern high-rise hotels that surround it. But a major renovation in 2001 transformed this aging charmer into a sophisticated, stylish, and surprisingly affordable SoMa lodging. Guest rooms are replete with original Victorian flourishes—bay windows, high ceilings, hand-carved moldings—that juxtapose well with the contemporary custom-designed furnishings, granite showers, stainless steel fixtures, ceiling fans, Frette linens, and modern electronics. The Mosser even houses Studio Paradiso, a state-of-the-art recording studio. The location is excellent as well—three blocks from Union Square, two blocks from the SFMoMA and Moscone Convention

Center, and half a block from the cable-car turn-around.

If there's a pet in your entourage... A number of San Francisco hotels make special provisions for pooches, ranging from simply tolerating their presence to greeting them in the lobby with a doggie biscuit. For the lowdown on off-leash parks and beaches, as well as restaurants and cafes that will allow you to bring Rover in with you, get *Dog Lover's Companion to the Bay Area* by Lyle York and Marcia Goodavage, available at Amazon.com. Lodgings that accept pets (call ahead to check limitations) include some lower-priced motel properties such as the **Laurel Inn** in Pacific Heights, as well as big mass-market chain properties such as the immense **San Francisco Marriott** and even, surprisingly, a couple of top-end luxury hotels—the **Westin Saint Francis** and the **Campton Place Hotel.** The small but distinctive **Hotel Monaco** offers a "Bone A Petit" package that includes, among other things, Evian water and a liver biscotti at turndown. Always call in advance for pet policies and required deposits.

> **Sleeping Seaside**
> *You would think that a city surrounded on three sides by water would have a slew of seaside hotels. Oddly enough, it has very few, one of which is the **Seal Rock Inn**. It's about as far from Union Square and Fisherman's Wharf as you can place a hotel in San Francisco, but that just makes it all the more unique (see map on p. 14). The motel fronts Sutro Heights Park, which faces Ocean Beach. Most rooms in the four-story structure have at least partial views of the ocean; at night, the sounds of the surf and distant foghorns lull guests to sleep. The rooms, although large and spotless, are basic, with rose and teal floral accents. Only some rooms have kitchenettes, but phones, TVs, fridges, covered parking, and use of the enclosed patio and pool area are standard. On the ground floor of the inn is a small old-fashioned restaurant serving breakfast and lunch. Golden Gate Park and the Presidio are both nearby, and the Geary bus—which snails its way to Union Square and Market Street—stops right out front. The Seal Rock Inn is located at 545 Point Lobos Ave., at 48th Avenue (Tel 888/732-5762 or 415/752-8000; fax 415/752-6034; www.sealrockinn.com). Double rooms range from $95 to $153.*

Euro-style lodgings... San Francisco's abundance of European-inspired small hotels and guesthouses are part of the ambience that has led people to call it "the Paris of the West." The **Andrews Hotel** (Union Sq.) is a prime example. The small, family-owned Victorian is rich in history, going back to its incarnation as the Sultan Turkish baths, a turn-of-the-20th-century men's club. Owner Henry Andrews oversees every detail, from the fluffy down comforters and fresh flowers in each guest room to the gourmet continental breakfast set up on each floor every morning. *Insider tip:* Ask for a "sunny bay king" room—they have beautiful bay windows and are larger than standard rooms, but they cost only two or three dollars more.

With just 10 guest rooms, **Jackson Court** is not exactly a hotel, but staying in this historic mansion in Pacific Heights will make you feel like European royalty. (In fact, many of the residents of this exclusive neighborhood are probably richer than royals.) Just around the corner, the 43-room **Hotel Drisco** makes you feel as though you're staying at the pied-à-terre of a friend—a very wealthy friend with fabulous taste and the thickest towels in town. If you can afford it, stay in the city/bay suite on the fourth floor, where huge bay windows on both sides of the suite provide views of the Golden Gate and Bay bridges as well as a sweeping panorama of the city itself. Bonus: If you want to go into town to work or shop, the hotel offers free morning car service.

Luscious love nests... *Town and Country* said a night at the **Archbishop's Mansion** is "like a night in a well-written romance novel," which is ideal if you like romance novels. It's probably the only hotel in the city where you'll find a huge bathroom with a working fireplace and a claw-foot bathtub in the middle of the room, smelling of perfume and just waiting for a candlelit soak for two. (Do you hear that mood music yet?) The next morning you can keep the spark alive as long as nature allows—the mansion staff will serve you breakfast in bed. If that whole Danielle Steel thing bores you, perhaps the passion of the opera will get your motor running. Couples have been known to hold intimate wedding dinners in front of the fire at the Ovation restaurant at **Inn at the Opera,** then walk across the street to pump up the volume with a fervent aria at the Opera House. The Inn at the Opera is the most sumptuous small hotel in the city, and I do mean small—the entire building is only 25 feet wide, which kind of makes you wonder how Luciano Pavarotti keeps from feeling cramped when he stays there. Still, the sense is one of airy coziness, partially because all of the windows open for real fresh air. If you've got that "truly, madly, deeply" kind of thing going on, and you're willing to prove it with some serious money, take your amour across the bay to the lush, 22-acre **Clare-mont Resort Hotel & Spa** and book a telescope suite, where San Francisco's lights will twinkle just for you all night long. It's one of the best views of San Francisco you'll ever find. The picture window is as big as a movie screen and is fitted with a wide, wraparound window seat custom-made for those spontaneous harmonic convergences.

Provident penthouses... You don't have to spend $12,500 a night at the Fairmont to stay in an enchanting penthouse. For $155 a night, you can have your own little cottage and sundeck at the **San Remo Hotel** in North Beach. True, it's perched on a tarpaper roof and is more like a goofy house-boat than a luxury apartment, but the location and the view are great. Unfortunately, this little gem is no longer a secret, so you may need to book about 5 or 6 months in advance. On the other hand, not many people know about the gorgeous terrace penthouses at the **Maxwell Hotel** near Union Square. If you ever want to impress your asso-ciates or entertain your friends, this is the place to splurge. There is no cheesy gold-plated anything, no marble floors, nothing froufrou at all—the decor is modern but luxurious, sort of high-end Pottery Barn. The view is to die for. Going up the scale, the **Prescott Hotel,** also in Union Square, has a more opulent penthouse: two fireplaces (including one in the bedroom), a baby grand piano, a state-of-the-art stereo system, and a dining room that seats eight for a private dinner catered by Wolfgang Puck's Postrio restaurant.

I'm with the band... You don't have to be on assignment for *Rolling Stone* to be curious about rock stars, but you do have to know where they stay at night if you want to sneak a peek. We'll tell you some of the best spots, but you have to promise to follow the two cardinal rules of stargazing: 1) Don't stare; and 2) Don't ask, "Aren't you...?" **The Phoenix Hotel** is the supreme hot spot for rock stars and other non-conformist celebrities. Originally a kind of futuristic, sleek motel in the 1950s, then a hooker hotel in the '70s and

'80s, it was bought in 1987 by Chip Conley, who managed to snag his first celebrity guest, Brenda Lee, when she stopped one day to ask for directions to another hotel. After that came Arlo Guthrie and a few others, and the celebrity guest register mushroomed. Sinéad O'Connor, Wim Wenders, the Sex Pistols, Nirvana, the Red Hot Chili Peppers, M.C. Hammer, k.d. lang, R.E.M., John Waters, Dr. John, Etta James, River Phoenix, Keanu Reeves, Chubby Checker, David Bowie, Bonnie Raitt, Bo Diddley, and the Cowboy Junkies are just a few of the stars who have lounged by the infamous mural-bottomed swimming pool in the Tenderloin. Celebrity guests at the **Inn at the Opera** are more along the lines of opera stars, artists, and dancers—Mikhail Baryshnikov, Twyla Tharp, David Hockney, Plácido Domingo, Oscar de la Renta, Robert Rauschenberg, Philip Glass, Herbie Hancock, and the principal dancers of the American Ballet Theatre—but there are a few surprises to round out the list, such as home-run king Hank Aaron and Gaylord Perry, the Hall of Famer who was known to throw a spitball or two. This superb hotel is very popular; reserve well in advance.

It's modern art, dear... A number of hotels are worth visiting strictly for the interior design of the lobbies. **Hotel Triton** has an "Alice in Wonderland on LSD" feeling that doesn't go away when you walk out the door and face the huge, ornate dragon on the gate to Chinatown. Some of the desk clerks could use a little less attitude, but then again, they're used to acting unimpressed by guests like Lily Tomlin, Sharon Stone, and Courtney Love. **Hotel Diva** is a different kind of fantasy, namely stainless steel and cobalt. Sounds like an operating room, but it's actually more like Zen sculpture—sleek, simple, and serene. If you'd like to spend the night at the Museum of Modern Art, this is your spot. The Diva's sister, **Hotel Metropolis,** did its lobby in acid green, tangerine, ice blue, and aluminum. The effect is spare and elemental, but the rooms are warmer, with lots of wood, color, and rich fabrics. The **Commodore Hotel** looks like a film set for a Picasso-meets-Popeye *Love Boat* episode. There are aqua lines painted around imaginary portholes on the front doors, through which Keanu Reeves, Jon Bon Jovi, and other celebs have entered the lobby. While staying at the Commodore, Jon Bon Jovi loved hanging out in the attached

Red Room cocktail lounge so much, he volunteered to bartend one night. A little less eccentric but equally popular is the **Hotel Palomar** just footsteps away from the Museum of Modern Art.

We gotta get outta this place... Fog getting to you? Think you'll scream if you see one more panhandler on Market Street? Here's the cure: Get a car, and drive across the Golden Gate Bridge and then another 12 miles to Mill Valley, one of those cozy little towns that forces you to use the word "quaint" to describe it. (It was, however, the setting for the 1970s satire *Serial,* starring Martin Mull, Sally Kellerman, and a flotilla of hot tubs; luckily, most of the Marin County stereotypes that inspired this book and the 1980 movie have gone to spawn elsewhere.)

Get a balcony room at the **Mill Valley Inn** and mingle with the locals—half of them are screenwriters and you know how they love to talk. After that, calm down a bit at Tea Garden Springs with a massage and an herbal elixir. Then get back in the car, head farther up the coast to Point Reyes National Seashore, and check into **Manka's Inverness Lodge & Restaurant,** a hunting lodge built in 1917 and later transformed into a romantic inn; the extraordinary restaurant here serves game grilled in the fireplace and local line-caught fish. Try to get one of the private cabins, and whatever you do, don't miss dinner in the restaurant.

If you have time, it's definitely worth driving another 2 hours to Mendocino, where a host of cozy seaside inns will soothe your spirit. Among the most unusual is **Stanford Inn by the Sea,** a working organic garden and farm on 10 acres between the Big River and the Pacific Ocean. A herd of animals, including a gaggle of llamas, roams near the garden, which supplies produce for the inn's innovative vegetarian restaurant. And guests roam all around the river, beaches, and village on mountain bikes provided free by the inn. The rooms—each with a wood-burning fireplace—have all the amenities of a luxury hotel yet feel as snug as a family cabin. The inn's romance and comfort draw many celebrities looking for an escape and who have become family friends of innkeepers Joan and Jeff Stanford.

Map 2: Union Square & Nob Hill Accommodations

Sansome St.

Leidesdorff St.

Montgomery St.

2nd St.

BART/Muni
Montgomery St.
Station

New Montgomery St.

SFMoMA

16

Jessie St.

3rd St.

Stevenson St.

Sacramento St.

Pine St.

California St.

Kearny St.

St. Mary's
Square

Claude Ln.

CHINATOWN

19 20

Sutter St.

Grant Ave.

22

Bush St.

Harlan Pl.

Geary St.

Post St.

Campton Pl.

Maiden Ln.

SOMA

Yerba Buena
Gardens

Stockton St. 24 Tunnel

23

Joice St.

17

Stockton St.

Union
Square

Market St.

4th St.

15

14

BART/Muni
Powell St. Station

Dashiell
Hammett St.

Powell St.

Powell St.

M

5th
St.

Pine St.

18

C. Magnin St.

26

25

Sacramento St.

Huntington
St.

Mason St.

UNION
SQUARE

7

9

11

Mason St.

12

13

27

Huntington
Park

5

6

O'Farrell St.

Ellis St.

Eddy St.

Grace
Cathedral

NOB HILL

Taylor St.

4

3

Cosmo Pl.

Shannon St.

Taylor St.

10

Turk St.

Jones St.

Geary St.

Jones St.

2

Post St.

Leavenworth St.

Sacramento St.

California St.

Hyde St.

Pine St.

Bush St.

Sutter St.

1

100 yds

100 m

M - BART/Muni
···· - Cable Car

0

0

Larkin St.

The Index

$$$$$	over $300
$$$$	$200–$300
$$$	$150–$200
$$	$100–$150
$	under $100

Price ratings are based on the lowest price quoted for a standard double room, including taxes and charges. Note that air-conditioning is usually unnecessary in Fog City, so if you want it, you'll need to stay at one of the $200-and-up hotels.

The following abbreviations are used for credit cards:

AE	American Express
DC	Diners Club
DISC	Discover
MC	MasterCard
V	Visa

Andrews Hotel (p. 30) UNION SQUARE This cozy, family-run inn near Union Square preserves many Victorian details.... *Tel 415/ 563-6877 (800/926-3739). Fax 415/928-6919. www.andrews hotel.com. 624 Post St., 94109. Powell–Mason cable car. 48 rooms. AE, DC, MC, V. $$$*

See Map 2 on p. 34.

Archbishop's Mansion (p. 22) WESTERN ADDITION This bed-and-breakfast inn has been hailed as the most spectacular place to stay in the city and as the most elegant in-city hotel in the United States.... *Tel 415/563-7872 (800/543-5820). Fax 415/885-3193. www.thearchbishopsmansion.com. 1000 Fulton St., 94117. MUNI bus 5. 10 rooms, 5 suites. AE, DC, MC, V. $$$–$$$$$*

See Map 1 on p. 14.

Campton Place Hotel (p. 29) UNION SQUARE This small luxury hotel is noted for its elegance and comfortable intimacy. *Tel 415/ 781-5555 (800/235-4300). Fax 415/955-5536. www.campton place.com. 340 Stockton St., 94108. Powell–Hyde or Powell–Mason cable car; MUNI buses 2, 3, 4, 30, or 45. 100 rooms, 10 suites. AE, DC, MC, V. $$$$–$$$$$*

See Map 2 on p.34.

Central YMCA (p. 17) TENDERLOIN This reliable standard in cheap lodgings is an especially good deal when you consider the rooms are private (some with private bath) and include use of the health club and pool. Dormitory accommodations are also available.... *Tel 415/345-6700. Fax 415/885-5439. www.central ymcasf.org. 220 Golden Gate Ave., 94109. Civic Center BART/ MUNI Metro stop; MUNI bus 15. 106 rooms, plus one 12-bed and two 4-bed dormitories. No TV or in-room phone. AE, DISC, MC, V,. $*
See Map 1 on p. 14.

Claremont Resort Hotel & Spa (p. 31) BERKELEY The 22 acres of landscaped grounds are just the backdrop for the landmark Victorian hotel (1915), the premier private tennis club, and a $6 million holistic health and beauty spa.... *Tel 510/843-3000 (800/551-7266). Fax 510/549-8582. www.claremontresort.com. 41 Tunnel Rd., 94705. Rockridge BART station (plus a cab). 279 rooms. AE, DC, DISC, MC, V. $$$$–$$$$$*

Commodore Hotel (p. 32) UNION SQUARE You have to go by here just to check out the lobby. It's a goofball version of a cruise ship, with a lobby full of furniture that looks like it came out of a cartoon.... *Tel 415/923-6800 (800/338-6848). Fax 415/923-6804. www.thecommodorehotel.com. 825 Sutter St., 94109. California St. cable car. 110 rooms. AE, DC, DISC, MC, V. $$$*
See Map 2 on p. 34.

The Donatello (p. 21) UNION SQUARE The standard rooms may be the largest in the city, with 10-foot ceilings and huge windows; terrace suites open to lushly landscaped private decks.... *Tel 415/441-7100 (800/227-3184). Fax 415/885-8842. 501 Post St., 94109. Powell–Mason cable car. 94 rooms. AE, DC, DISC, MC, V. $$$$*
See Map 2 on p. 34.

The Edwardian San Francisco Hotel (p. 25) HAYES VALLEY A wide green awning welcomes you to this red-brick Victorian perched at the crossroads of the Mission District, the Hayes Valley, and Upper Market Street. You'll drool over the Gay Paree/ French Quarter motif: wrought-iron fire escapes on the front and white wood railings surrounding the rooftop.... *Tel 415/864-1271 (888/864-8070). Fax 415/861-8116. www.edwardiansfhotel.com. 1668 Market St., 94102. Van Ness Ave. MUNI Metro station; MUNI bus 7. 36 rooms. AE, DC, DISC, MC, V. $–$$*
See Map 1 on p. 14.

Fairmont Hotel (p. 16) NOB HILL This is probably the most famous hotel in San Francisco, at the tip-top of Nob Hill, yet it's not incredibly expensive if you don't stay in a suite.... *Tel 415/772-5000 (800/441-1414). Fax 415/772-5086. www.fairmont. com. 950 Mason St., 94108. California St. cable car. 591 rooms. AE, DC, DISC, MC, V. $$$$–$$$$$*
See Map 2 on p. 34.

Grant Plaza (p. 24) CHINATOWN This bargain hotel in Chinatown is clean and comfortable. The rooms are a bit dreary, but the windows are large and let in lots of light.... *Tel 415/434-3883 (800/472-6899). Fax 415/434-3886. www.grantplaza.com. 465 Grant Ave., 94108. MUNI buses 15, 30, or 45. 72 rooms. AE, DC, DISC, MC, V. $$–$$$*

See Map 2 on p. 34.

Green Tortoise Guest House (p. 24) NORTH BEACH This non-smoking facility attracts lots of young people and has a sauna, laundry, free breakfast and Internet access, and organized tours.... *Tel 415/834-1000 (800/867-8647). Fax 415/956-4900. www.greentortoise.com. 494 Broadway, 94133. MUNI buses 15 or 30. 100 beds, 17 rooms with shared bath. No in-room phone. No credit cards. $*

See Map 1 on p. 14.

Hostelling International San Francisco—Downtown (p. 24) UNION SQUARE This hostel is in the heart of Union Square and features several rooms with private baths for families as well as the normal dorm facilities.... *Tel 415/788-5604 (888/GOHIUSA). Fax 415/788-3023. www.sfhostels.com. 312 Mason St., 94102. Powell–Mason cable car; MUNI buses 7B or 38. 105 rooms (39 private, 241 dorm beds). No TV or in-room phone. MC, V. $*

See Map 2 on p. 34.

Hostelling International San Francisco—Fisherman's Wharf (p. 17) FORT MASON Fort Mason is the hub of the beautifully scenic Golden Gate National Recreation Area, and this dormitory hostel is right in the thick of it.... *Tel 415/771-7277 (888/GOHIUSA). Fax 415/771-1468. www.sfhostels.com. Building 240, 94123. Powell–Hyde cable car; MUNI buses 30 or 42. 170 beds. Shared baths, no TV or in-room phone. MC, V. $*

See Map 1 on p. 14.

Hotel Astoria (p. 24) CHINATOWN This super-cheap Chinatown hotel has plain, but not shabby, rooms, some with shared bath. Airport pickup and some business services are provided.... *Tel 415/434-8889 (800/666-6696). Fax 415/434-8919. www. hotelastoria-sf.com. 510 Bush St., 94108. MUNI buses 30 or 45. 80 rooms. AE, DC, DISC, MC, V. $$*

See Map 2 on p. 34.

Hotel Bijou (p. 16) UNION SQUARE A shrine to the silver screen, this small hotel in the heart of the theater district looks like an old-time movie palace and features movie-themed guest rooms.... *Tel 415/771-1200 (800/771-1022). Fax 415/346-3196. www. hotelbijou.com. 111 Mason St., 94102. Powell–Mason cable car. 65 rooms. AE, DC, DISC, MC, V. $$$*

See Map 2 on p. 34.

Hotel Bohème (p. 17) NORTH BEACH This Parisian-style beatnik villa is comfortable and chic at the same time. It's in the heart of North Beach, but the rooms are surprisingly quiet.... *Tel 415/433-9111. Fax 415/362-6292. www.hotelboheme.com. 444 Columbus Ave., 94133. MUNI buses 15, 30, or 45. 15 rooms. AE, DC, DISC, MC, V. $–$$$*

See Map 1 on p. 14.

Hotel des Arts (p. 28) UNION SQUARE Considering the price (rooms with a shared bathroom start at $59) and artistic themes throughout, it's quite possibly the best budget hotel in the city.... *Tel 415/956-3232 (800/956-4322). Fax 415/956-0399. www.sfhoteldesarts.com. 447 Bush St., at Grant St., 94108. Powell–Hyde or Powell–Mason cable car. 51 rooms, 26 with private bath. AE, DC, MC, V. $–$$*

See Map 2 on p. 34.

Hotel Diva (p. 16) UNION SQUARE If you love the look of sleek stainless steel beds but crave the feel of luxurious linens, join the artsy types who love this super-chic, ultramodern urban retreat.... *Tel 415/885-0200 (800/553-1900). Fax 415/885-3268. www.hoteldiva.com. 440 Geary St., 94102. MUNI bus 38. 115 rooms. AE, DC, DISC, MC, V. $$$–$$$$*

See Map 2 on p. 34.

Hotel Drisco (p. 30) PACIFIC HEIGHTS Find out why the richest people in San Francisco choose to live in Pacific Heights by staying at this sumptuous, intimate hotel.... *Tel 415/346-2880 (800/634-7277). Fax 415/567-5537. www.hoteldrisco.com. 2901 Pacific Ave., 94115. MUNI bus 3. 48 rooms. AE, DC, DISC, MC, V. $$$$–$$$$$*

See Map 1 on p. 14.

Hotel Metropolis (p. 16) UNION SQUARE This 1930s landmark colonial revivalist building was renovated in 1998 with "vivid color and modern materials." Despite the inescapable artiness of the lobby, the rooms are down-to-earth and comfy. There is one special room just for kids (with bunk beds and Nintendo).... *Tel 415/775-4600 (800/553-1900). Fax 415/775-4606. www.hotelmetropolis.com. 25 Mason St., 94102. Powell–Mason cable car; MUNI bus 38. 105 rooms. AE, DC, DISC, MC, V. $$$$*

See Map 2 on p. 34.

Hotel Monaco (p. 16) UNION SQUARE This impeccably refurbished 1910 Beaux Arts landmark is now a four-star hotel with all the amenities that attract discriminating nonmainstream types.... *Tel 415/292-0100 (800/214-4220). Fax 415/292-0111. www.monaco-sf.com. 501 Geary St., 94102. Powell–Mason cable car; MUNI bus 38. 201 rooms. AE, DC, DISC, MC, V. $$$$*

See Map 2 on p. 34.

Hotel Nikko (p. 25) UNION SQUARE This Japanese hotel is perilously close to the Hilton, and it has rubbed off. Most of the rooms are very Western, though the traditional Japanese suites are beautiful.... *Tel 415/394-1111 (800/645-5687). Fax 415/394-1106. www.hotelnikkosf.com. 222 Mason St., 94102. Powell St. BART/MUNI Metro station; Powell–Mason or Powell–Hyde cable car; MUNI bus 38. 500 rooms. AE, DC, DISC, MC, V. $$$$–$$$$$*

See Map 2 on p. 34.

Hotel Palomar (p. 33) SOMA Once you get past the typical San Francisco interior design fuss, there are some really good things about this hotel: cordless phones, 27-inch TVs in every room, Fuji spa tubs in the suites, and package deals that include everything from a luscious spa to art tours.... *Tel 415/348-1111 (877/294-9711). Fax 415/348-0302. www.hotelpalomar.com. 12 Fourth St., 94103. Market St. near Union Sq. Powell St. BART station. 198 rooms. AE, DC, DISC, MC, V. $$$$–$$$$$*

See Map 2 on p. 34.

Hotel Rex (p. 16) UNION SQUARE This arts and literary salon/hotel draws artists and writers for book-signings and conversation.... *Tel 415/433-4434 (800/433-4434). Fax 415/433-3695. www.thehotelrex.com. 562 Sutter St., 94102. Powell–Mason or Powell–Hyde cable car. 94 rooms. AE, DC, DISC, MC, V. $$$$*

See Map 2 on p. 34.

Hotel Triton (p. 16) UNION SQUARE Plush, upholstered chairs sit next to the modern, angular front desk; huge columns rise out of the royal-blue carpet. The guests look as arty as the decor.... *Tel 415/394-0500 (800/800-1299). Fax415/394-0555. www.hoteltriton.com. 342 Grant Ave., 94108. MUNI buses 30 or 45. 140 rooms. AE, DC, DISC, MC, V. $$$$–$$$$$*

See Map 2 on p. 34.

Huntington Hotel (p. 26) NOB HILL Rooms are exquisitely—and individually—appointed, with museum-quality works of art and a blend of antique and custom-designed furniture.... *Tel 415/474-5400 (800/227-4683). Fax 415/474-6227. www.huntington hotel.com. 1075 California St., 94108. California St. cable car; MUNI bus 1. 135 rooms. AE, DC, DISC, MC, V. $$$$–$$$$$*

See Map 2 on p. 34.

Inn at the Opera (p. 17) CIVIC CENTER This tiny, 25-foot-wide Victorian jewel is the most distinguished small luxury hotel in the city and one of the most romantic.... *Tel 415/863-8400 (800/590-0157). Fax 415/861-0821. www.innattheopera.com. 333 Fulton St., 94102. Civic Center BART/MUNI Metro station; MUNI buses 5, 21, 47, or 49. 46 rooms. AE, DC, DISC, MC, V. $$$$*

See Map 1 on p. 14.

InterContinental Mark Hopkins (p. 21) NOB HILL Sometimes overshadowed by its Nob Hill neighbor, the Fairmont, this classic 19-story luxury hotel should not be overlooked. Every room has a marvelous view.... *Tel 415/392-3434 (800/327-0200). Fax 415/ 421-3302. www.san-francisco.intercontinental.com. 1 Nob Hill, 94108. California St. cable car. 380 rooms. AE, DC, DISC, MC, V. $$$$–$$$$$*

See Map 2 on p. 34.

Jackson Court (p. 30) MARINA DISTRICT Reserve at least 6 weeks in advance for this 10-room brownstone mansion in elite Pacific Heights. Somewhat ornate in parts, it's also warm and homey, with very comfortable beds.... *Tel 415/929-7670. Fax 415/929-1405. www.jacksoncourt.com. 2198 Jackson St., 94115. MUNI bus 12. 10 rooms. AE, DC, DISC, MC, V. $$$–$$$$*

See Map 1 on p. 14.

Laurel Inn (p. 29) PACIFIC HEIGHTS This recently remodeled motel has a great location plus rooms with kitchens, a complimentary continental breakfast, and free lemonade and cookies in the afternoon. Parking is free and pets are welcome.... *Tel 415/567-8467 (800/552-8735). Fax 415/928-1866. www. thelaurelinn.com. 444 Presidio Ave., 94115. MUNI bus 3. 49 rooms. AE, DC, DISC, MC, V. $$$*

See Map 1 on p. 14.

The Mandarin Oriental (p. 23) FINANCIAL DISTRICT All guest rooms are between the 38th and 48th floors of a high-rise with extraordinary panoramic views of the bay and city.... *Tel 415/ 276-9888 (800/622-0404). Fax 415/433-0289. www.mandarin oriental.com. 222 Sansome St., between Pine and California sts., 94104. MUNI Metro J, K, L, or M to Montgomery. All Market St. buses. 158 rooms. DC, DISC, MC, V. $$$$–$$$$$*

See Map 1 on p. 14.

Manka's Inverness Lodge & Restaurant (p. 33) INVERNESS Locals rave about this cheerful, rustic, little oceanside inn, with its remarkable restaurant, less than an hour from the city.... *Tel 415/669-1034. www.mankas.com. 30 Callendar Way, on Point Reyes National Seashore, 94937. 14 rooms. MC, V. $$$–$$$$$*

Maxwell Hotel (p. 31) UNION SQUARE You can't miss the sculpture of a shopper outside this restored 1908 Art Deco masterpiece, a tribute to the high-end shopping nearby in Union Square. The spacious guest rooms are done in deep, rich colors with plush fabrics and hand-painted lampshades.... *Tel 415/986-2000 (888/734-6299). Fax 415/986-2193. www.maxwellhotel.com. 386 Geary St., 94102. Powell–Mason cable car; MUNI bus 38. 153 rooms. AE, DC, DISC, MC, V. $$$$–$$$$$*

See Map 2 on p. 34.

Mill Valley Inn (p. 33) MILL VALLEY This three-story European-style pensione looks like a cross between an Italian villa and a California Colonial lodge, at the foot of Mount Tamalpais, alongside a redwood grove.... *Tel 415/389-6608 (800/595-2100). Fax 415/389-5051. www.jdvhospitality.com. 165 Throckmorton Ave., 94941. 25 rooms, 2 cottages, 1 executive suite. AE, DC, DISC, MC, V. $$$$*

The Mosser (p. 28) SOMA A "hip on the cheap" hotel that fuses Victorian architecture with modern interior design.... *Tel 415/986-4400 (800/227-3804). Fax 415/495-7653. www.themosser. com. 54 Fourth St., at Market St., 94103. BART/MUNI Metro station F. 166 rooms. AE, DC, MC, V. $-$$*
See Map 1 on p. 14.

Nob Hill Lambourne (p. 16) NOB HILL This sleek hotel looks like another ritzy, oh-so-spare hotel for the rich and private, but it's actually a reasonably priced lodging that attracts business travelers.... *Tel 415/433-2287 (800/274-8466). Fax 415/433-0975. www.nobhilllambourne.com. 725 Pine St., 94108. Powell St. BART station. 14 rooms, 6 suites. AE, DC, DISC, MC, V. $$$$-$$$$$*
See Map 2 on p. 34.

The Palace Hotel (p. 26) SOMA This San Francisco landmark has now been restored to its turn-of-the-century distinction but with all the modern conveniences.... *Tel 415/512-1111 (800/325-3589). Fax 415/543-0671. www.sfpalace.com. 2 New Montgomery St., 94105. Montgomery St. BART/MUNI Metro station; MUNI buses 7, 15, 30, or 45. 552 rooms. AE, DC, DISC, MC, V. $$$$$*
See Map 2 on p. 34.

The Phoenix Hotel (p. 16) CIVIC CENTER One of the most wacked-out and popular lodgings in the city, this Tenderloin/Civic Center motel is best known for its famous guests. The decor is sort of psychedelic kitsch.... *Tel 415/776-1380 (800/248-9466). Fax 415/885-3109. www.thephoenixhotel.com. 601 Eddy St., 94109. MUNI buses 19, 31, or 38. 44 rooms. AE, DC, MC, V. $$-$$$*
See Map 1 on p. 14.

Prescott Hotel (p. 16) UNION SQUARE This luxurious boutique hotel features massive cherrywood furniture in the guest rooms. Guests get preferred seating at Wolfgang Puck's chic Postrio restaurant.... *Tel 415/563-0303 (800/283-7322). Fax 415/563-6831. www.prescotthotel.com. 545 Post St., 94102. Powell St. BART station; Powell-Mason or Powell-Hyde cable car; MUNI buses 2, 3, 4, or 38. 164 rooms. AE, DC, DISC, MC, V. $$$$$*
See Map 2 on p. 34.

The Queen Anne Hotel (p. 23) PACIFIC HEIGHTS A majestic 1890 Victorian building that was once a finishing school for upper-class young women.... *Tel 415/441-2828 (800/227-3970). Fax 415/775-5212. www.queenanne.com. 1590 Sutter St., between Gough and Octavia sts., 94109. MUNI buses 2, 3, or 4. 48 units. AE, DC, DISC, MC, V. $$–$$$*

See Map 1 on p. 14.

Radisson Miyako Hotel (p. 25) JAPANTOWN One of the most tranquil, gracious hotels in the city. Opt for the luxurious traditional Japanese suites. Continental breakfast is included.... *Tel 415/922-3200 (800/333-3333). Fax 415/921-0417. www.radisson.com/sanfranciscoca_miyako. 1625 Post St., near Geary Blvd. and Laguna St., 94115. MUNI bus 38. 218 rooms. AE, DC, DISC, MC, V. $$$$$*

See Map 1 on p. 14.

Red Victorian Bed, Breakfast & Art (p. 22) UPPER HAIGHT There should be a sign in front of this lovely and eccentric Haight-Ashbury inn that reads welcome back to 1967. Each room has its own theme.... *Tel 415/864-1978. Fax 415/863-3293. www.redvic.com. 1665 Haight St., 94117. MUNI buses 7, 66, 71, or 73. 18 rooms. AE, DISC, MC, V. $$–$$$$*

See Map 1 on p. 14.

The Ritz-Carlton San Francisco (p. 27) NOB HILL Handsome rooms, Italian-marble bathrooms, plush terry bathrobes, and twice-daily maid service are just some of the comforts here. Fully equipped fitness center, too.... *Tel 415/296-7465 (800/241-3333). Fax 415/986-1268. www.ritzcarlton.com. 600 Stockton St., 94108. Stockton St. BART station. 336 rooms. AE, DC, DISC, MC, V. $$$$$*

See Map 2 on p. 34.

San Francisco Marriott (p. 29) SOMA You can't miss this gigantic building, looming like a huge parking meter over the Financial District. Decor is typical Chain Hotel Moderne. Unbelievable views of both the bay and the Golden Gate.... *Tel 415/896-1600 (800/228-9290). Fax 415/486-8101. www.sfmarriott.com. 55 Fourth St., 94103. Powell St. BART/MUNI Metro station; Powell St. cable-car turnaround. 1,500 rooms. AE, DC, DISC, MC, V. $$$$$*

See Map 2 on p. 34.

San Remo Hotel (p. 17) NORTH BEACH The rooms at this delightful, clean, European-style hotel are furnished with antiques and have comfortable beds, big windows, and ceiling fans. The shared bathrooms on each floor are sparklingly clean and well kept.... *Tel 415/776-8688 (800/352-7366). Fax 415/776-2811. www.sanremohotel.com. 2237 Mason St., 94133. Powell–Mason cable car; MUNI buses 15 or 30. 62 rooms. No TV. AE, DC, MC, V. $–$$*

See Map 1 on p. 14.

Stanford Inn by the Sea (p. 33) MENDOCINO Movie and TV stars flock to this smoke-free, vegetarian, Mendocino hideaway to escape from the poisonous air and attitude of Hollywood. The tranquil seaside inn manages to remain totally unpretentious despite the splendid accommodations.... *Tel 707/937-5615 (800/331-8884). Fax 707/937-0305. www.stanfordinn.com. Coast Hwy. and Comptche Ukiah Rd., 94560. 41 rooms. AE, DC, DISC, MC, V. $$$$$*

24 Henry Guesthouse (p. 25) CASTRO This intimate little Victorian guesthouse is in the Castro District.... *Tel 415/864-5686 (800/900-5686). Fax 415/864-0406. www.24henry.com. 4080 18th St., 94114. J Church MUNI Metro. 10 rooms. AE, DC, DISC, MC, V. $$–$$$*

See Map 1 on p. 14.

Westin Saint Francis (p. 21) UNION SQUARE Perhaps the most venerable grande dame, the Saint Francis is in the Union Square area. Rooms in the original old building are preferable to those in the bland modern tower.... *Tel 415/397-7000 (800/WESTIN-1). Fax 415/774-0124. www.westin.com. 335 Powell St., 94102. Powell–Hyde or Powell–Mason cable car; MUNI buses 2, 3, 4, 30, 45, or 76. 1,195 rooms. AE, DC, DISC, MC, V. $$$$–$$$$$*

See Map 2 on p. 34.

York Hotel (p. 26) UNION SQUARE The hotel's formal script logo, emblazoned on deep-green awnings, belies the relaxed atmosphere that prevails at the York.... *Tel 415/885-6800 (800/808-9675). Fax 415/885-2115. www.yorkhotel.com. 940 Sutter St., 94109. Powell–Mason or Powell–Hyde cable car; MUNI bus 38. 96 rooms. AE, DC, DIS, MC, V. $$*

See Map 2 on p. 34.

ING

2

Map 3: San Francisco Dining

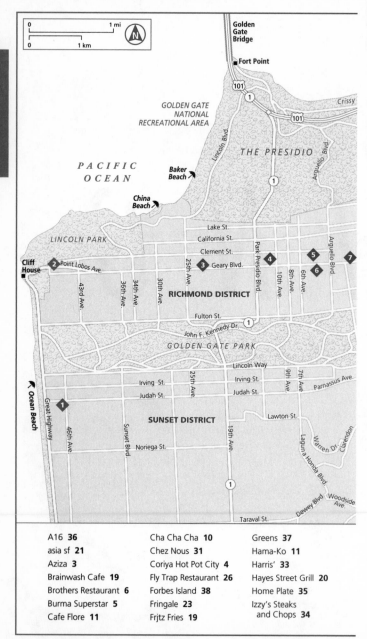

A16 **36**	Cha Cha Cha **10**	Greens **37**
asia sf **21**	Chez Nous **31**	Hama-Ko **11**
Aziza **3**	Coriya Hot Pot City **4**	Harris' **33**
Brainwash Cafe **19**	Fly Trap Restaurant **26**	Hayes Street Grill **20**
Brothers Restaurant **6**	Forbes Island **38**	Home Plate **35**
Burma Superstar **5**	Fringale **23**	Izzy's Steaks
Cafe Flore **11**	Frjtz Fries **19**	and Chops **34**

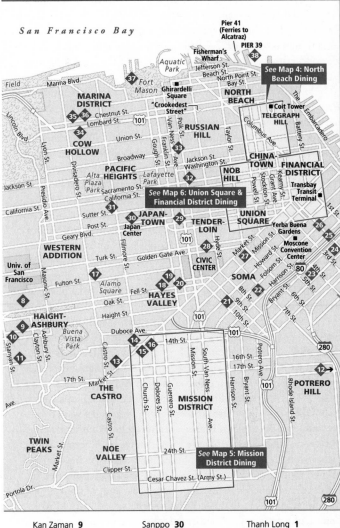

San Francisco Bay

Pier 41
(Ferries to
Alcatraz)
PIER 39
38

Fisherman's
Wharf
Aquatic
Park
Jefferson St.
Beach St.
North Point St.
Bay St.

See Map 4: North
Beach Dining

Field
Marina Blvd.
37 Fort
Mason
Ghirardelli
Square
NORTH
BEACH

MARINA
DISTRICT
"Crookedest
Street"
Coit Tower
TELEGRAPH
HILL

35 36 Chestnut St.
Lombard St.
Polk St.
RUSSIAN
HILL
Columbus Ave.
The Embarcadero

34
Union St.
Taylor St.
Battery St.

COW
HOLLOW
Broadway
CHINA-
TOWN
FINANCIAL
DISTRICT

PACIFIC
HEIGHTS
Alta
Plaza
Park
Franklin St.
Gough St.
Van Ness Ave.
Jackson St.
Washington St.
Lafayette
Park
32
NOB
HILL
Kearny Ave.
Grant Ave.
Stockton St.
Powell St.
Transbay
Transit
Terminal

Jackson St.
Divisadero St.
Sacramento St.
California St.
See Map 6: Union Square &
Financial District Dining
1st St.

California St.
Sutter St.
31
UNION
SQUARE
26

WESTERN
ADDITION
30 JAPAN-
TOWN
29 TENDER-
LOIN
Post St.
Geary Blvd.
Japan
Center
Fillmore St.
101
28
Hyde St.
Market St.
Mission St.
Howard St.
Folsom St.
Yerba Buena
Gardens
Moscone
Convention
Center
25
24
3rd St.

Univ. of
San
Francisco
Masonic Ave.
Turk St.
Golden Gate Ave.
CIVIC
CENTER
27
SOMA
Harrison St.
23
80
5th St.

8
Fulton St.
17
Alamo
Square
19
18 20
Fell St.
22
8th St.
Bryant St.
7th St.

HAIGHT-
ASHBURY
Oak St.
HAYES
VALLEY
21
9th St.
280

9
Buena
Vista
Park
Haight St.
101
10th St.

10
Ashbury St.
Clayton St.
Duboce Ave.
14 14th St.
Potrero Ave.
Rhode Island St.
12
POTRERO
HILL

11
Stanyan St.
Castro St.
15
16
16th St.
17th St.

17th St.
THE
CASTRO
Church St.
Dolores St.
Guerrero St.
Mission St.
South Van Ness Ave.
Harrison St.
101

Ave.
13
MISSION
DISTRICT

TWIN
PEAKS
Castro St.
Market St.
NOE
VALLEY
24th St.
See Map 5: Mission
District Dining

Clipper St.
Cesar Chavez St. (Army St.)
280

Portola Dr.

Basic Stuff

It's official: San Francisco is the best food town in America. New York had to accept the backseat when the City by the Bay first won all of the top James Beard awards (the Oscars of the restaurant world) in 1997—and the city's chefs continue to dazzle food critics and draw the rising stars of the chef kingdom from all over the planet.

And it's not just critics who love the food here. Readers of *Bon Appetit,* the world's largest-circulation epicurean magazine, have named San Francisco their favorite American city for dining out several years running. With more than 3,500 restaurants representing every cuisine on earth (and a few from outer space), the city that spawned California cuisine has become North America's ground zero for ingenious chefs. They are drawn not only to the creative freedom that has always defined San Francisco but also to the year-round abundance of fresh fruits, vegetables, herbs, fish, and seafood that are Northern California's unique bounty. And the dot-com invasion—which had San Francisco teeming with rich Internet start-up companies and deep-pocket cybernerds—spawned even more restaurants that continue to thrive (though many have gone belly-up since the easy money dried up).

Oddly enough, it took local cooks until nearly the end of the 20th century to figure out there was more to culinary life than steak and seafood, at which point they immediately went berserk with outlandish combinations of exotic ingredients and trickled raspberry vinegar on absolutely everything. Fortunately, most food fads—including that one—have the life span of a disposable razor, but there are some things you can always count on when you dine in San Francisco: a mélange of authentic ethnic eateries that is probably the most diverse in America; cafes, bistros, and formal dinner houses that serve extraordinary French food; a solid core of world-class restaurants inspired by California cuisine in all its transmutations; and, of course, the traditional grill fare that has been a staple since the gold rush. You could spend your entire vacation—and most of your money—eating at high-profile spots, but the best way to enjoy San Francisco's lavish feast is to explore the nation's most exotic variety of ethnic foods. Often the most interesting food is far less expensive than "see-and-be-seen" fare. There are far too many excellent restaurants to mention here, but the samples offered here will get you started on your own irreverent dining adventure.

Only in San Francisco

The sunny Mission District has long been famous for its authentic Mexican restaurants and storefront taquerias, where locals take for granted lunchtime feasts of *carnitas* (barbecued pork) and *carne asada* (grilled steak) for less than the price of a Big Mac. A steady stream of immigrants and refugees from Guatemala, El Salvador, Nicaragua, Chile, and Peru has brought dozens of new restaurants to the neighborhood. While you're there, you'll notice an infusion of chic, upscale eateries along Valencia and Guerrero streets, an area that food critics have dubbed "the Valencia corridor" to distinguish it from the barrio that surrounds it. If you get past the snobby euphemism—and San Francisco's interminable preoccupation with interior design—you can settle into food heaven without ever leaving the neighborhood. Chinese food is also synonymous with San Francisco, but you can find that in almost every city. The true gems are the harder to find Asian/Pacific cuisines, such as Cambodia's complex mingling of coconut milk, lemongrass, lime, and classical French fish sauce; or Singapore's exotic seafood dishes that combine European, Indian, Chinese, and Malaysian influences.

Supper clubs are still the favored late-night haunts for gourmets, where swanky drinks, as well as the locally fermented Anchor Steam beer and Gordon Biersch brews, are high on the locals' list of favorite beverages (get it on tap, not bottled). Beer has been big in the city since the raucous Barbary Coast days, when the San Francisco Brewing Company pub (corner of Columbus and Pacific aves.) first opened its doors. After Prohibition, the 1907 establishment started legally producing its own beer, which is available only at the pub or in extremely limited bottled batches at two neighborhood liquor stores (the Jug Shop, 1576 Pacific Ave., and Coit Liquors, 585 Columbus Ave.). Don't try to take it home as a souvenir—the beer is not pasteurized, so it must be refrigerated to last even 2 weeks. Finally, though Irish coffee is far from a local invention, a visit to the Buena Vista Cafe (2765 Haight St.), a National Historic Landmark for a cup of it—especially on a foggy late afternoon— is a time-honored tradition among locals and tourists alike.

How to Dress

Jackets and ties are rarely mandatory at San Francisco restaurants, but common sense should dictate the obvious: If you're going to a fancy place, dress up a bit. You'll probably need some sort of jacket, anyway, because it's so cool at night, even in summer. At casual establishments, anything goes. As long as you don't look like you just climbed out of a dumpster, you'll probably be acceptable no matter what you're wearing.

When to Eat

San Franciscans tend to dine out before they go to the opera or ballet, not afterwards, which means you need to reserve weeks in advance if you want to have dinner before 8pm in any popular restaurant near a major theater or concert hall. After 8:30pm, however, you can get a table on the spot at the **Hayes Street Grill** or other popular "opera ghetto" restaurants (those clustered near the performing arts mecca centering on City Hall and the War Memorial Opera House). Very few restaurants serve dinner after 10pm, so get your grazing over with before you go out on the town or you may be stuck with burgers or all-night coffee-shop food (see "Eating with insomniacs," on p. 71). Most breakfast places serve all day, with specials often ending at 11:30am, and lunch tends to be whatever you feel like eating between then and mid-afternoon, when many restaurants begin to gear up for dinner. Mexican food seems to work for breakfast, lunch, and dinner, so you'll never have to go hungry if you can find your way to the **Mission District.**

Eating at the Bar

There is little doubt that dining out is the favorite pastime of San Franciscans. Getting a table—or even a short-notice reservation—at a popular spot can be frustrating if not impossible. So do what locals do: Skip that and park yourself on a barstool. You can get in almost anywhere at the last minute, and the service is often quicker and more relaxed than in the dining room. Occasionally there is a special bar menu, but typically the offerings are identical to the fare served at the tables. A bonus for travelers is that bar diners are usually quite sociable, so you'll get a chance to schmooze with the locals on equal footing. Try **Aqua, Fringale, Harris', Moose's, Rose Pistola,** all the hip spots on Valencia Street, or anywhere else with bar seating and a waiting list to get in.

Cafe Society

When you hear people raving about the cafe scene in San Francisco, they're not referring to the posh bistros calling themselves cafes just to horn in on the French tradition of charging a small fortune for a dab of *je ne sais quoi*. They're talking about coffeehouses with names like **Muddy Waters Coffee House**—neighborhood caffeine dens that are often much more popular than bars as places to meet, hear music, listen to poetry, read, write, talk about art and politics, or just sit and watch the general buzz. The best cafes are basically ongoing block parties.

In recent years, Seattle has often been mislabeled by the media as America's gourmet-coffee center—primarily due to the success of the Starbucks coffee chain—but the problem with this perception is that coffee by itself is utterly insignificant. Seattle could sell enough coffee beans to fill up Mount St. Helens, yet it would still never be San Francisco. San Francisco's coffeehouses and cafes are the hearts and souls of their communities. Such small cafes have been the center of the city's vital bohemian scene since the turn of the 20th century; they have enticed some of the world's most interesting artists and writers to not only visit, but also stay.

Navigating the Coffee Trail

In many of San Francisco's neighborhoods, there are at least two cafes per block—parts of the Mission District and the Haight average twice that many. North Beach has been a bohemian stronghold for more than a century, known best for the Beat movement that originated there in the '50s, when Jack Kerouac and Allen Ginsberg were regulars at **Caffe Trieste** and **Enrico's Sidewalk Cafe.** One of the last remaining originators of the Beat movement, Lawrence Ferlinghetti still hangs around—and displays his paintings—at Enrico's and Caffe Puccini. There are more than 20 cafes in one six-block area alone—bordered by Union Street and Broadway on the north and south and Grant and Powell streets on the east and west. The coffee and pastries are very Italian, as is the opera music commonly heard on the jukeboxes, and the customers range from neighborhood residents having their afternoon coffee break to visitors from all over the world.

The **Mission District** cafe scene used to be totally funky, neighborhood oriented, and the command post of alternative lifestylers. Though the scene has become a tad less unorthodox, very few tourist types make it out to Valencia Street's coffeehouses. Locals, however, come from all over the city to take in the live music and spoken-word performances—and to congregate with young, anti-fashion fashion-setters. Most of the cafes (and bars) are concentrated in the area bordered by 16th and 24th streets on the north and south and by Mission and Valencia streets on the east and west.

The **Haight** is still a hippie haven of sorts, but the postpunk species is better suited than its flower-child predecessors to hours of angst-ridden malingering at local coffee joints. The neighborhood isn't all nose rings, purple hair, and Jerry Garcia murals, though. You'll find cafes for every taste, from tranquil pastry shops to ultra-hip hangouts vibrating from the blare of loud music and the jolt of caffeine. Walk along Haight Street from Central to Stanyan streets, and don't neglect to venture a block or two up or down the side streets.

Other cafes I mention are in three areas where you'd expect to find the city's cafe culture well represented: **Hayes Valley,** a small, sunny neighborhood perfect for strolling because it comprises only a few blocks along Hayes Street (between Franklin and Buchanan sts.) with an occasional side-street detour; **South of Market** (SoMa), an industrial neighborhood where artists, architects, multimedia gurus, filmmakers, and musicians live and work in warehouse lofts (below Market St., between Second and Tenth sts.); and the **Castro** district, San Francisco's famous gay mecca (mostly south of Market to about 20th St., between Castro and Sanchez sts.).

Finally, there are the refuges—cafes that provide escapes from neighborhoods that are often overrun by tourists or other consumption-crazed breeds. The ones mentioned in this chapter are located in the **Financial District** (Grant Ave. at Sutter St.) and the gentrified section of **Fillmore Street** (near Steiner St.).

The Lowdown

Grills in the mist... Long before there was California cuisine or nouvelle anything, mesquite-grilled seafood was the most popular item at **Tadich Grill,** where mesquite has been the charcoal of choice since the 1920s. This turn-of-the-20th-century Financial District landmark still entices the tourist trade and local traditionalists, but the surly waiters are no longer charming to diners who prefer to get their steaks before they're cold and their fries before they are soggy. As you'll learn if you go on any of the Dashiell Hammett walking tours, **John's Grill** is the place where Sam Spade ate his chops (actually rack of lamb) while in pursuit of the Maltese Falcon. A replica of the black bird, donated by Warner Brothers, sits in a display case outside John's small Hammett museum. Founded in 1908, this downtown dinner house has wood-paneled walls, period furnishings, and perfectly grilled, tender steaks.

South of Market's **Fly Trap Restaurant** has moved a few blocks away from its original 1898 address, where fly-paper was tacked to the tables to keep the horses' pesky companions off the steaks, but it still bases its menu on traditional San Francisco grill fare. The decor is conventional but not stuffy—small cloth-covered tables with cafe chairs and a variety of maps and architectural drawings on the walls—and its comfort-food specialties follow suit.

Fish and seafood are the mainstays of the **Hayes Street Grill** menu—which changes daily—and they may be sautéed or mesquite-grilled with a Mexican, American, French, Italian, or Asian accent, depending on which vegetables are freshest that day. Grilled Alaskan king salmon and pan-fried Hama-Hama oysters are favorites. Some purists bemoan the loss of the older, funkier decor—creaky floors and cafe chairs—to the carpeting and chic little banquettes of the improved Hayes Street Grill, but the food is just as good as ever.

For committed carnivores... The best pure-and-simple steakhouse in town is definitely **Harris',** midway between Russian Hill and Pacific Heights on Van Ness Avenue, where luscious cuts of Midwestern corn-fed beef are dry-aged on the premises, killer martinis flow by the barrel, and the gigantic booths can swallow you whole. Everybody who's anybody carves flesh here; Robin Williams has been known to have steaks sent to him by taxi when he couldn't make it to the restaurant in person. For more exotic flesh feasts, try the Texas antelope, Wyoming Buffalo, or locally raised ostrich. **Izzy's Steaks and Chops** is also a meat-eater's dream, but its true glory is its status as a lively Marina watering hole. The steaks, though tender and delicious, may not be quite as luxurious as those at Harris', but they cost a lot less.

Seafood supremo... Many tourists leave San Francisco without discovering that there's more to its seafood restaurants than the fish joints around Fisherman's Wharf. Don't make the same mistake. One of the city's finest seafood restaurants is the elegant, understated **Aqua** in the Financial District. The decor is sleek and simple, adorned only by lush exotic-flower arrangements. The ahi tartare—my favorite all-time rendition, period—is mixed tableside with pears, pine nuts, quail egg, and spices. Glazed Chilean sea bass with mushrooms, scallops, shiso tortellini, and miso broth is heavenly, while the sculptural grilled medallions of ahi tuna with foie gras in Pinot sauce is beyond decadent.

Pizza perfection... I agree that there's no such thing as bad pizza, but there's nothing like diving into really good pizza, and here's three of my favorites. When the bars are hopping in North Beach you'll always find a crowd of inebriated sots savoring steamy slices of wondrously gooey pizza at **Golden Boy Pizza.** The big, doughy squares of Italian-style pizzas, each enticingly placed in the front windows (the aroma alone is deadly), attract both locals and tourists who are looking to fill up on one of the cheapest and cheesiest meals in town. Way on the other side of town on a dreary strip of busy Divisadero Street is **Little Star Pizza,** a bohemian speakeasy with dark-colored walls, low ceilings, and jukebox, and an oven that cranks out the best deep-dish cornmeal-crust pizza in town. These babies take about 20 minutes to bake, which is a great excuse to order chicken wings and a glass of wine for the wait. If the yuppie in you is feeling up, head to the Marina to **A16.** This sleek and lively spot features Neapolitan-style pizza from the region of Campania. Its secret weapon is chef Christophe Hille, who whips up outstanding appetizers, pizza, and entrees that are so good, A16 has quickly become one of San Francisco's best and busiest restaurants.

Affordable Euro-chic eats... Lord know I don't get paid enough to eat at those fancy French restaurants all the time, but I can still take my taste buds on a European vacation with a trip to **Ti Couz** (say "Tee Cooz"). It's one of the most architecturally stylish and popular restaurants in the Mission, and the delicate, paper-thin crepes—made with more than 30 choices of fillings such as smoked salmon, mushrooms, sausage, ham, scallops, and onions—are hefty enough to be an inexpensive meal-in-one. Another favorite is **Chez Nous,** a bright, cheery, small, and bustling restaurant on Fillmore serving delicious and affordable French tapas. Most of its Mediterranean dishes taste so clean and fresh you can't wait to come back and dine here again. Start with the soup, whatever it is; don't skip tasty french fries with *harissa* (Tunisian hot sauce) aioli; savor the lamb chops with lavender sea salt; and save room for their famed dessert, the minicustard-cakelike canneles de Bordeaux. If you like french fries (and who doesn't?), you'll love **Frjtz Fries.** This funky-artsy "Belgian fries, crepes, and DJ/Art teahouse" in Hayes Valley features killer, fat french fries with a barrage of exotic dipping sauces as well as fine sandwiches and salads. Grab a bag of the addictively crisp and thick fried potatoes—perhaps with chipotle rémoulade or balsamic mayo—and wash it down with Belgian ale.

See-and-be-scenes... Where you go to be seen depends largely on whom you hope to see—and how long it takes the trendies to get bored with the place. For years, Jeremiah Tower's Stars (near Civic Center) was the easiest place for commoners to rub shoulders with celebrities. But the place went belly-up, and namedroppers had to move on. One of the new prime spots is **MoMo's** (across from the Giants' ballpark), where the bar is jammed with hard-drinking Multimedia Gulch types and the crowded patio is known for celebrity sightings. It's also known for the terrific heaters that keep it warm and comfy even on the foggiest days. The food is mercifully unfussy, the martinis are legendary, and if you can't get a table (reservations are strongly recommended), you can eat at the bar. **Moose's** (North Beach) is a good place to go to stare at fashion models and young Republicans. The best people-watching is on crowded weekend nights, when the long wait for a table leaves people milling around in the foyer near the bar. **Enrico's Sidewalk Cafe** in North Beach has always been a great place to people-watch, and nightly jazz makes it even more fun. You can have a full dinner or just stop in for a drink (try the lip-puckering mojito).

DINING

The "Valencia corridor"... Depending on who you talk to, the recent infusion of upscale restaurants on Valencia Street is either the best thing that has happened to the food scene in years or one more nail in the gentrification coffin that is burying San Francisco's funky neighborhood culture alive. Either way, the area's newest sleek, chic eateries are a wet dream for interior designers and food critics alike. Take BART or a cab to 16th Street and walk up Valencia to 24th, pop into alleys and side streets, and stop wherever the notion strikes you. It's tough to go wrong in this eight-block stretch, from an authentic Spanish-Basque tapas feast at **Ramblas Tapas Bar** to an antidotal bite of Japanese fast-food at **We Be Sushi.** Ramblas is just one stop on the neighborhood's fantastic tapas tour (see "Tantalizing tapas," below), but it was voted best in the Bay Area by the *Bay Guardian.* For the record, the building that houses Ramblas is a perfect example of the gentrification of the Mission District—it was formerly an appliance repair shop. **Firecracker** is still a hot spot for northern Chinese cuisine (see "Some like it hot," later in the chapter).

Tantalizing tapas... Cities everywhere have gone a bit mad for those little Spanish tidbits that are more than an appetizer but less than a main dish. They're so *ne plus* trendy in San Francisco that every chef in town has some little signature tidbit on the menu. It's just a matter of time before they offer a tasting menu at Taco Bell. Until that happens, I'm sticking with my tried-and-true favorites such as **Bocadillos,** a trendy yet casual Financial District space that's the latest addition from Fringale chef and owner Gerald Hirigoyen. The Spanish-influenced small plates here are flat-out fabulous. Hirigoyen celebrates his Basque roots with outstanding calamari, caramelized quail, and decadent foie gras sushi rolls. **Ramblas Tapas Bar** in the Mission still serves some of the best Basque tapas in town. It's a good thing, as Martha Stewart would say, because the guy who opened it also owns the Thirsty Bear, a microbrewery with great beer but decidedly mediocre tapas and truly regrettable service. The service is iffy at Ramblas, but nobody cares because the food is so good. Try the house-cured salmon, *patatas bravas* (a tapas dish made with potatoes and tomatoes), and spinach Catalan, and wash it down with some microbrew or sangria. (Hint: If you feel like lingering a bit after dinner, avoid paying your bill until you're definitely ready to leave. Otherwise you'll risk getting the evil eye from your waiter and all the hungry diners waiting in line.)

Just around the corner, **Esperpento,** a boisterous little spot decorated like somebody's surrealistic dream about a childhood piñata party, is always packed—for good reason. It wins the purist award for the most authentic Spanish tapas in town. And the paella—a steaming mountain of shellfish, pork, chicken, and saffron-flavored rice—is to die for. Order it with a variety of tapas and share it family-style. The noisy Caribbean-psychedelic-voodoo-queen atmosphere at **Cha Cha Cha** makes it the perennial favorite among tapas lovers who can't decide what they like more: the fiery food or the endless supply of potent sangria that flows from the bar. Fortunately for them, the place is so crowded they often have to sit at the bar for an hour or more before a table is avail-

> ### The Sun on Your Face at Belden Place
>
> *San Francisco has always been woefully lacking in the alfresco dining department. One exception is Belden Place, an adorable little brick alley in the heart of the Financial District that is open only to foot traffic (see map on p. 77). When the weather is agreeable, the restaurants that line the alley break out the big umbrellas, tables, and chairs, and voilà—a bit of Paris just off Pine Street. A handful of Euro-style cafes line Belden Place and offer a variety of cuisine. There's* **Cafe Bastille,** *22 Belden Place (Tel 415/986-5673), a classic French bistro and fun speakeasy basement serving excellent crepes, mussels, and French onion soup; it schedules live jazz on weekends.* **Cafe Tiramisu,** *28 Belden Place (Tel 415/421-7044), is a stylish Italian hot spot serving addictive risottos and gnocchi.* **Plouf,** *40 Belden Place (Tel 415/986-6491), specializes in big bowls of mussels slathered in a choice of seven sauces, as well as fresh seafood.* **B44,** *44 Belden Place (Tel 415/986-6287), serves up a side order of Spain alongside its revered paella and other seriously zesty Spanish dishes.*

able. Why not just eat at the bar? You'll save your taste buds, plus the bartenders are a major hoot.

No, man, it's an island... Been there and done that in every San Francisco dining room? Then it's time for **Forbes Island,** a wonderfully ridiculous floating restaurant disguised as an island (complete with lighthouse and real 40-ft. palm trees) and unknown to even most locals. The idea's kitschy, but the execution's actually wonderful. Here's how it works: Arrive at the dock next to PIER 39, call the restaurant via the courtesy phone, climb aboard their pontoon boat that takes you on a 2-minute journey to the "island" located 75 feet from the city's famed sea lions, and climb into the island's bowels to find a surprisingly classy, Tudor-like wood-paneled dining room. Warmed by a fireplace with fish swimming past the portholes (yes, the dining room is a wee bit under water), guests dine on surprisingly well-prepared classic French food such as a decadent ragout of wild mushrooms with toasted brioche and soft goat cheese, and roasted half rack of lamb with herb brioche crust and tomato lamb jus. But be warned: The menu is very limited, the wine list features your basic big-name producers without listing the vintage, it's impossible to get away from spending lots of money, and the "island" does gently rock (landlubbers need not apply). That said, anyone looking for something completely different will revel in this fantastic and completely unique find. One annoyance: a mandatory $3 shuttle fee since the only other way to get there is to swim.

Hold the hype... No matter how endlessly food critics lavish praise on the super-restaurants, there are some sacred cows, like Berkeley's **Chez Panisse,** that aren't always

●●

Aw, Shuckit!

Offering nearly a century of faithful service to Bay Area chowderheads, the ***Swan Oyster Depot*** *is classic San Francisco, a unique dining experience you shouldn't miss. Opened in 1912, this tiny hole-in-the-wall run by the city's friendliest servers is little more than a narrow fish market that decided to slap down some bar stools. There are only 20 or so seats, jammed cheek-by-jowl along a long marble bar. Most patrons come for a cup of chowder or a plate of oysters on the half shell that arrive chilling on crushed ice. The menu is limited to fresh crab, shrimp, oyster, clam cocktails, Maine lobster, and Boston-style clam chowder, all of which are exceedingly fresh. It's not much of a bargain for such a fast and light meal, but the experience is priceless. Note: Don't let the lunchtime line dissuade you—it moves fast. It's open Monday to Saturday from 8am to 5:30pm and is located at 1517 Polk St., between California and Sacramento streets (Tel 415/673-1101). See map on p. 47. Reservations aren't accepted, and they don't take credit cards.*

●●

worth the money and effort. To give credit where it's due, Chez Panisse has been the most important restaurant in the Bay Area's culinary development in the past two decades, and chef/owner Alice Waters was honored as the 1997 Humanitarian of the Year by the James Beard Foundation. But sometimes students surpass their teachers, and these days there are plenty of other restaurants with more innovative chefs and less expensive tabs. The fact that you have to reserve a month in advance for a weekend dinner may be a testament to the restaurant's reputation, but it's also a pain in the neck, especially when you don't know if you'll be in the mood for the set menu when the day finally arrives.

DINING

Some like it hot... San Francisco's hottest addition to the four-alarm category is **Firecracker,** a stylish Chinese restaurant that's right at home with its fiery hot Latin neighbors in the Mission District. Chef Phil Lee denies the California-fusion label that is often applied to his low-oil, low-sugar cooking: His cuisine is actually true to traditional Beijing cookery, in which the scarcity of oil was compensated by lots of garlic and spice. Firecracker's environment is also contemporary, yet faithful, to Chinese history, with old photographs on the walls and Chinese opera music mixed in with modern jazz.

For authentic Thai food that's unbelievably delicious, and not watered down for uninitiated Western tongues, the Upper Haight's **Thep Phanom** can't be beat. The Thai waitstaff, whose traditional garb suits the gracious, antiques-laden dining room, usually tries to warn you when a dish is hot. Believe them. The super-hot delicacies include *larb ped* (duck salad with mint, hot chili peppers, red onion, and lemon); even the milder dishes, such as charbroiled catfish or deep-fried quail, are served with a variety of hot dipping sauces. For cooler options, try any of the mild curries, especially those made with coconut milk.

Cha Cha Cha is still a Haight hot spot and now has a second location in the Mission District. It's an exhaustingly popular place, especially if you indulge in the house sangria in the funky bar area during your inevitable wait for a table. (You may find yourself in line behind regulars like Chris Isaak.) And the Cajun/Caribbean food (mostly tapas) is absolutely fiery. That's saying something in San Francisco, where Mexican food has numbed most locals to anything cooler than a jalapeño.

Pass the dumplings, darling... The other little morsels that make parking tickets bearable are served from dim sum carts—tender shrimp wrapped in paper-thin dumplings, tiny crab cakes, octopus with hot peppers, and dozens of other Chinese delicacies. For exceptionally delicate dumplings, **Yank Sing** has long been a local favorite on the weekends, but nearby **Harbor Village** is a more serene and majestic alternative at lunchtime (11am–2:30pm). You won't find any unidentified steamed objects on their carts; instead you'll find dozens of authentic delicacies served by a meticulous waitstaff. Every porcelain dish and carved chopstick reflects the Imperial aesthetic Harbor Village claims to have brought from Hong Kong, and the dim sum tradition allows you to enjoy all its refinement without the high tab of its exquisite dinners.

Best Chinese in Chinatown... Most locals know that the best Chinese food in the city isn't in Chinatown. That said, **R & G Lounge** serves probably the best food in China-town. The dining room used to be in the basement of a commercial building, but a brighter upstairs room has opened to accommodate the burgeoning clientele drawn primarily by super-fresh seafood. If you think Maine has a corner on the lobster market, try a live one from R & G's tank. One huge plus is that the waiters will gladly translate the Chinese menu for Westerners, which expands the choices considerably.

Ultra-chic Chinoise... You usually don't think of donning a dinner jacket to chow down on Chinese food, but it's not a bad idea at **Tommy Toy's,** where elaborate meals are served by an army of tuxedoed waiters who will pick up your nap-kin before you realize you've dropped it. Unquestionably the most elegant Chinese restaurant in San Francisco, it's the top choice for local and visiting celebrities, as the entryway gallery of Clint Eastwood memorabilia will attest. Whole bright-red lobsters, trimmed and served tableside, are the house specialty.

South of the border in the Mission... The Mission District is crammed with Central and South American food that often outdoes native versions, thanks to the fresh ingredients that abound in San Francisco. Even the most ordinary taqueria beats a fast-food lunch by a mile. Start with my suggestions, then graze your way through the neighborhood. **Los Jarritos** makes wonderful fresh tortillas and other home-cooked Mexican standards for a loyal following, many of whom travel across the city—and sometimes the bridges—for its food and friendly ambience. Call in advance to find out when they'll be serving *posole* (a spicy chicken-and-pork stew that takes all day to prepare and is rarely available outside of home kitchens). If you want to get in a good mood fast, go to **La Rondalla.** It serves standard Mexican fare such as enchiladas, *chiles rellenos* (stuffed chili peppers baked in egg batter), and other dishes, but there's nothing standard about the atmosphere, from the year-round Christmas ornaments to the strolling mariachis who serenade on weekends. **La Taqueria** is an immaculate neighborhood favorite famous for its *carnitas* (shredded pork), which fill soft, fluffy tortillas to make the perfect taco.

Modest **El Nuevo Frutilandia** is one of the few places in the city to get home-cooked Puerto Rican and Cuban food (the fresh fruit shakes are wonderful, as are the Puerto Rican dumplings made of crushed plantain and yuca, filled with shredded pork). The odds of running into a horde of tourists here are slim. Next door you can get one of the best dinner deals in town at **El Trebol,** a Formica-table kind of place that serves Salvadoran/Nicaraguan treats like *pupusas* (handmade corn patties stuffed with cheese or meat or both) for less than a dollar and full meals (including rice and beans) for less than $4.

Talented transvestites in tights... Another only-in-SF dining experience—gourmet Asian cuisine served by sexy she-males—is an evening at **asia sf.** Part restaurant, part gender illusionist musical review, asia sf always manages to be an entertaining experience and highly recommended no matter how square you are. The centerpiece of the restaurant is the Chinese-red runway that provides a platform for the evening's entertainment. A cadre of transvestites—mostly Asian men dressed very convincingly as women—lip-sync show tunes on the runway in between serving guests surprisingly good Cal-Asian cuisine. You'll enjoy the food as well: grilled shrimp and herb salad; baby back pork ribs with honey tamarind glaze, pickled carrots, and sweet potato crisps; filet mignon with Korean dipping sauce, miso eggplant, and fried potato stars. The full bar, *Wine Spectator* award-winning wine list, and sake list only add to the festivities. Fortunately, the food and the atmosphere are as colorful as the staff, which means a night here is more than a meal—it's a very happening event.

Seoul food... At do-it-yourself Korean barbecue joints, the food is as much fun to cook as it is to eat. You barbecue marinated beef and pork on grills built into the tables, wrap the meat in a lettuce leaf and add whatever condiments you like—kind of a Korean burrito. **Brothers Restaurant,** one of many popular Korean eateries along Geary Boulevard (Richmond District), caters to a primarily Korean clientele—it's probably the most popular Geary Boulevard place with local Koreans, and the staff sometimes proves its own authenticity when you're making reservations in English. You can grill meats at your table's wood-fired hibachi or sample from the rest of the small menu. Brothers' *kim chee* (spicy pickled cabbage) is outstanding. The Taiwanese hot pot food at nearby **Coriya Hot Pot City** (Clement St.) has been described as a cross between Japanese shabu-shabu and Korean barbecue. Each table has a hot pot and a grill, so you can steam or sauté beef, pork, chicken, seafood, and vegetables to your heart's content. Again, you're the chef. The place is loud, crowded, festive, and does not serve parties of one.

Asian adventures... One of the first destinations on your San Francisco ethnic-food adventure tour should be **Angkor Borei,** the perfect place to sample Cambodia's intricate cuisine at the modest price tag locals have come to expect in the Mission District. The combination of spices in most any dish on the menu is intriguing—typically, sweet basil and tangy lemongrass are first to hit the tongue, then a short blast of hot chili pepper bursts through, and finally, soothing coconut milk brings the whole blend together.

Geary Boulevard's tropical, romantic **Straits Cafe** features extraordinary food from Singapore—an exotic hybrid of European, Indian, Chinese, and Malaysian tastes that mixes spicy-hot peanut sauces with cool cucumbers and coconut-milk curries. Chef Chris Yeo uses all these flavors and textures to create extraordinary dishes like *laksa* (tamarind-scented broth with fish, chili peppers, onions, and rice noodles) and satays.

Thanh Long is a San Francisco secret, an out-of-the-way Sunset District Vietnamese standout known for excellent roasted crab and addictive garlic noodles. Since the owners, the An family, have become rather famous for their aforementioned signature dishes now that they're served in sister restaurants Crustacean in LA, Vegas, and SF, suffice it to say the crab's out of the bag. But this location is still far enough on the outskirts of the city to keep it from becoming too overcrowded.

Although it's only a few blocks off Union Square, the walk to **Pho Hóa** Vietnamese restaurant in the downtrodden Tenderloin District is quite an adventure, often characterized by crack-smoking loiterers (literally) and plenty of people down on their luck. Thing is, the folks along the way are usually friendly enough and the arrival promises huge, killer bowls of Vietnamese soup with all the classic fixings (basil, bean sprouts, and so on) at absurdly low prices. For a cheap, hearty, but light meal, this is my favorite downtown option, and could be yours, too. In the same area is the **Saigon Sandwich Shop,** a Civic Center takeout deli with incredible Vietnamese sandwiches— baguettes full of pork or chicken with spicy sauces, cilantro, and peppers, or the popular Vietnamese-style meatball sandwiches—both for around $3.

If you haven't tried Burmese cuisine yet, consider a trip to **Burma Superstar.** This basic dining room garners true superstar status by offering exceptional Burmese food at rock-bottom prices. Unfortunately, the allure of the tealeaf salad, clay-pot chicken curry, and sweet-tangy sesame beef is one of the city's worst-kept secrets. Add to that a no-reservations policy and you can count on waiting in line for up to an hour.

Japanese jewels... There are more than 75 sushi bars in San Francisco, but for a variety of Japanese country-style food—fluffy tempura, savory noodles, and dumplings—go to **Sanppo** in the heart of Japantown, a favorite of local Japanese, where you may be asked to share a table when the regular crowd elbows in. Sanppo's rustic, homelike decor is instantly cozy. The tempura is excellent, and the *gyoza nabe* (pot stickers in a savory broth with noodles and bean curd) is a wonderful meal in itself. For the freshest sushi in town,

Amazing Grazing

There's no better way to enjoy breakfast on a sunny San Francisco morning than strolling the Ferry Plaza Farmers Market and snacking your way through breakfast on some of America's finest organic produce. While poking among the 100 stalls crammed with northern California fruit, vegetable, bread, shellfish, and dairy items, you're bound to bump elbows with the dozens of Bay Area chefs (such as Alice Waters) who do their shopping here. The enthusiastic vendors are always willing to educate visitors about the benefits of organic produce, and often provide free samples. But wait, there's more: On Saturdays the market operates a Shop with the Chef program in which a guest restaurant chef browses the market for ingredients, and then conducts a free cooking class at 10:30am (with free samples, of course). Several local restaurants, such as North Beach's Rose Pistola, also have food stalls promoting their organic cuisine, so skip breakfast before you come. You can also pick up locally made vinegars and oils, which make wonderful gifts. The Farmers Market takes place year-round, rain or shine, every Saturday and Sunday from 8am to 2pm, Tuesdays from 10am to 2pm, and Thursdays from 3 to 7pm at the Ferry Building, on the Embarcadero at the foot of Market Street (about a 15-minute walk from Fisherman's Wharf). Call or visit their website for more information (Tel 415/353-5650; www.ferry plazafarmersmarket.com).

call in advance to **Hama-Ko,** a gracious little Cole Valley restaurant, and ask chef Ted Kashiyama to prepare his special deluxe meal of hot and cold dishes; the exact contents depend on what local fishermen have available that morning. There are two **We Be Sushi** locations within a few blocks of each other on Valencia Street (16th and 22nd sts.). They're both usually crowded at night with locals who know the sushi is both good and cheap—$10 to $15 for an ample dinner.

If you're really on a tight budget, consider **Nippon Sushi.** The lack of exterior signage inspired the locals to call this small, plain sushi restaurant "No Name." But even with its intentionally low profile, for over 10 years the tiny room has had a line out the door. What's the big deal? Since its beginnings it's been one of the cheapest sushi houses in town. How cheap? Try a vegetable roll for $2.05, a California roll for $3.60, or a melt-in-your-mouth tekka maki for $3.40. It ain't the best in town by far, but for the price, you can't beat it.

Total dives you can't resist... Anyone can enjoy an expensive meal at a fancy restaurant. The real talent is discovering a total dive of a restaurant that rocks. Two of my favorites are **Tommy's Joynt** and **Tú Lan.** With its colorful mural exterior, it's hard to miss Tommy's Joynt, a half-century-old haven for cholesterol-be-damned hold-outs and a late-night favorite for those in search of a cheap and hearty meal. The restaurant's exterior is tame in comparison to the interior, which looks like a Buffalo Bill museum that imploded: a wild collage of stuffed birds, a mounted buffalo head, an ancient piano, rusty firearms, fading prints, a beer-guzzling lion, and Santa Claus masks. The hofbrau-style buffet offers a cornucopia of rib-clinging a la carte dishes such as their signature buffalo stew (the meat from a buffalo ranch in Wyoming), which resides under heat lamps among the stainless steel trays of turkeys, hams, sloppy joes, oxtails, corned beef, meatballs, mashed potatoes, and other classics. There's also a slew of seating on two levels, almost 100 varieties of beer, and a most interesting clientele of almost exclusively 50-some-thing pre-cardiac-arrest males. It's all good stuff in a 'mer-ican kind of way, the kind of place you take grandpappy when he's in town just to show him that San Francisco's not entirely prissy.

Even more of a dive is Tú Lan. You'll have to brave the winos, weirdos, and street stench to get to this greasy Vietnamese diner bordering Union Square and SoMa, but the reward for such bravery is a chance to feast on out-of-this-world imperial rolls. Even Julia Child (whose face graced the greasy old menus) was once spotted pulling up a chair at this down-and-dirty shack of a restaurant, dining on—what else?—imperial rolls on a bed of rice noodles, lettuce, peanuts, and mint (around $5), as well as other regional dishes served from the grease-stained grill. You'll feel brave just eating here, and don't even think about using the bathroom. *Bon appetit.*

The French connection... **Fleur de Lys** is San Francisco's true gem among classic French restaurants. Chef/owner Hubert Keller—who was the first guest chef in White House history when he cooked for President Clinton—was named best chef in California by the James Beard Founda-tion (1997). It's tough to find anything critical to say about this romantic, elegant Union Square restaurant, where the regularly changing menu is full of dishes like boneless quail stuffed with Swiss chard and pine nuts, enhanced with foie gras and a rich Merlot sauce. This is the very best of French dining—without the snotty waiters. Three bits of advice: Reserve well in advance, try the "Symphony of Fleur de Lys Appetizers," and don't be surprised if a dinner for two costs as much as your plane ticket.

And if you really want to go out of your way for great food, take a 90-minute trip from the city to **French Laundry,** up in Yountville, a wine-country village. You'll have to reserve months in advance, but it's worth the drive, the wait, and the money. Fleur de Lys's Hubert Keller was named best chef in California, but French Laundry's Thomas Keller snagged the title of best chef in the country that same year and has been the center of rave reviews all over the nation ever since. An enthusiastic California chef, Keller grows at least half of what he cooks in three gardens on the premises of this tiny three-star restaurant that has the feel of a private country home. He oversees every bite that ends up on a diner's plate.

You'll find far less expensive French food in more modest bistros such as **Fringale** (South of Market). Fringale's menu reflects the chef's Basque origins and his classic training; the place is reasonably priced and so friendly and comfortable that you never feel self-conscious, despite the studied indifference of much of the too-hip-for-words clientele. The frisée salad with warm bacon dressing and croutons is exquisite—soft but not soggy—and the pork tenderloin with onion and apple marmalade is rich and velvety without being overly sweet. If you want to feel as though you're in Paris, stop in at a Financial District treasure, **Cafe Claude,** where every fixture, chair, dish, and spoon have been imported from France. It's jammed with a lively, youngish crowd who come to enjoy both the atmosphere and the inexpensive but oh-so-French sandwiches along with a glass or two of Rhine, Beaujolais, or Mâcon Blanc wine.

Super supper clubs... You don't have to line up and wait an hour just to get in the door of a supper club anymore, but the best ones are still extremely popular, and new ones that hope to last longer than a Kleenex have to be both good restaurants and good nightclubs at the same time. The atmosphere at **Mecca** is a perfect fit for its Upper

● ●
TENT SHOW

*Hungry for dinner and a good show? It ain't cheap, but **Teatro ZinZanni** is a rollicking ride of food, whimsy, drama, and song within a stunningly elegant 1926 tent on the Embarcadero. Part musical theater and part comedy show, the 3¹/₂-hour dinner theater includes a surprisingly good five-course meal served by dozens of performers who weave the audience and astounding physical acts (think Cirque du Soleil) into their wacky and playful world. Anyone in need of a night of laughs should definitely book a table here. Shows are held Wednesday through Sunday and tickets are $110 to $135 including dinner. The tent is located at Pier 29 on the Embarcadero at Battery Street. Call or log on to their website for more details (Tel 415/438-2668; www.teatrozinzanni.org).*

● ●

DINING

Market address. The circular bar is the centerpiece of the restaurant, which features gender-illusionist cabaret shows and an eclectic mix of live music ranging from soul to classic jazz. But forget about the great atmosphere—the food alone is reason enough to make a pilgrimage to Mecca. Chef Stephen Barber mixes Creole and Asian influences with California cuisine, and the result is unforgettable. Try the fresh stone crab legs with spicy rémoulade for an appetizer and follow it up with rock shrimp pad Thai rice noodles (tons of shrimp, peanuts, carrots, asparagus, and cilantro) or a grilled pork chop with apple and date chutney. And save room for the unbelievably delicious desserts. Union Square's **Biscuits and Blues** isn't quite as funky as it sounds, though it definitely takes pride in presenting down-home Southern-style cooking. Some of the best blues acts in the country keep the crowds coming, however (see the Nightlife chapter).

Vegging out... The Mother of All Vegetarian Restaurants once was **Greens,** where there's up to a 2-week waiting list to sample the fare that has spawned several cookbooks, international acclaim, and a devoted following. This is no hippie-veggie-health-food cafe; it is meatless haute cuisine, combining the best of French, Mediterranean, and California cookery. Unfortunately, the service has become inconsistent, and the menu has lost its edge. Still, it retains its status as a classic and is worth a visit for breakfasts and romantic late-night desserts—the dining room's view of the marina and the bay is stunning. For a spectacular vegan meal, you're better off at **Millennium.** Even carnivores have given rave reviews to this hip, beautiful Union Square restaurant. Chef Eric Tucker, a lifelong vegan, is a daredevil in the kitchen, concocting exotic entrees and outlandish, architectural-looking, scrumptious desserts. The staff is knowledgeable but never stuffy.

A feast from the Middle East... An evening dining at **Kan Zaman** is one of those quintessential Haight-Ashbury experiences that you can't wait to tell your friends about back home. As you pass through glass-beaded curtains, the hostess leads you to knee-high tables under a billowed canopy tent. Shoes removed, you sit cross-legged with your friends in cushioned comfort. The most adventurous of your group requests an *argeeleh*, a large hookah pipe filled with fruity honey or apricot tobacco. Reluctantly at first, everyone simultaneously sips the sweet smoke from the cobralike tendrils emanating from the hookah. Then dinner arrives—inexpensive platters offering a variety of classic Middle Eastern cuisine: smoky baba ghanouj, *kibbee* (cracked wheat with spiced lamb) meat pies, Casablanca beef couscous, spicy hummus with pita bread, succulent lamb and chicken kabobs. The spiced wine is starting to take effect, just in time for the beautiful, sensuous belly dancers who glide across the dining room, mesmerizing the rapt audience with their seemingly impossible gyrations. The evening ends, the bill arrives: $17 each. Perfect.

If Kan Zaman isn't exotic enough for you, head deep into the Avenues for a taste of Morocco at **Aziza.** Chef-owner Mourad Lahlou creates an excellent dining experience through colorful and distinctly Moroccan surroundings and his modern but still authentic take on the food of his homeland. In any of the three opulently adorned dining rooms you can indulge in the very affordable five-course tasting menu ($39) or individual treats such as kumquat-enriched lamb shank, saffron Cornish hen with preserved lemon and olives, or lavender honey-braised squab.

North Beach classics... Columbus Avenue's main strip (between Broadway and Washington Sq.) is loaded with calzone joints and trattorias, and one of the classics in San Francisco's "little Italy" is **Rose Pistola.** It continues to attract the rich and famous as well as the hungry. Superstar guests range from Kirk Hammett (Metallica) to Francis Ford Coppola. The sleek decor might have been out of place in the midst of North Beach's unpretentious little cafes, but owner Reed Hearon (who previously turned a South of Market warehouse into the loud and trendy Restaurant Lulu) has managed to keep the place warm and inviting with a friendly bar and sidewalk tables for people-watching. The menu runs from snacks to full meals, so you can stop for a minute or stay for as long as you want. Try the *cioppino*, a classic fish soup that was originally brought by Italian immigrants to San Francisco, where local Dungeness crab became the central ingredient.

Another North Beach classic is **Capp's Corner**. Capp's is a place of givens: It's a given that some high-spirited regulars are hunched over the bar, that Sinatra's on the jukebox, and that you'll be served huge portions of Italian fare at low prices in a raucous atmosphere that prevails until closing. The overworked waitresses are usually brusque and bossy, but always with a wink. Long tables are set up for family-style dining: bread, soup, salad, choice of around 20 classic main dishes (herb-roasted leg of lamb, spaghetti with meatballs, osso buco with polenta, fettuccine with prawns and white-wine sauce), and dessert—all for $15 to $17 or so per person. You might have to wait a while for a table, but if you want fun and authentic old school dining without pomp or steep prices you'll agree that Capp's is well worth the wait.

The rest of the world... You'd be missing out on three of San Francisco's most fun—and unusual—dining experiences if you bypassed **Suppenküche** or **Helmand**. Fans of German food may find Suppenküche one of the only places in town to satisfy their appetite. A small, spirited Hayes Valley beer hall and cafe, it serves delicious German food and drink to a good-humored, youngish crowd. The staples, served at plain wood tables, are variations of sauerkraut and sausage—flanked by baskets full of fresh-baked breads or mounds of buttery Bavarian-style mashed potatoes—supplemented by the more refined choices on the daily special chalkboard. The Helmand River flows out of Iran through Afghanistan; the formal dinner house Helmand rests on the shores of Broadway, which flows from

North Beach to Pacific Heights. The Afghani food here is exquisite, with flavors from Central Asia, India, and the Middle East, and owner Mahmood Karzai has done Westerners the favor of removing much of the fat from the traditional recipes. I recommend *aushak,* a delicate, triangular-shaped wheat dumpling filled with leek and served in a yogurt-mint or beef sauce reminiscent of the Far East, and *chowpan seekh,* a grilled rack of lamb on Iranian-style flatbread; or try *kaddo borawni,* an appetizer of baked pumpkin with garlic-yogurt sauce.

Kid pleasers... Dining with the family can be tricky business, especially if your children vary in age, but you're always safe in any of the neighborhood eateries in the Mission District, where there is usually at least one six-year-old running between tables while apologetic parents try to pull in the reins. **El Nuevo Frutilandia** (24th St.) is an especially good choice, because the fruit shakes will appeal to all ages, even if the Puerto Rican food is a bit too spicy for some younger palates. **La Rondalla** (Valencia St.) is fun for lunch or early dinner because of the goofy decorations and the traditional Mexican food, familiar to most kids—and not too fiery. (Later in the evening, the bar livens up and the atmosphere is less suitable for younger children.) If the kids do like hot-and-spicy treats, take them to **Coriya Hot Pot City** (Richmond District), where they can have a ball playing chef and cooking their own meat on the grills.

Where to seal a deal... This, of course, depends upon the client. The Old Boy network tends to be wary of fancy food and effusive waiters, which you'll never find at **Harris'** (Van Ness Ave.). Old-school attorneys love the **Fly Trap Restaurant,** the traditional San Francisco grill (with a few culinary updates) across from the courthouse. If your clients are food lovers who don't want to be bothered with trendy trappings, take them to my favorite small French bistro, **Fringale** (South of Market).

Cheap eats... The Mission District is jammed with great food at inexpensive prices, but the best buy of all is **El Trebol** (24th St.), where a full Salvadoran dinner including rice and beans comes in at around $4. You'll also find good food for next to nothing at **La Taqueria** (Mission St. near

24th St.), a family-oriented Mexican cafe, and **El Nuevo Frutilandia** (24th St.), where the fruit shakes are as popular as the Puerto Rican food. The best Vietnamese deli in the city is the **Saigon Sandwich Shop** (near Civic Center), where $3 buys a delectable pork or chicken sandwich with spicy sauce.

Eating with insomniacs... Every true San Francisco party hound knows where the late-night diners are in each district. Very handy for those 2am munchies in North Beach or Chinatown is **Sam Wo,** a total dive that's well known among hard-partying locals. The restaurant's two pocket-size dining rooms are on top of each other, on the second and third floors—take the stairs past the first-floor kitchen. You'll probably have to share a table, but this place is for mingling almost as much as for eating (the bossy waitresses are pure comedy). The house specialty is *jook,* known as congee in its native Hong Kong—a thick rice gruel flavored with fish, shrimp, chicken, beef, or pork; the best is Sampan, made with rice and seafood. Try sweet-and-sour pork rice, wonton soup with duck, or a roast-pork/rice-noodle roll. More traditional fried noodles and rice plates are available, too, but I always end up ordering the addictive tomato beef with noodles and house special chow mein. Another popular place to eat after the bars close is **Sparky's Diner,** a 24-hour Church Street diner that serves a decent burger and a hearty breakfast to Castro and Upper Market locals. The lights are a tad too bright and the waitstaff a bit too dim, but at least the breakfasts here avoid the white-bread toast and frozen-hash-brown-type food substance that seem to be standard issue at all-night coffee shops. It was good enough for Queen Latifah when she was in town.

The morning after... Four breakfast stops are mandatory when you visit San Francisco—Sear's and Dottie's near Union Square, Home Plate in the Marina District, and the Seal Rock Inn near the ocean. **Sear's Fine Foods** is best visited after 9am on weekday mornings, when the Financial District crowd has had time to get to work. Its coin-size Swedish pancakes are marvelous—thin and sweet like the best French crepes—and you get almost a million of them (well, 18) stacked high on your plate.

Dottie's True Blue Café is my favorite downtown diner, located on the edge of the seedy Tenderloin (all the drunks sleep until noon, so they won't hassle you). The staff is quite the eclectic bunch, and everyone is welcomed with a hearty hello and steaming mug of coffee. Dottie's serves superb American morning fare (big portions of French toast, pancakes, bacon and eggs, omelets, and the like, some of the best I've ever tasted) delivered to blue-and-white checkerboard tablecloths on rugged, diner-quality plates. Whatever you order arrives with delicious house-baked bread, muffins, or scones, as well as house-made jelly. Expect a long wait on warm weekend mornings, but persevere—Dottie's is that good.

Dollar for dollar, **Home Plate** just may be the best breakfast place in San Francisco. Many Marina residents kick off their hectic weekends by carbo-loading here on big piles of buttermilk pancakes and waffles smothered with fresh fruit, or hefty omelets stuffed with everything from applewood–smoked ham to spinach. You'll always start off with a plate of freshly baked scones, best eaten with a bit of butter and a dab of jam. Be sure to look over the daily specials scrawled on the little green chalkboard before you order. And as every fan of this tiny cafe knows, it's best to call ahead and ask to have your name put on the waiting list before you slide into Home Plate.

A family-owned coffee shop attached to a small inn, **Seal Rock Inn** is one of those breakfast places you can go to on a Saturday or Sunday morning and see who slept with whom the night before. The scenic location is unbeatable (2 blocks from the Pacific Ocean, near the Cliff House), the eggs Benedict and omelets are a local legend, and you can actually find a place to park on the street. There is also patio dining. If you don't have a night-before paramour, take your kids here and walk down afterward to the Musée Mécanique at the Cliff House.

Wake-up call... When you're up and at 'em at the crack of dawn and you need a serious caffeine jolt, only a select number of cafes are open before 8am and ready to pamper you with a perfectly frothy cappuccino or cafe au lait, airy croissants, and the morning paper to boot. If you're staying in a downtown hotel, try the Financial District's **Cafe de la Presse,** a subdued French-owned refuge that is also an international newsstand. In North Beach, **Caffe Greco, Caffe Trieste,** and **Stella Pastry Cafe** are early-morning favorites.

How about a little fresh air?... San Francisco's narrow sidewalks leave little room for outdoor seating, and some neighborhoods strictly enforce ordinances against al fresco impediments to pedestrian traffic. A typical sidewalk seat is a bench—sans tables—in front of the building. There are some notable exceptions, however. At the granddaddy of the city's sidewalk cafes, **Enrico's Sidewalk Cafe** (North Beach), huge awnings overhang a table-seating area that provides Broadway's best people-watching—you feel as though you have box seats at the opera. Then there's the elevated wooden deck outside the gay hangout **Cafe Flore** in the Castro. On a foggy day, it's like being in one of those pensive French movies. On a sunny day, it's like being on the French Riviera. But no matter what the weather, it's almost impossible to get

> ### Bayside Basking
> *If you're lucky enough to be in San Francisco on one of those rare hot days, then don't waste those fleeting sunny moments lunching inside. Call for directions and head to* **The Ramp,** *a favorite bayside hangout among in-the-know locals. The fare is of the basic pub grub variety—burgers, sandwiches, salads, and soups from $8 to $13—but the rustic boatyard environment and patio seating make this a relaxing place to dine in the sun. In summer, the place really rocks when live bands perform (4:30–7:30pm Fri–Sun April–Oct) and when tanned, cocktailing singles prowl the area. It's open for lunch Monday through Thursday from 11am to 3:30pm and Friday 11am to 4pm, and for brunch Saturday and Sunday from 8:30am to 4pm. The bar is open Monday through Friday from 11am to 8pm, Friday and Saturday from 8:30am to 8pm. From April to October, outdoor barbecue is offered Saturday and Sunday from 4 to 8pm; on nonbarbecue days, appetizers are featured daily from 5:30 to 8pm. Take bus 22 or 48, or just ask the cabbie to take you to The Ramp, 855 China Basin St., at the end of Mariposa Street (Tel 415/621-2378). See map on p. 47.*

a deck seat unless you're there at opening time (7am) or have the patience to wait for someone to leave—and can sprint to the open table faster than anyone else.

All-day hangouts... One of the unwritten rules of cafe life is that customers get to linger as long as they wish, even if all they buy is one cup of coffee. But certain places are more conducive than others to the all-day, write-in-your-journal type of pause. **Cafe La Bohème** (Mission District) is the ultimate spot to waste a day—dozens of unemployed poets, artists, and general layabouts have made a career of it. If you sit there long enough, you'll see—and maybe meet—people of all ages, ethnic backgrounds, professions, and talents. (You'll probably also be asked for spare change a dozen times.) The location of **South Park Cafe** makes it possible to hang out all day within arm's length of an espresso without having to stay inside the whole time. It's one of a Victorian necklace of stylish eateries that circles the oval lawn of South Park.

Live music... The North Beach institution **Enrico's Sidewalk Cafe** (also see the Nightlife chapter) presents live jazz 7 nights a week, ranging from Brazilian, bebop, and swing to Dixieland and jump 'n' jive. For opera buffs, North Beach's **Caffe Trieste** has live opera music on Sunday afternoons. Another cafe that occasionally presents live music is **Brainwash Cafe.**

Jack Kerouac woke up here... Legendary writers have scribbled all over North Beach. Jack Kerouac and Allen Ginsberg were regulars at **Caffe Trieste;** Richard Brautigan hawked homemade copies of his poems and stories there. Francis Ford Coppola drafted a screenplay at one of the tables at **Mario's Bohemian Cigar Store Cafe.** Lawrence Ferlinghetti is a regular at **Caffe Puccini,** where every seat is a window seat.

Hippie holdouts... One of the few true hippie cafes left over from the 1960s—it was a crash pad then—is **Sacred Grounds Cafe,** a Haight-Ashbury classic that will make you want to tie-dye your entire wardrobe. The atmosphere is gentle but not nostalgic. The Mission District's **Cafe La Bohème** welcomes virtually everybody, and always has its share of customers who look like extras from Woodstock.

Map 4: North Beach Dining

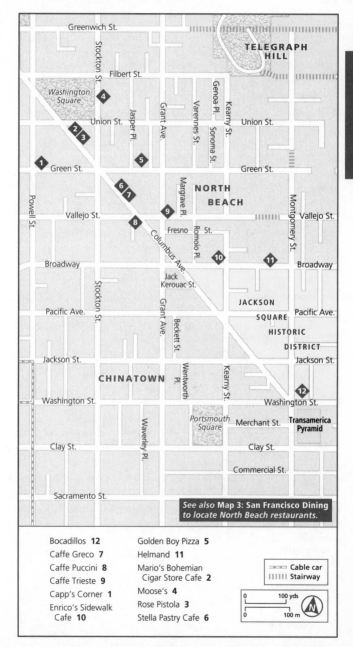

See also **Map 3: San Francisco Dining** *to locate North Beach restaurants.*

Bocadillos **12**
Caffe Greco **7**
Caffe Puccini **8**
Caffe Trieste **9**
Capp's Corner **1**
Enrico's Sidewalk Cafe **10**

Golden Boy Pizza **5**
Helmand **11**
Mario's Bohemian Cigar Store Cafe **2**
Moose's **4**
Rose Pistola **3**
Stella Pastry Cafe **6**

⊐⊂⊐ Cable car
‖‖‖‖ Stairway

0   100 yds
0   100 m

Map 5: Mission District Dining

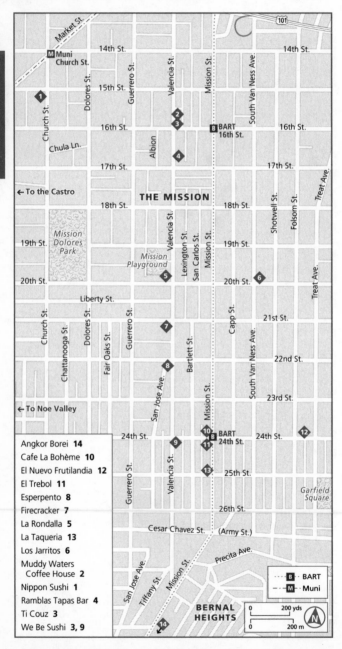

Angkor Borei **14**
Cafe La Bohème **10**
El Nuevo Frutilandia **12**
El Trebol **11**
Esperpento **8**
Firecracker **7**
La Rondalla **5**
La Taqueria **13**
Los Jarritos **6**
Muddy Waters
  Coffee House **2**
Nippon Sushi **1**
Ramblas Tapas Bar **4**
Ti Couz **3**
We Be Sushi **3, 9**

Map 6: Union Square & Financial District Dining

DINING

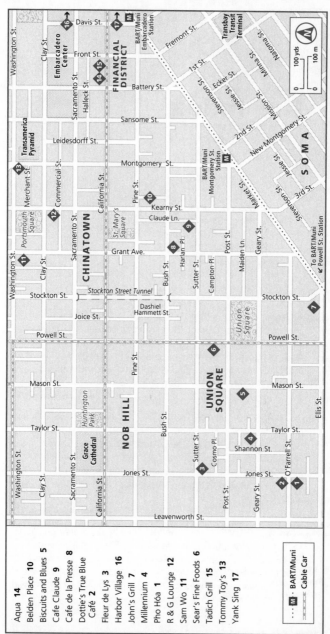

Aqua **14**
Belden Place **10**
Biscuits and Blues **5**
Cafe Claude **9**
Cafe de la Presse **8**
Dottie's True Blue Café **2**
Fleur de Lys **3**
Harbor Village **16**
John's Grill **7**
Millennium **4**
Pho Hóa **1**
R & G Lounge **12**
Sam Wo **11**
Sear's Fine Foods **6**
Tadich Grill **15**
Tommy Toy's **13**
Yank Sing **17**

▥ - BART/Muni
✕✕✕ - Cable Car

The Index

$$$$	over $30
$$$	$18–$30
$$	$10–$17
$	under $10

Prices given are per person for entrees only.

The following abbreviations are used for credit cards:

AE	American Express
DC	Diners Club
DISC	Discover
MC	MasterCard
V	Visa

Angkor Borei (p. 62) MISSION DISTRICT *CAMBODIAN* This small, unpretentious neighborhood restaurant serves fine cuisine at Mission District prices. Try the delicate vegetable-filled spring rolls to warm up, then go for a spicy noodle dish.... *Tel 415/550-8417. 3471 Mission St., at Courtland Ave. MUNI buses 14 or 49. AE, DISC, MC, V. Daily 11am–10pm.* $

See Map 5 on p. 76.

Aqua (p. 50) FINANCIAL DISTRICT *SEAFOOD* Celebrity lovebirds and hungry powerbrokers frequent this elegant seafood restaurant.... *Tel 415/956-9662. www.aqua-sf.com. 252 California St., near Battery St. Embarcadero BART/MUNI Metro station; MUNI bus 42. Reservations highly recommended. AE, DISC, DC, MC, V. Mon–Fri 11:30am–2pm, Mon–Sat 5:30–10:30pm, Sun 5:30–9:30pm.* $$$–$$$$

See Map 6 on p. 77.

asia sf (p. 61) SOMA *ASIAN* "Gender illusionists" serve pan-Asian food and perform hourly at this very hot South of Market club.... *Tel 415/255-2742. www.asiasf.com. 201 Ninth St., (at Howard St. Civic Center BART/MUNI Metro station; MUNI buses 9, 12, or 47. Reservations recommended. AE, DC, DISC, MC, V. Mon–Wed 6–10pm, Thurs–Sun 5–10pm.* $$

See Map 3 on p. 46.

A16 (p. 54) MARINA DISTRICT *ITALIAN* One of San Francisco's best and busiest restaurants featuring Neapolitan-style pizza and cuisine from the region of Campania.... *Tel 415/771-2216. www.a16sf.com. 2355 Chestnut St., between Divisadero and Scott sts. Buses 22, 30, or 30X. Reservations recommended. AE, DC, MC, V. Wed–Fri 11:30am–2:30pm, Sun–Thurs 5–10pm, Fri–Sat 5–11pm. $$–$$$*

See Map 3 on p. 46.

Aziza (p. 68) RICHMOND DISTRICT *MOROCCAN* Wonderful and distinctly Moroccan surroundings and cuisine make the drive deep into the Avenues worth the trip.... *Tel 415/752-2222. www.aziza-sf.com. 5800 Geary Blvd., at 22nd Ave. Buses 29 or 38. Reservations recommended. MC, V. Wed–Mon 5:30–10:30pm. $$–$$$*

See Map 3 on p. 46.

Biscuits and Blues (p. 67) UNION SQUARE *SOUTHERN* The dressed-up, down-home menu at this supper club includes treats like yam fries, along with jambalaya, chicken, catfish, and, of course, biscuits.... *Tel 415/292-BLUE. www.biscuitsandblues. com. 401 Mason St., at Geary St. Union Sq., Powell–Mason, or Powell–Hyde cable car; Powell St. BART/MUNI Metro station; MUNI bus 38. MC, V. Tues–Thurs 5:30–10pm, Fri–Sat 5:30–11pm. $$–$$$*

See Map 6 on p. 77.

Bocadillos (p. 56) FINANCIAL DISTRICT *TAPAS* Spanish-influenced small plates served in a very sexy setting (the hostesses are HOT) have made this casual Financial District tapas bar a smash hit... *Tel 415/982-2622. www.bocasf.com. 710 Montgomery St., at Washington St. Buses 15, 30X, or 41. AE, MC, V. Mon–Fri 7am–11pm, Sat 5–11pm. $$*

See Map 4 on p. 75.

Brainwash Cafe (p. 74) SOMA *CAFE* Hang with the post-punkers or go online while you wash 'n' dry.... *Tel 415/861-3663. www. brainwash.com. 1122 Folsom St., near Seventh St. Civic Center BART station; MUNI buses 12 or 19. MC, V. Daily 7am–10pm. $*

See Map 3 on p. 46.

Brothers Restaurant (p. 62) RICHMOND DISTRICT *KOREAN* This Korean barbecue spot has wood-fired hibachis at each table, plus a host of other dishes for those who choose not to barbecue.... *Tel 415/387-7991. 4128 Geary Blvd., at Fifth Ave. MUNI bus 38. Reservations recommended. MC, V. Daily 11am–2am. $$*

See Map 3 on p. 46.

Burma Superstar (p. 63) RICHMOND DISTRICT *BURMESE* Exceptional food at rock-bottom prices—order the clay-pot chicken curry and you'll see what I mean.... *Tel 415/387-2147. www. burmasuperstar.com. 309 Clement St., at 4th Ave. Buses 2, 4, 38, or 44. MC, V. Mon–Thurs 11am–9:30pm, Fri–Sat 11am–10pm, Sun 11am–9:30pm. $–$$*

See Map 3 on p. 46.

Cafe Claude (p. 66) FINANCIAL DISTRICT *CAFE* This great lunch spot tucked away in the Financial District is the most authentic Parisian-style cafe in the city. It serves wonderful sandwiches and wines by the glass.... *Tel 415/392-3515. www.cafeclaude.com. 7 Claude Lane, near Bush and Kearny sts. Montgomery St. BART/MUNI Metro station; MUNI bus 38. AE, DC, DISC, MC, V. Mon 11:30am–5:30pm, Tues–Wed 11:30am–10pm, Thurs–Sat 11:30am–10:30pm.* $

See Map 6 on p. 77.

Cafe de la Presse (p. 72) UNION SQUARE *CAFE* Escape from the shopping frenzy of Union Square into this oh-so-French cafe.... *Tel 415/398-2680. 352 Grant Ave., near Sutter St. MUNI buses 2, 3, 4, or 76. AE, DC, DISC, MC, V. Daily 7am–11pm.* $

See Map 6 on p. 77.

Cafe Flore (p. 73) CASTRO *CAFE* The food is good (a bit pricey) and the outside sundeck is one of the prime people-watching spots in the Castro District.... *Tel 415/621-8579. 2298 Market St., at Noe St. Castro St. MUNI Metro station; MUNI buses 8, 24, or 37. MC, V. Sun–Thurs 7am–11:30pm, Fri–Sat 7am–midnight.* $

See Map 3 on p. 46.

Cafe La Bohème (p. 74) MISSION DISTRICT *CAFE* Share big, wooden tables with artistic and often terminally unemployed cafe-dwellers at this all-day hangout.... *Tel 415/643-0481. 3318 24th St., at Mission St. 24th St. BART station. MC, V. Mon–Thurs 6am–10pm, Fri 6am–10:30pm, Sat 7am–11pm, Sun 7am–10pm.* $

See Map 5 on p. 76.

Caffe Greco (p. 73) NORTH BEACH *CAFE* One of North Beach's most popular coffeehouses, offering peerless espresso.... *Tel 415/397-6261. 423 Columbus Ave., between Green and Vallejo sts. MUNI buses 15, 30, 41, or 45. MC, V. Mon–Fri 7am–midnight, Sat–Sun 7am–1am.* $

See Map 4 on p. 75.

Caffe Puccini (p. 74) NORTH BEACH *CAFE* This cafe is truly Italian and manages to avoid becoming a trend trap despite its fair share of noted patrons and artistic types.... *Tel 415/989-7033. 411 Columbus Ave., between Green and Vallejo sts. MUNI buses 15, 30, 41, or 45. MC, V. Daily 6am–11:30pm.* $

See Map 4 on p. 75.

Caffe Trieste (p. 51) NORTH BEACH *CAFE* One of the last remaining beatnik haunts—Jack Kerouac and Allen Ginsberg were regulars—this legendary little cafe is a must for visiting coffee-hounds.... *Tel 415/392-6739. www.caffetrieste.com. 601 Vallejo St., at Grant St. MUNI buses 15 or 41. No credit cards. Sun–Thurs 6:30am–11pm, Fri–Sat 6:30am–midnight.* $

See Map 4 on p. 75.

Capp's Corner (p. 69) NORTH BEACH *ITALIAN* Authentic old-school Italian family-style dining: huge portions of straightforward fare served at long tables in a raucous atmosphere.... *Tel 415/989-2589. www.cappscorner.com. 1600 Powell St., at Green St. MUNI buses 15, 30, or 41. AE, DC, MC, V. Daily 11:30am–2:30pm, Sun–Thurs 4:30–10:30pm, Fri–Sat 4:30–11pm. $$*

See Map 4 on p. 75.

Cha Cha Cha (p. 57) UPPER HAIGHT/MISSION DISTRICT *CUBAN* Every dish in this funky joint is a tongue-burner, as it should be in a Cuban/Cajun restaurant that looks like it was decorated by a voodoo queen on a sangria binge.... *Haight: Tel 415/386-7670; www.cha3.com; 1801 Haight St., at Shrader St; MUNI buses 6, 7, 33, 66, or 71. Mission: Tel 415/648-0504; 2327 Mission St. 24th St. BART/MUNI Metro station. Daily 11am–4pm, Sun–Thurs 5–11pm, Fri–Sat 5–11:30pm. MC, V. $*

See Map 3 on p. 46.

Chez Nous (p. 55) FILLMORE DISTRICT *MEDITERRANEAN* This friendly and fast-paced neighborhood haunt serves the city's best Mediterranean small plates—the lamb chops with lavender sea salt are divine.... *Tel 415/441-8044. 1911 Fillmore St., between Pine and Bush sts. Buses 22, 41, or 45. Reservations recommended. AE, MC, V. Daily 11:30am–2:45pm and 5:30–10pm (Fri–Sat until 11pm). $$.*

See Map 3 on p. 46.

Chez Panisse (p. 58) BERKELEY *NEW AMERICAN* Among restaurant reviewers, Berkeley's Chez Panisse is held sacred, but locals will tell you that it isn't consistent.... *Tel 510/548-5525. 1517 Shattuck Ave., at Cedar St. Berkeley, North Berkeley BART station and a cab. Reservations essential. AE, DISC, MC, V. Mon–Sat seatings at 6–6:30pm, 8:30–9:30pm. $$$*

Coriya Hot Pot City (p. 61) RICHMOND DISTRICT *KOREAN* Load up your trays with the makings of a hearty meal, then play chef at your own table, where hot pots and grills are built in. You'll have to wait in line on weekends.... *Tel 415/387-7888. 852 Clement St., at 10th Ave. MUNI bus 38. MC, V. Sun–Thurs noon–11:30pm, Fri–Sat noon–1am. $*

See Map 3, on p. 46.

Dottie's True Blue Café (p. 72) TENDERLOIN *AMERICAN* My favorite breakfast diner, the kind of place you'd expect to see off Route 66, where most customers are on a first-name basis with the staff.... *Tel 415/885-2767. 522 Jones St., at O'Farrell St. Union Sq., Powell–Mason cable car. MUNI buses 2, 3, 4, 27, or 38. DISC, MC, V. Wed–Mon 7:30am–3pm. $*

See Map 6 on p. 77.

El Nuevo Frutilandia (p. 61) MISSION DISTRICT *LATIN* This is one of the few places in San Francisco that serves authentic Puerto Rican and Cuban home cooking.... *Tel 415/648-2958. 3077 24th St. at Folsom St. 24th St. BART/MUNI Metro station. MC, V. Mon–Sun noon–3pm and 5–8:45pm. $*

See Map 5 on p. 76.

El Trebol (p. 61) MISSION DISTRICT *LATIN* This delightful little Salvadoran/Nicaraguan eatery in the Castro District is one of the best deals in the city.... *Tel 415/285-6298. 3324 24th St., at Mission St. 24th St. BART station. No credit cards. Mon–Fri noon–9pm, Sat noon–8pm. $*

See Map 5 on p. 76.

Enrico's Sidewalk Cafe (p. 51) NORTH BEACH *CAFE* New owners resurrected what may be the city's favorite cafe and transformed it into a casual supper club.... *Tel 415/982-6223. www.enricossidewalkcafe.com. 504 Broadway, at Kearny St. MUNI buses 15, 30, 41, 45, or 83. Reservations recommended for dinner (essential on weekends). AE, MC, V. Sun–Thurs 11:30am–11pm, Fri–Sat 11:30am–midnight; bar daily 11:30am–1:30am or earlier depending on patronage. $$*

See Map 4 on p. 75.

Esperpento (p. 57) NORTH BEACH *SPANISH* You'll find authentic, inexpensive Spanish paella and tapas in a jam-packed Mission District storefront.... *Tel 415/282-8867. 3295 22nd St., at Valencia St. 24th St. BART station; MUNI bus 26. Reservations recommended. No credit cards. Mon–Fri 11am–3pm and 5–10pm, Sat 11am–10:30pm, Sun 3–10pm. $*

See Map 5 on p. 76.

Firecracker (p. 56) MISSION DISTRICT *CHINESE* In case the name didn't make it obvious, the exquisite Mandarin food here is hot and spicy.... *Tel 415/642-3470. 1007½ Valencia St., at 21st St. 24th St. BART station. MC, V. Mon–Thurs 5:30–10:30pm, Fri–Sat 5:30–11pm. $$–$$$*

See Map 5 on p. 76.

Fleur de Lys (p. 65) UNION SQUARE *FRENCH* The ultimate for a major splurge. Critics and customers call it the best classic French restaurant in the city.... *Tel 415/673-7779. www.fleurdelyssf.com. 777 Sutter St., at Taylor St. Powell–Mason or Powell–Hyde cable car. Reservations essential. AE, DC, MC, V. Mon–Thurs 6–9:30pm, Fri–Sat 5:30–10:30pm. $$$$*

See Map 6 on p. 77.

Fly Trap Restaurant (p. 53) SOMA *AMERICAN* A long history of good humor and a menu based on traditional San Francisco grill food make this institution a refreshing choice amid the glut of tony, food-fad eateries.... *Tel 415/243-0580. 606 Folsom St., at Second St. Montgomery St. BART/MUNI Metro station; MUNI bus*

15. Reservations recommended. AE, DC, MC, V. Mon–Thurs 11:30am–10pm, Fri 11:30am–10:30pm, Sat 5:30–10:30pm. $$
See Map 3 on p. 46.

Forbes Island (p. 57) SAN FRANCISCO BAY *FRENCH* A floating restaurant disguised as an island, complete with lighthouse and real 40-foot palm trees. Climb aboard.... *Tel 415/951-4900. www.forbesisland.com. Water shuttle is just left of PIER 39. Reservations recommended. Powell–Hyde cable car; MUNI buses 15, 30, 42, or 69. MC, V. Wed–Sun 5–10pm. $$$*
See Map 3 on p. 46.

French Laundry (p. 66) NAPA VALLEY *FRENCH* Thomas Keller, named 1997's best chef in the country by the James Beard Foundation, presides over this small gem out in the wine country.... *Tel 707/944-2380. 6640 Washington St., Yountville. Reservations essential. AE, MC, V. Mon–Thurs 5:30–9:30pm, Fri–Sun 11am–1pm, 5:30–9:30pm. $$$$*

Fringale (p. 50) SOMA *FRENCH/BASQUE* A curved blond-wood bar greets you the moment you open the door of this chic South of Market bistro. The food is delightful.... *Tel 415/543-0573. www.fringalesf.com. 570 Fourth St., between Brannan and Bryant sts. MUNI buses 30, 45, or 76. Reservations recommended. AE, MC, V. Tues–Fri 11:30am–3pm, Mon–Thurs 5:30–10pm, Fri–Sat 5:30–10:30pm. $$*
See Map 3 on p. 46.

Frjtz Fries (p. 55) HAYES VALLEY *BELGIAN* Addictive fries served in a paper cone with a barrage of exotic dipping sauces are the reason I can't get enough of this funky-artsy DJ/Art teahouse.... *Tel 415/864-7654. www.frjtzfries.com. 579 Hayes St., at Laguna St. Bus 21. AE, DC, DISC, MC, V. Mon–Thurs 9am–10pm, Fri 9am–midnight, Sat 10am–midnight, Sun 10am–9pm. $*
See Map 3 on p. 46.

Golden Boy Pizza (p. 54) NORTH BEACH *PIZZA* Heavenly squares of wondrously gooey pizza have both tourists and locals following their noses to the front windows of this North Beach favorite.... *Tel 415/982-9738. 542 Green St., between Stockton St. and Grant Ave. Buses 15, 30, 45, 39, or 41. No credit cards. Sun–Thurs 11:30am–11pm, Fri–Sat 11:30am–2am. $*
See Map 4 on p. 75.

Greens (p. 67) FORT MASON *VEGETARIAN* More than a decade ago there was a 6-month waiting list for reservations here. Three cookbooks and a couple of chefs later, Greens can usually accommodate guests with just 2 weeks' notice.... *Tel 415/771-6222. www.greensrestaurant.com. Building A, Buchanan St., at Marina Blvd. MUNI bus 28. Tues–Sat noon–2:30pm, Sun 10:30am–2pm, Mon–Sat 5:30–9pm. Greens To Go Mon–Thurs 8am–8pm, Fri–Sat 8am–5pm, Sun 9am–4pm. DISC, MC, V. $$*
See Map 3 on p. 46.

DINING

THE INDEX

Hama-Ko (p. 64) COLE VALLEY *JAPANESE* Chef Ted Kashiyama's Cole Valley restaurant offers a limited sushi-bar menu; for a full meal, order in advance.... *Tel 415/753-6808. 108 Carl St., at Cole St. MUNI bus 37 or 43. Reservations essential except for sushi bar. MC, V. Tues–Sun 6–10pm. $$*

See Map 3 on p. 46.

Harbor Village (p. 60) FINANCIAL DISTRICT *CHINESE* The dinners are exquisite, but the real reason to go to Harbor Village is for the dim sum, served only at lunch.... *Tel 415/781-8833. www. harborvillage.net. 4 Embarcadero Center, at Drumm St. between Sacramento and Clay sts. Embarcadero BART/MUNI Metro station; MUNI buses 15, 45, or 76. Reservations recommended. AE, DC, DISC, MC, V. Mon–Fri 11am–2:30pm, Sat–Sun 10:30am–2:30pm, daily 5:30–9:30pm. $$–$$$*

See Map 6 on p. 77.

Harris' (p. 50) RUSSIAN HILL *STEAKS* Anne Harris cooks and serves damn fine steaks. The best steakhouse in the city.... *Tel 415/673-1888. www.harrisrestaurant.com. 2100 Van Ness Ave., at Pacific Ave. MUNI buses 42, 47, 49, or 76. Reservations recommended. AE, DC, DISC, MC, V. Mon–Thurs 5:30–9:30pm, Fri 5:30–10pm, Sat 5–10pm, Sun 5–9:30pm. $$$*

See Map 3 on p. 46.

Hayes Street Grill (p. 50) HAYES VALLEY *SEAFOOD* Superb fish and seafood are the mainstays of the menu. They're sautéed or mesquite-grilled with a Mexican, American, French, Italian, or Asian accent.... *Tel 415/863-5545. www.hayesstreetgrill.com. 320 Hayes St., near Franklin St. Civic Center BART/MUNI Metro station; MUNI bus 21. Reservations essential for tables before 8:30pm. AE, DC, DISC, MC, V. Mon–Fri 11:30am–2pm, Mon–Thurs 5–9pm, Fri 5–10:30pm. Sat 5:30–10:30pm. Sun 5–8:30pm. $$*

See Map 3 on p. 46.

Helmand (p. 69) NORTH BEACH *AFGHANI* A formal dinner house on a stretch of Broadway between North Beach and Pacific Heights. Owner Mahmood Karzai's menu incorporates tastes of Central Asia, India, and the Middle East.... *Tel 415/362-0641. 430 Broadway, between Montgomery and Kearny sts. MUNI buses 15, 30, or 45. Reservations recommended. AE, MC, V. Sun–Thurs 5:30–10pm, Fri–Sat 5:30–11pm. $*

See Map 4 on p. 75.

Home Plate (p. 72) MARINA DISTRICT *BREAKFAST* You'll always start off with a coveted plate of freshly baked scones, and breakfast just keeps getting better.... *Tel 415/922-HOME. 2274 Lombard St., at Pierce St. MUNI buses 28, 30, 43, or 76. DC, DISC, MC, V. Daily 7am–4pm. $*

See Map 3 on p. 46.

Izzy's Steaks and Chops (p. 53) MARINA DISTRICT *STEAKS* The steaks are thick, the drinks stiff and plentiful, the waitstaff very friendly.... *Tel 415/563-0487. 3345 Steiner St., at Lombard St. MUNI buses 10, 20, 30, 43, 60, 70, or 80. Reservations recommended. AE, DC, DISC, MC, V. Daily 5:30–10pm. $$*

See Map 3 on p. 46.

John's Grill (p. 53) FINANCIAL DISTRICT *AMERICAN* Now 97 years old, this is a classic old-school place to get a juicy steak or have a late afternoon cocktail.... *Tel 415/986-0069. 63 Ellis St., between Powell and Stockton sts. Powell St. BART/MUNI Metro station. Reservations recommended. AE, DISC, MC, V. Mon–Sat 11am–10pm, Sun 5–10pm. $$*

See Map 6 on p. 77.

Kan Zaman (p. 68) UPPER HAIGHT *MIDDLE EASTERN* A quintessential Haight-Ashbury experience: billowed canopy tents, knee-high tables, hookah pipe, sensuous belly dancers, and classic Middle Eastern cuisine.... *Tel 415/751-9656. 1793 Haight St., at Shrader St. MUNI Metro: N. MUNI Buses 6, 7, 66, 71, or 73. MC, V. Mon–Thurs 5pm–midnight, Fri 5pm–2am, Sat noon–2am, Sun noon–midnight. $$*

See Map 3 on p. 47.

La Rondalla (p. 61) MISSION DISTRICT *MEXICAN* The fare is tasty and substantial, a perfect prelude to a few gigantic margaritas at the crowded, lively bar.... *Tel 415/647-7474. 901 Valencia St., at 20th St. 16th or 24th St. BART station; MUNI bus 26. No credit cards. Sun–Thurs 5pm–midnight, Fri–Sat 5pm–3am. $–$$*

See Map 5 on p. 76.

La Taqueria (p. 61) MISSION DISTRICT *MEXICAN* This Mission District favorite has a clean, comfortable cantina-style atmosphere.... *Tel 415/285-7117. 2889 Mission St., at 25th St. 24th St. BART station; MUNI buses 14 or 49. No credit cards. Mon–Sat 11am–9pm, Sun 11am–8pm. $*

See Map 5 on p. 76.

Little Star Pizza (p. 54) WESTERN ADDITION *PIZZA* A little-known bohemian speakeasy on a dreary strip of busy Divisadero Street that serves the city's best deep-dish cornmeal-crust pizzas.... *Tel 415/441-1118. www.littlestarpizza.com. 846 Divisadero St., at McCallister St. Buses 5 or 24. MC, V. Daily 5–10pm. $–$$*

See Map 3 on p. 47.

Los Jarritos (p. 61) MISSION DISTRICT *MEXICAN* Anything you order at this friendly Mexican eatery will be authentic and tasty, but make sure you don't miss the homemade tortillas.... *Tel 415/648-8383. 901 South Van Ness Ave., at 20th St. 16th or 24th St. BART station; MUNI bus 33. MC, V. Daily 8am–10pm. $*

See Map 5 on p. 76.

Mario's Bohemian Cigar Store Cafe (p. 74) NORTH BEACH *CAFE* This is my favorite North Beach cafe, not just because it has the best focaccia sandwiches in the city, but because it's still a closet-size corner cafe (and there are hardly any tourists)…. *Tel 415/362-0536. 566 Columbus Ave., at Union St. MUNI buses 15, 30, 41, or 45. MC, V. Daily 10am–11pm. $*

See Map 4 on p. 75.

Mecca (p. 66) CASTRO *ECLECTIC* Cozy into a black-leather booth and be pampered by the attentive waitstaff while you enjoy jazz or cabaret at this sensual supper club…. *Tel 415/621-7000. www.sfmecca.com. 2029 Market St., between Dolores and 14th sts. Any Market St. MUNI bus. Reservations recommended. AE, DC, MC, V. Sun and Tues–Thurs 5–11pm, Fri–Sat 5pm–midnight, bar remains open later. $$$*

See Map 3 on p. 47.

Millennium (p. 68) UNION SQUARE *VEGAN* This stylish restaurant's inventive menu is the culinary equivalent of a world-beat concert…. *Tel 415/345-3900. www.millenniumrestaurant.com. 580 Geary St., between Taylor and Jones sts. Powell–Hyde cable car; MUNI buses 2, 3, 4, 30, 45, or 76. AE, DC, MC, V. Sun–Thurs 5:30–9:30pm, Fri–Sat 5:30–10pm. $$–$$$*

See Map 6 on p. 77.

MoMo's (p. 55) SOMA *AMERICAN* The best part about this trendy scene across the street from SBC Park is that you can eat, drink, and be merry on the outdoor patio day and night—major heaters keep the chill off…. *Tel 415/227-8660. www.sfmomos.com. 760 Second St., at King St. MUNI bus 15, 30, or 42. AE, DC, MC, V. Sun–Wed 11:30am–9pm, Thurs–Sat 11:30am–10pm. $$–$$$*

See Map 3 on p. 47.

Moose's (p. 50) NORTH BEACH *AMERICAN* Proprietor Ed Moose's innovative menu—combining Southwestern, Italian, and Californian delicacies—is exceptional, and the scene is glam…. *Tel 415/989-7800 (800/28-MOOSE). www.mooses.com. 1652 Stockton St., between Filbert and Union sts. MUNI bus 15 or 30. Reservations essential. AE, DC, MC, V. Mon–Wed 5:30–10:30pm, Thurs 11:30am–10:30pm, Fri 11:30am–11pm, Sat 11:30am–2:30pm and 5:30–11pm, Sun 10am–2:30pm and 5–10:30pm, Thurs–Sun bar menu 2:30–5:30pm. $$–$$$*

See Map 4 on p. 75.

Muddy Waters Coffee House (p. 51) MISSION DISTRICT *CAFE* The atmosphere is funky, bohemian, punked-out cybernerd—with an eclectic clientele to match…. *Tel 415/863-8006. 521 Valencia St., near 16th St. 16th St. BART station; MUNI bus 26. No credit cards. Mon–Fri 6am–midnight, Sat 7am–midnight, Sun 7am–11pm. $*

See Map 5 on p. 76.

Nippon Sushi (p. 64) CASTRO *SUSHI* For more than 10 years this tiny, dumpy restaurant has had a line out the door for cheapest sushi in town. BYO beer—Nippon has no liquor license.... No telephone. 314 Church St., at 15th St. Buses 8, 22, or 37. No credit cards. Mon–Sat noon–10pm. $

See Map 5 on p. 76.

Pho Hóa (p. 63) TENDERLOIN *VIETNAMESE* This cafeteria-style restaurant serves huge, killer bowls of pho soup that are a cheap and healthy four-course meal.... *Tel 415/673-3163. 431 Jones St., between O'Farrell and Ellis sts. Buses 27, 31, or 38. Reservations accepted. No credit cards. Daily 8am–7pm. $*

See Map 6 on p. 77.

Ramblas Tapas Bar (p. 56) MISSION DISTRICT *TAPAS* The Spanish tapas served in this extremely popular Mission District restaurant were voted best in the Bay Area by the *Guardian*..... *Tel 415/565-0207. 557 Valencia St., at 17th St. 16th St. BART/ MUNI Metro station. Reservations strongly recommended. MC, V. Sun–Thurs 5–11pm, Fri 5pm–1am, Sat 11am–1am, Sun 11am– 11pm. $$–$$$*

See Map 5 on p. 76.

R & G Lounge (p. 60) CHINATOWN *CHINESE/SEAFOOD* The name sounds like a booze joint where a guy named Sam might be playing the piano, but it's actually a Chinatown restaurant offering some of the best seafood in the area.... *Tel 415/982-7877. 631 Kearny St., at Clay St. MUNI buses 15, 30, or 45. AE, DC, DISC, MC, V. Mon–Thurs 11am–9:30pm, Fri 11am–10pm, Sat 11:30am– 10pm, Sun 11:30am–9:30pm. $–$$*

See Map 6 on p. 77.

Rose Pistola (p. 50) NORTH BEACH *ITALIAN* This trattoria was voted best new restaurant in the country in 1997 by the James Beard Foundation, and it's still going strong.... *Tel 415/399- 0499. 532 Columbus Ave., between Union and Green sts. MUNI buses 15 or 30. AE, DC, DISC, MC, V. Sun–Thurs 11:30am–11pm, Fri–Sat 11:30am–midnight. $$–$$$*

See Map 4 on p. 75.

Sacred Grounds Cafe (p. 74) UPPER HAIGHT *CAFE* This 1960s throwback—eclectic furnishings and works by local artists share the room with fine, Victorian-style wood paneling—is still a vital part of the Haight-Ashbury scene.... *Tel 415/387-3859. 2095 Hayes St., at Cole St. MUNI bus 21. No credit cards. Daily 7am–10pm. $*

See Map 3 on p. 47.

Saigon Sandwich Shop (p. 63) CIVIC CENTER *VIETNAMESE* Not a full-fledged restaurant, but it makes the best Vietnamese sandwiches in town—for around $2. Lunch only.... *Tel 415/474- 5698. 560 Larkin St., at Turk St. Civic Center BART/MUNI Metro station; MUNI buses 19, 31, or 38. No credit cards. Mon–Sat 7am–5pm, Sun 7am–4:30pm. $*

See Map 3 on p. 47.

Sam Wo (p. 71) CHINATOWN *CHINESE* Very handy for late-nighters, Sam's is a total dive that serves addictive tomato beef with noodles.... *Tel 415/982-0596. 813 Washington St., by Grant Ave. MUNI buses 9x, 15, 30, or 45. No credit cards. Mon–Sat 11am–3am. Open Sun 11am–9:30pm in summer and on holidays.* $

See Map 6 on p. 77.

Sanppo (p. 63) JAPANTOWN *JAPANESE* Comfortable, inexpensive, and very good.... *Tel 415/346-3486. Japan Center, 1702 Post St., at Laguna St. MUNI bus 38. MC, V. Open daily 11:30am–midnight.* $

See Map 3 on p. 47.

Seal Rock Inn (p. 72) RICHMOND DISTRICT *BREAKFAST* Join the regulars or perhaps Carlos Santana for breakfast at this neighborhood coffee shop just footsteps away from Sutro Park, which overlooks the Pacific Ocean.... *Tel 415/752-8000. 545 Point Lobos Ave., at 47th Ave. MUNI bus 38. AE, DC, MC, V. Mon–Fri 6:30am–4pm, Sat–Sun 6:30am–6pm.* $–$$

See Map 3 on p. 47.

Sear's Fine Foods (p. 71) UNION SQUARE *AMERICAN* If you're anywhere near Union Square at breakfast time, it is mandatory to eat at Sear's diner, beloved for its teeny-tiny, rich, sweet Swedish pancakes.... *Tel 415/986-0700. www.searsfinefood.com. 439 Powell St., between Post and Sutter sts. Powell St. BART/MUNI Metro station; any Powell St. cable car; MUNI bus 76. No credit cards. Daily 6:30am–10pm (breakfast until 3pm).* $

See Map 6 on p. 77.

South Park Cafe (p. 74) SOMA *FRENCH* This little South of Market spot starts as a casual cafe in the morning, then turns into a super-hip lunch bistro, then goes back to its casual cafe persona for the rest of the day.... *Tel 415/495-7275. 108 South Park, near Second and Bryant sts. Montgomery St. BART station; MUNI buses 15, 30, or 45. AE, MC, V. Mon–Fri 7:30am–10pm, Sat 6–10pm.* $$

See Map 3 on p. 47.

Sparky's Diner (p. 71) CASTRO *AMERICAN* The wee-hours crowd at Sparky's can be a bit eccentric—and sometimes a tad inebriated—but just mind your own business and pass the ketchup.... *Tel 415/621-6001. 242 Church St., at Market St. Church St. MUNI Metro station. AE, MC, V. Open 24 hours.* $

See Map 3 on p. 47.

Stella Pastry Cafe (p. 73) NORTH BEACH *CAFE* Owner Franco Santucci will be happy to expound on the virtues of his patented Sacripantina, one of many delectable pastries baked on Stella's premises.... *Tel 415/986-2914. 446 Columbus Ave., at Green St. MUNI buses 15, 30, 41, or 45. Cash only. Mon–Thurs 7:30am–7pm, Fri–Sat 7:30am–midnight, Sun 8:30am–7pm.* $

See Map 4 on p. 75.

Straits Cafe (p. 62) RICHMOND DISTRICT *SINGAPOREAN* The coconut-milk chicken curry is as exotically delicious as the Singapore-style decor.... *Tel 415/668-1783. www.straitsrestaurants.com. 3300 Geary Blvd., at Parker St. MUNI bus 38. Reservations recommended. AE, DC, MC, V. Mon–Thurs noon–2:30pm and 5:30–10pm, Fri–Sat noon–11pm, Sun noon–10pm. $$*

See Map 3 on p. 47.

Suppenküche (p. 69) HAYES VALLEY *GERMAN* This small, inviting (often crowded and noisy) Hayes Valley beer hall/dining room steadily attracts a young crowd looking for good food, good beer, and good company all in the same place. The weekend brunch (Sun 10am–2:30pm) is a special treat.... *Tel 415/252-9289. 601 Hayes St., at Laguna St. Civic Center BART/MUNI Metro station; MUNI bus 21. AE, MC, V. Mon–Sun 5–10pm, Sat–Sun 10am–2:30pm. $$*

See Map 3 on p. 47.

Tadich Grill (p. 52) FINANCIAL DISTRICT *STEAKS/SEAFOOD* This landmark grill has been run by the same family since the turn of the 20th century..... *Tel 415/391-1849. 240 California St., between Battery and Front sts. Embarcadero St. BART/MUNI Metro station. MC, V. Mon–Fri 11am–9:30pm, Sat 11:30am–9:30pm. $$–$$$*

See Map 6 on p. 77.

Thanh Long (p. 63) SUNSET DISTRICT *VIETNAMESE* This out-of-the-way Sunset District standout is worth the drive for the excellent roasted crab and addictive garlic noodles.... *Tel 415/665-1146. www.anfamily.com. 4101 Judah St., at 46th Ave. Streetcar N. Reservations recommended. MC, V. Sun–Tues and Thurs 4:30–9:30pm, Fri–Sat 4:30–10:30pm. $$*

See Map 3 on p. 47.

Thep Phanom (p. 59) LOWER HAIGHT *THAI* It's a good thing Thep Phanom is located in California, land of a zillion chili farmers, because it uses tons of the red-hot peppers in its fiery Thai food. Keep plenty of water at your table—you'll need it.... *Tel 415/431-2526. www.thepphanom.com. 900 Waller St., at Fillmore St. MUNI buses 3, 6, 7, 22, 66, or 71. AE, DC, DISC, MC, V. Daily 5:30–10:30pm. $–$$*

See Map 3 on p. 47.

Ti Couz (p. 54) MISSION *CREPERIE* One of the most hip, popular, and mispronounced restaurants in the Mission specializes in delicate, paper-thin crepes with more than 30 choices of fillings (Nutella anyone?).... *Tel 415/252-7373. 3108 16th St., at Valencia St. BART: 16th and Mission; Buses 14, 22, 26, 33, 49, or 53. MC, V. Mon 11am–10pm, Tues–Thurs 5–10pm, Fri 11am–11pm, Sat 10am–11pm, Sun 10am–10pm. $*

See Map 5 on p. 76.

Tommy's Joynt (p. 65) CIVIC CENTER *AMERICAN* A half-century-old haven for cholesterol-be-damned holdouts, this hofbrau-style buffet looks like a Buffalo Bill museum that imploded.... *Tel 415/775-4216. www.tommysjoynt.com. 1101 Geary St., at Van Ness Ave. MUNI buses 2, 3, 4, or 38. No credit cards. Daily 10am–2am. $*

See Map 3 on p. 47.

Tommy Toy's (p.60) FINANCIAL DISTRICT *CHINESE* This chi-chi dinner house is a favorite of visiting dignitaries and Hollywood stars.... *Tel 415/397-4888. www.tommytoys.com. 655 Montgomery St., at Clay and Washington sts. BART/MUNI Metro station: Montgomery St. Reservations highly recommended. AE, DC, DISC, MC, V. Mon–Fri 11:30am–2:30pm, daily 5:30–9:30pm. $$$–$$$$*

See Map 6 on p. 77.

Tú Lan (p. 65) SOMA *VIETNAMESE* You'll have to brave the winos, weirdos, and street stench to get to this greasy diner, but the out-of-this-world imperial rolls are worth it.... *Tel 415/626-0927. 8 Sixth St., at Market St. Powell–Mason or Powell–Hyde cable car; F, J, K, L, M, or N MUNI Metro; MUNI buses 6, 7, 27, 31, 66, or 71. No credit cards. Mon–Sat 11am–9pm. $*

See Map 3 on p. 47.

We Be Sushi (p. 56) MISSION DISTRICT *SUSHI* The two We Be Sushi locations on Valencia Street are jammed with hip locals at dinnertime.... *Location 1: 538 Valencia St. 16th St. BART station. Tel 415/565-0749. Location 2: 1071 Valencia St. 24th St. BART station. Tel 415/826-0607. No credit cards. Daily 5–10pm, Mon–Fri 11:45am–2:30pm. $–$$*

See Map 5 on p. 76.

Yank Sing (p. 60) EMBARCADERO *CHINESE* A guidebook staple that's worth the trip. The dim sum is always satisfying, especially the dumplings, which include many vegetarian options.... *Tel 415/957-9300. 101 Spear St., at Mission St. at Rincon Center. Embarcadero BART/MUNI Metro station. AE, DC, MC, V. Mon–Fri 11am–3pm, Sat–Sun 10am–4pm. $$*

See Map 6 on p. 77.

SIONS

3

Map 7: Major San Francisco Attractions

Asian Art Museum **31**

Boudin Sourdough Bakery **9**

Cable Car Museum **23**

Cartoon Art Museum **25**

Coit Tower **17**

Exploratorium **1**

Fisherman's Wharf **6**

Gino & Carlo **16**

Glide Memorial United
Methodist Church **29**

Golden Gate Ferry **10**

Golden Gate Fortune
Cookie Factory **22**

Good Vibrations **4**

Hard Rock Cafe **12**

Harrington's
Bar & Grill **24**

Lyle Tuttle's
Tattoo Museum **13**

Maritime Museum **5**

The Metreon **28**

Musée Mécanique **7**

Nick's Lighthouse **7**

North Beach Museum **15**

Palace of Fine Arts **2**

Pier 23 Cafe **18**

PIER 39 **11**

Precita Eyes
Mural Center **32**

San Francisco Museum
of Modern Art **26**

San Francisco Zoo
& Children's Zoo **3**

Specs' Adler
Museum Cafe **19**

Tosca Cafe **20**

Vesuvio **21**

Washington Square
Bar & Grill **14**

Yerba Buena Center
for the Arts **27**

Zeum **30**

DIVERSIONS

GOLDEN GATE
NAT'L REC. AREA

MARINA
DISTRICT

Bay St.

Francisco St.

Chestnut St.

Lombard St.

Greenwich St.

Filbert St.

COW
HOLLOW

Union St.

Divisadero St.

Scott St.

Pierce St.

Steiner St.

Fillmore St.

Webster St.

Buchanan St.

Laguna St.

Octavia St.

Gough St.

Franklin St.

Pacific Ave.

Jackson St.

Alta Plaza
Park

Washington St.

Clay St.

PACIFIC
HEIGHTS

Lafayette
Park

Sacramento St.

California St.

Pine St.

Bush St.

To the
Richmond
District

Sutter St.

JAPANTOWN

Post St.

Japan Center

Geary St.

O'Farrell St.

Ellis St.

Eddy St.

Turk St.

Pierce St.

WESTERN
ADDITION

Fillmore St.

Webster St.

Buchanan St.

Laguna St.

Golden Gate Ave.

McAllister St.

Steiner St.

Fulton St.

Alamo
Square

Grove St.

Ivy St.

Hayes St.

HAYES
VALLEY

Octavia Blvd.

Gough St.

Franklin St.

Fell St.

Oak St.

Page St.

Divisadero St.

Scott St.

Haight St.

Waller St.

Hermann St.

Duboce
Park

Duboce Ave.

Castro St.

14th St.

Noe St.

Sanchez St.

Church St.

Market St.

Dolores St.

Guerrero St.

Valencia St.

Mission St.

Gough St.

To the Castro
& Noe Valley

14th St.

To the Mission
District

15th St.

0   1/4 mi

0   0.25 km

N

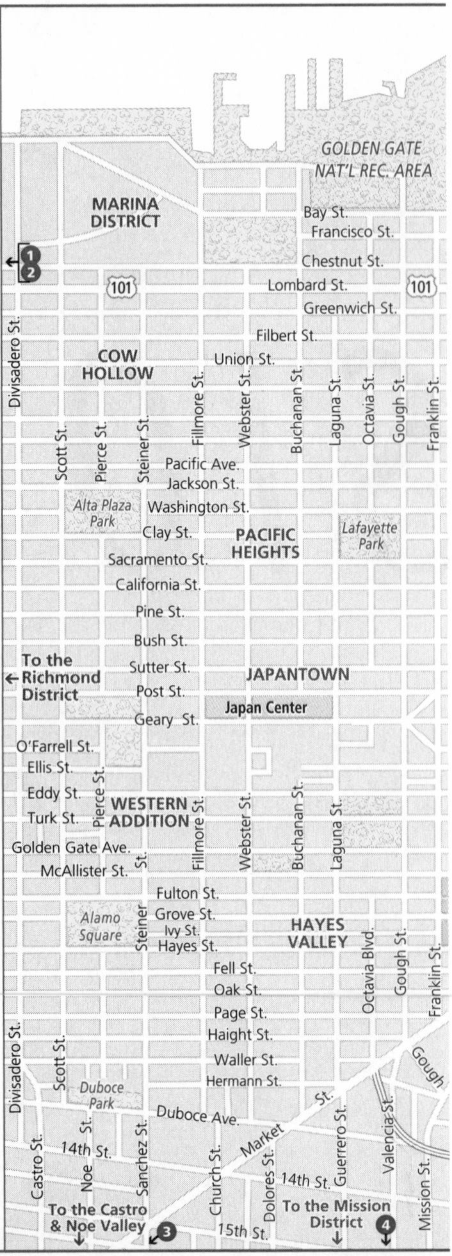

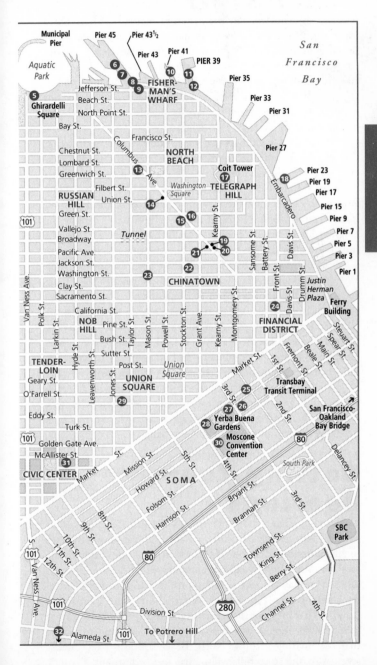

Municipal Pier

Pier 45

Pier 43½

Pier 43

Pier 41

PIER 39

San Francisco Bay

Aquatic Park

Jefferson St.
Beach St.
North Point St.
Bay St.

Ghirardelli Square

FISHER-MAN'S WHARF

Pier 35

Pier 33

Pier 31

Francisco St.

Chestnut St.
Lombard St.
Greenwich St.

NORTH BEACH

Pier 27

Coit Tower

Filbert St.
Union St.

Washington Square

TELEGRAPH HILL

Pier 23
Pier 19
Pier 17

RUSSIAN HILL

Green St.
Vallejo St.
Broadway

Tunnel

Pier 15
Pier 9

Embarcadero

Pier 7
Pier 5

Pacific Ave.
Jackson St.
Washington St.
Clay St.
Sacramento St.

Kearny St.

Sansome St.
Battery St.

Pier 3
Pier 1

Justin Herman Plaza

CHINATOWN

Davis St.

Front St.

Drumm St.

Ferry Building

California St.

NOB HILL

Pine St.
Bush St.

Van Ness Ave.
Polk St.
Larkin St.
Hyde St.
Leavenworth St.

Mason St.
Powell St.
Stockton St.
Grant Ave.
Kearny St.
Montgomery St.

FINANCIAL DISTRICT

Davis St.

Steuart St.
Spear St.
Main St.
Beale St.

TENDER-LOIN

Geary St.
O'Farrell St.

Sutter St.
Post St.

Union Square

Market St.

1st St.

Fremont St.

Eddy St.
Turk St.

Jones St.

UNION SQUARE

3rd St.

Transbay Transit Terminal

2nd St.

San Francisco-Oakland Bay Bridge

Golden Gate Ave.
McAllister St.

CIVIC CENTER

Yerba Buena Gardens

Moscone Convention Center

Mission St.
Howard St.
Folsom St.
Harrison St.

4th St.
5th St.

SOMA

Bryant St.
Brannan St.

South Park

3rd St.

Delancey St.

8th St.
9th St.
10th St.
11th St.
12th St.

SBC Park

Townsend St.
King St.
Berry St.

Van Ness Ave.

Division St.

To Potrero Hill

Alameda St.

Channel St.

4th St.

Basic Stuff

First words of advice: Stay away from Fisherman's Wharf. Ditto for PIER 39 and the cable-car turnarounds. That is, unless your purpose in traveling all the way to San Francisco is to rub elbows with throngs of tourists, shivering in their shorts and souvenir tank tops despite repeated warnings about how cold it is in July. If you brought the kids, you may have to surrender, but get your wharf duty out of the way as quickly as possible so you can move on to the city's true delights.

There are a few things that are so utterly San Francisco that they absolutely must be experienced at some point during your visit—a cable-car ride to the Buena Vista Cafe for a cup of Irish coffee, a trip to Coit Tower, a walk across the Golden Gate Bridge, the view from the elevator at the top of the Fairmont Hotel—but the best way to get to know the city is to explore the neighborhoods where people actually live. Skip the taxicabs (unless it's after dark or you're in a questionable neighborhood): Take a bus or a streetcar instead, then poke around on foot. Wander around the Haight and count the shrines to Jerry Garcia. Take in the Spoken Word or a cha-cha band at a hip side-street bar in the Mission District. Practice your tai chi with the Chinese seniors in Washington Square (North Beach). Gawk at the mansions in Pacific Heights. Visit the Castro for an undiluted dose of the predominant—and wonderfully irreverent—influence gay culture has on every aspect of life in San Francisco.

No matter what neighborhood you visit, the best seat in the house is any table at a cozy cafe (see the Dining chapter). Pull up a chair and order a frothy cappuccino. There is plenty of time for that trip to the museum—mañana.

Getting Your Bearings

Get a map. There's no other way to visualize San Francisco's irregular layout. The city is not one big grid like Manhattan; it's totally akimbo with sub-grids that skirt its many hills and valleys in a roundabout way. You can rarely see what's over the next hill, so you may not realize that North Beach is the uphill next-door neighbor of Fisherman's Wharf (north) and Chinatown (south). That may not seem important to you yet, but when you think you're trapped at PIER 39, you'll be relieved to realize that the inviting cafes of North Beach are just a few blocks away. Also, the steep hills will punish lost pedestrians.

When it comes to maps, you need two kinds—an overall view of the neighborhoods in relation to each other, and a comprehensive street map. A neighborhood map will show clearly, for example, that Haight-Ashbury is right next to Golden Gate Park, which stretches from the middle of the city all the way to the Pacific Ocean (at Ocean Beach, near the Cliff House). You'll see that the Castro and the Mission District—right next to each other, and not too far east of Haight-Ashbury—are both south of Market Street, but the neighborhood officially known as South of Market is quite a distance farther east, in the downtown area.

You'll also see that San Francisco—a city and county unto itself—is at the northern tip of a peninsula flanked by the San Francisco Bay on the east and the Pacific Ocean on the west. The Financial District sits on the eastern shore of the city, which curves northward as the Embarcadero passes North Beach and Fisherman's Wharf, eventually turning almost due west to the Golden Gate, where the Pacific Ocean meets the bay. If you stand just about anywhere in the city, you can see a red-and-white radio and television tower that looks like a miniature space needle sitting atop Twin Peaks, the geographical center of the city.

The front section of the San Francisco Yellow Pages has several excellent maps, including transit maps, but if you want to get your bearings in advance, log onto the San Francisco Convention and Visitors Bureau's website (www.sfvisitor.org). If you simply need specific information faxed to you, you can call (Tel 800/220-5747); follow the prompts to receive information by fax only. You can also pick up a copy of a visitor map for free at the Visitor Center when you arrive. It's located at 900 Market St., at Powell Street, on the lower level of Hallidie Plaza. While you're here also purchase a $2 MUNI transit map. It includes all MUNI routes (cable cars, buses, and Metro streetcars), regional transit connections, frequency guide, travel hints, and points of interest. Transit maps, fares, schedules, and tours are also downloadable for free (www.sfmuni.com).

The Lowdown

Must-sees for first-time visitors... There is one sure-fire perfect way to spend your first afternoon in San Francisco—take $5 out of your pocket, walk a few blocks up Powell from Market Street (away from the turnaround), and hop on the Powell–Hyde cable car. Don't think about not doing it because it seems too "touristy"—locals have been known to invite out-of-town guests purely for an excuse to take this ride. The Powell–Hyde line is my favorite because it ends up just steps away from the Buena Vista Cafe, 2765 Hyde St. (Tel 415/474-5044), a National Historic Landmark where a post-cable-car Irish coffee is an esteemed tradition, especially on a foggy afternoon. (The first Irish coffees served in America were mixed at the Buena Vista in 1952.) The ride itself twists through the city, climbing "halfway to the stars" atop Nob Hill, then plummeting back down on a breathtaking roller-coaster ride that levels out around the famous crooked section of Lombard Street before coasting down to the bay. No post-card can capture what it feels like the first moment you glimpse those million-dollar views.

Another mandatory awe-inspiring adventure is a bracing 15-minute walk across the Golden Gate Bridge. There is simply no other way to truly appreciate its immense scale and beauty. The best part is that the weather is absolutely predictable—it always feels cold and windy on the bridge (wear layers). To get an unbelievable view before you actually set foot on the bridge, take the MUNI bus 28 to Fort Point—a brick-and-granite stronghold built in 1861—where you can climb up to the roof and behold the bridge above you before you set out on the pedestrian walkway. Once you are on the bridge, you'll feel it sway and vibrate as gusty ocean winds whip through its cables. Don't be alarmed. The bridge is not about to collapse. It held up under the ballast of more than a hundred thousand revel-ers who congregated there to celebrate its 50th anniversary (1987), and it didn't flinch during the 1989 earthquake.

Unless you take the lazy—and boring—way out (MUNI buses 30, 39, or 45), you'll probably need to fuel up for the steep hike to **Coit Tower.** I suggest starting out with a cup of super-strength coffee at Caffe Trieste, 601 Vallejo St. (Tel 415/392-6739; see the Dining chapter), because it's right on the corner of Grant Street, the most interesting route to the famous fire-hose-nozzle spire atop Telegraph Hill (where you turn right and head up the hill to the tower). Then head up Grant to Greenwich Street. Once you've actually begun the ascent, you may want to distract yourself from the daunting incline by imagining the tower's namesake—Lillie Hitchcock Coit (1843–1929)—dressed as a fireman and racing around town with the volunteer brigade. Rumor has it that Ms. Coit found men's clothes appealing in other circumstances as well, particularly when she wanted to get into places where "ladies" weren't allowed. Though Ms. Coit's greatest achievement was to be made mascot of Engine Company 5—a reward for her help in fighting a fire—we love to think of Ms. Coit as San Francisco's most famous cross-dresser. No one really knows if Coit Tower was deliberately designed in the shape of a fire-hose nozzle. Up close, it doesn't matter. The Depression-era murals inside the lobby are haunting images of Americans at labor, and the 360-degree view from the top of the tower (elevator ride $3.75) is unbeatable.

Only in San Francisco... San Francisco is full of sights and sounds that simply don't exist in other cities. Where else do you hear foghorns, barking sea lions, the ringing of cable car bells, and the continuous clackety-clack of the cable-car pulleys winding underneath the streets? The rolling fog and steep hills are San Francisco's natural treasures as well.

One of the best ways to enjoy the trademark topography is to hike down some of the stairways that have been built into the city's steep sidewalks and pathways. Allow at least an hour or two to walk the Filbert Street Steps (between Sansome St. and Telegraph Hill), a romantic favorite with locals because the path feels hidden from urban clamor as it winds past 100-year-old cottages and lush gardens. The breathtaking view of the bay from the top of the hill has attracted artists, writers, and singers for years (Joan Baez and Armistead Maupin are among past residents). Start there, at Telegraph Hill Boulevard near Coit Tower, and work your way down. When you cross Montgomery Street to the lower steps, take a look at the Art Deco apartment complex at 1930 Montgomery—you might recognize it from the movie *Dark Passage* (Humphrey Bogart and Lauren Bacall). You may want to take a sidetrack along Napier Lane, a lovely wooden walkway that leads to the public Grace Marchant Gardens, a particularly enchanting sight on Halloween, when more than 200 jack-o'-lanterns light up the night for local trick-or-treaters.

DIVERSIONS

A billion Chinese can't all be wong... Chinatown is one of the most celebrated neighborhoods in San Francisco, but it has never become merely a tourist trap—above all else it is a place where people live; in fact, it's the largest Chinese community outside Asia. As soon as you cross under the ornate, dragon-crested gateway on Grant Avenue at Bush Street, you're no longer in the Western world. Street signs are marked in Chinese characters, lampposts are encircled by dragons, and store windows display strange medicinal herbs and animal parts you'd never find at a suburban drugstore. The best time to see this teeming neighborhood is early in the morning, when merchants deliver their wares in pushcarts and mothers rush down the street toting live chickens, gasping catfish, and very dead armadillos in pink plastic bags—*always* the pink plastic bags—for tonight's dinner (yes, I've seen boxes of dead armadillos for sale here).

Wander up Grant Avenue or Stockton Street to Sacramento and find Waverly Place. Also known as "The Street of Painted Balconies," this is Chinatown's most popular side street because of its painted balconies and colorful architectural details—a sort of Chinese-style New Orleans street. You can admire the architecture only from the ground because most of the buildings are private family associations or temples. One temple you can visit is the Tien Hon Temple, 125 Waverly Place, top floor. Accessible via a narrow stairway three floors up, this incense-laden sanctuary, decorated in traditional black-, red-, and gold-lacquered wood, is a house of worship for Chinese Buddhists, who come here to pray, meditate, and send offerings

Man with Hand in Pocket Feel Cocky
At 56 Ross Alley is the Golden Gate Fortune Cookie Factory, a tiny Chinatown storefront where, since 1962, three women sit at a conveyer belt, folding messages into thousands of fortune cookies as the manager invariably calls out to tourists, beckoning them to stroll in, watch the cookies being made, and buy a bag of 40 for about $3. Sure, there are other fortune cookie bakeries in the city, but this is the only one left where the cookies are still made by hand the old-fashioned way. You can purchase regular fortunes, unfolded flat cookies without fortunes, or, if you bring your own fortunes, they can create custom cookies (great for dinner parties) at around $6 for 50 cookies—a very cheap way to impress your friends. The factory is open daily 7am to 8:30pm; admission is free (Tel 415/781-3956).

to their ancestors and to Tin How, the Queen of the Heavens and Goddess of the Seven Seas. There are no scheduled services, but you are welcome to visit. Just remember to quietly respect those who are here to pray, and try to be as unobtrusive as possible (it's customary to give a donation or buy a bundle of incense during your visit).

The Chinatown Kite Shop, 717 Grant Ave., has an assortment of flying objects, including cool fish kites, nylon or cotton windsock kites, hand-painted Chinese paper kites, wood-and-paper biplanes, and pentagonal kites—all great for gifts and souvenirs. As you're walking along Grant Street, turn east on Washington Street and stop in at the Washington Bakery & Restaurant, 733 Washington St., and purchase a little culinary adventure to-go: snow red beans with ice cream. This sugary-sweet drink mixed with whole beans and ice cream is unlike any snack you've ever experienced. At 949 Grant Ave. is the Ten Ren Tea Co., Ltd., where you can sample a freshly brewed tea variety and check out the dozens of drawers and canisters labeled with more than 40 kinds of tea. Like Washington Bakery, Ten Ren also offers an unusual drink worth trying: hot or iced tapioca milk teas with giant black tapioca blobs or jelly. Try the black tea or green tea versions and enjoy the subtle flavors and the giant balls of tapioca slipping around in your mouth.

At the corner of Grant Avenue and Washington Street is a tiny bar with the single word BUDDHA on a sign over the door. Look inside. Old men with long braids and "thinking caps" may be sitting at the bar. You're not only on a different continent, you're in a different century. Another great Chinatown dive bar is the Li Po Cocktail Lounge, 916 Grant Ave., a dim, slightly spooky haunt that was once an opium den. Li Po's alluring character stems from its mishmash clutter of dusty Asian furnishings and mementos, including an unbelievably huge ancient rice-paper lantern hanging from the ceiling and a glittery golden shrine to Buddha behind the bar. The bartenders love to creep out patrons with tales of opium junkies haunting the joint.

Also worth a visit is the Great China Herb Co. at 857 Washington St. For centuries the Chinese have relied on shops like this one—which are full of exotic herbs, roots, and other natural elixirs—to buy what they believe will cure all types of ailments and ensure good health and long life. Thankfully, unlike owners in many similar area shops,

Mr. and Mrs. Ho speak English, so you will not be met with a blank stare when you inquire what exactly is in each box, bag, or jar arranged along dozens of shelves. (It's important to note that you should not use Chinese herbs without the guidance of a knowledgeable source such as an herb doctor. They may be natural, but they also can be quite powerful and are potentially harmful if misused.)

Some other great Chinese stores for gifts, souvenirs, or just poking around are the Canton Bazaar at 616 Grant Ave; The Wok Shop at 718 Grant Ave., where you can purchase just about any cleaver, wok, cookbook, or vessel you might need for Chinese-style cooking in your own kitchen; and Jade Galore at 1000 Stockton St., which purveys a fine jade jewelry. If all those aromas of Chinese food are making you hungry, I recommend lunch at the House of Dim Sum, 735 Jackson St. (Tel 415/399-0888)—nothing fancy, for sure, but the dumplings are fresh, cheap, and delicious, and owners Cindy and Ben Yee are friendly, which is a plus in this sometimes abrupt community. Order at the counter: pork, chive, and shrimp dumplings; sweet buns; turnip cake; and sweet rice with chicken wrapped in a lotus leaf. Unless they're taken, grab a seat at one of the two tables to enjoy your cheap feast. Two other great places to appease your appetite are the AA Bakery & Café at 1068 Stockton St.— try a mooncake—and Gourmet Delight B.B.Q., 1045 Stockton St., for a plate of barbecued duck and pig, or steamed pig and chicken feet (c'mon, live a little). Everything's to go here, so don't forget napkins.

Soaking up the sunset… If a ride on the Powell–Hyde cable car or the view from **Coit Tower** hasn't already made you fall hopelessly in love with San Francisco, perhaps what you need is a view of the sun melting into an orange-red-fuchsia pool as it sets on the blue Pacific. The ultimate spot is a window table at the pub in the Cliff House restaurant, 1090 Point Lobos Ave. (Tel 415/386-3330), facing directly out to sea. Even the most jaded urbanites ooh and ahh at the display, so be sure to go at least an hour before sundown for a good seat—or go outside and find a spot along the cliff.

If you have access to a car, don't leave the Bay Area without watching a sunset from the top of **Grizzly Peak** in the Berkeley Hills. Cars start lining up about a half-hour before sundown to watch the transformation from daylight to shimmering night lights—a magnificent sight in any weather, clear or foggy. The vista covers the entire bay, from San Mateo to the south, the city and the Golden Gate Bridge straight ahead, and Marin County to the north.

Morbid landmarks... For those who enjoy excursions to the dark side, here are a few points of interest that will never make it into San Francisco's public relations hall of fame.

The People's Temple, where Jim Jones gathered disciples before leading them to their eventual death at a tragic mass suicide in Guyana, still stands at 1859 Geary St. (It is now a Korean Presbyterian Church.)

It's hard to believe that Charles Manson recruited some of his deadliest "family" members—including Susan Atkins and Squeaky Fromme—during the peak of Haight-Ashbury's peace-and-love scene, but he lived at 636 Cole St. for a few months in 1967 before heading to Southern California to organize his horrifying killing spree.

San Quentin State Prison, fondly known to its residents simply as "Q," has hosted some of California's most notorious criminals, including the aforementioned Mr. Manson, Sirhan Sirhan, and William Harris (one of Patty Hearst's kidnappers). They don't give tours of death row or anything like that, but you can take a ferry to Larkspur and hoof it to the prison, where there is a small museum (gas-chamber mementos and such) and a gift shop that sells items made by prisoners (no license plates).

> **Soulful Sundays**
> *Every city has churches, but only San Francisco has the Glide Memorial United Methodist Church. An hour or so with Reverend Cecil Williams and his exuberant gospel choir will surely shake your soul and let the glory out, no matter what your religious beliefs may be—everybody leaves this Tenderloin church spiritually uplifted and slightly mist-eyed. Williams's non-dogmatic, fun Sunday services attract a diverse audience that crosses all socioeconomic boundaries. Go for an uplifting experience and some hand-clapping, shoulder-swaying gospel choir music—it's an experience you'll never forget. The church is located at 330 Ellis St., west of Union Square. Services are Sunday at 9 and 11am (Tel 415/674-6000; www.glide.org).*

Every hotel has gruesome moments it would rather not recall, but the Westin Saint Francis (see the Accommodations chapter) has a couple of whoppers—President Ford's assassination attempt (Sept 23, 1975) and Fatty Arbuckle's lost weekend (Labor Day weekend, 1921). President Ford was leaving the hotel when Sara Jane Moore whipped out a gun and fired at him from across the street, but an ex-Marine standing next to her grabbed her arm, redirecting the bullet. (It was the second assassination attempt in one 2-week trip to California.) Fatty Arbuckle was celebrating a multimillion-dollar movie contract inside the hotel at what has often been described as a drunken orgy when a young female guest was found unconscious in Room 1219. She died a few days later, and Arbuckle was tried three times for her murder before finally being acquitted.

The roar of the fish stalls, the smell of the crowd...
It has been decades since **Fisherman's Wharf** was actually a bustling fresh-fish market, and equally as long since **PIER 39** and the Port of San Francisco were a thriving part of the city's mercantile economy. Yet these two tourist traps are the first stop for most sightseers. (PIER 39, converted in the early 1980s to an outdoor mall of shops and restaurants, is third on the list of the world's top 10 attractions, with more than 10.5 million guests each year.) There are precious few reasons to go near either place, but if you must, here are some ways to make the best of it: Buy a fresh, whole crab at **Nick's Lighthouse** seafood stall (make sure it's still alive and wiggling), get them to cook and crack it for you on the spot, then pick up a sourdough baguette from **Boudin Sourdough Bakery,** and savor one of the best crab sandwiches around. Visit the sea lions—hundreds of them hang around PIER 39's K-Dock, where docents from the Marine Mammal Center (remember it from *Star Trek IV*?) give out free books and teach visitors all about the barking pinnipeds (11am–5pm). Then escape to **Pier 23 Cafe,** an almost-unnoticeable shack that attracts a local crowd with jazz, reggae, and calypso, as well as stiff drinks, outdoor seating, and a beautiful view.

Urban ferry tales... There are plenty of bay cruises that pick up tourists at Fisherman's Wharf and PIER 39, but it's more fun to go to the Ferry Building at the foot of Market Street and ride with the locals on an afternoon **Golden**

A DESIRE FOR STREETCARS

San Francisco's famous cable cars aren't the only rolling blast from the past. One of MUNI's Metro streetcar lines, the F-Market line, consists of several beautifully restored and beloved 1930s streetcars. The colorful, eye-catching line runs along Market Street from Castro to the Downtown district and is a quick and charming way to tour the city (that, and they make great photo ops).

Gate Ferry to the seaside village of Sausalito. You can do a 1-hour round-tripper or stop to explore Sausalito. There is really just one main street—Bridgeway—so it's easy to walk around the yuppie/nautical/ex-bohemian enclave and find a perfect spot to watch the sun set behind the San Francisco skyline. If sunsets aren't your thing, and you'd sooner toss back a pint at a rowdy tavern full of live music and boisterous baby boomers, try the **No Name Bar,** but don't drink too many happy-hour specials unless you intend to spend the night—the last ferry departs for San Francisco just after 7pm.

Cruising Golden Gate Park... The city's reigning playground, Golden Gate Park has been home to the 49ers football team and all the city's major hippie happenings (including Jerry Garcia's memorial service in 1995); it's still home to Sunday strollers, skaters, and joggers, to museums, to free operas, even a herd of buffalo. Then there are the gardens. The 5-acre Japanese Tea Garden is the oldest in America. When you enter through the hand-carved gate, you really feel as though you're in Japan. The bamboo-lined footpaths and bridges pass ponds full of koi fish, tiny bonsai trees, stone lanterns, Shinto shrines, and a serene 18th-century Buddha. In early spring, the garden is ablaze with cherry blossoms. (Go early in the morning to avoid crowds.) Cap your visit with a rest stop at the tea pavilion for a fortune cookie (they were first introduced there) and a relaxing cup of green tea served by women in traditional Japanese attire. The newly restored Conservatory of Flowers (on Conservatory Way, near Arguello Blvd.) is a massive glass Victorian greenhouse that was built in Ireland and shipped to San Francisco piece by piece. It is stunning from the outside and utterly magnificent on the inside, where beautiful exotic flowers and tropical trees are always in season.

Museum meccas outside Golden Gate Park... From a half block away, the huge circular skylight atop Swiss architect Mario Botta's **San Francisco Museum of Modern Art** (South of Market) looks like some sort of signaling device for extraterrestrial art collectors. Inside, earthlings have been known to be dazzled by the West Coast's most extensive collection of 20th-century art, which fills 50,000 square feet of gallery space. Botta's magnificent structure is a work of art in itself and one of the primary reasons to visit.

The city's ethnic diversity and social compassion fuel most of the art displayed in the celebrated **Yerba Buena Center for the Arts,** a multigallery center adjacent to the Museum of Modern Art. Exhibits have included panels from the NAMES Project Memorial Quilt and works by prison inmates and residents of local halfway houses. There is also a theater, which hosts a variety of local performances from multicultural groups.

The **Palace of Fine Arts** is a must-see, not just because it houses the Exploratorium, but because it looks just like an ancient Roman temple and it's the only building that remains from the 1915 Panama Pacific Exposition (held to celebrate the opening of the Panama Canal). A trip to the **Exploratorium** is also mandatory, particularly if you're toting along kids. Seasoned locals will assure you it's the most fun you can have without hallucinogenic drugs, especially if you crawl through the dark, sensual Tactile Dome or try any of the other hands-on games designed to totally twist your mind. You never know what the mad scientists will have in store for you at this wonderfully fun, interactive science museum—and the gift shop is the best place in the city to load up on brainy birthday and Christmas gifts.

San Francisco's cable-car system is still run out of a three-story red-brick barn, and you can watch it in action from several special spectator galleries at the highly entertaining (and always free) **Cable Car Museum.** If you've ever wondered how the cable-car system works, this nifty museum explains (and demonstrates) it all. Yes, this is a museum, but it's no stuffed shirt. It's the living powerhouse, repair shop, and storage place of the cable-car system that is in full operation every day year-round. Built for the Ferries and Cliff House Railway in 1887, the building underwent an $18-million reconstruction to restore its original gaslight-era look, install an amazing spectators' gallery and add a museum of San Francisco transit history. The exposed machinery, which pulls the cables under San Francisco's streets, looks like a Rube Goldberg invention. Stand in the mezzanine gallery and become mesmerized by the massive groaning and vibrating winches as they thread the cable that hauls the cars through a huge figure-eight and back into the system using slack-absorbing tension wheels. For a better view, move to the lower-level viewing room, where you can see the massive pulleys and gears operating underground. Also on display here is one of the first grip cars developed by Andrew S. Hallidie, operated for the first time on Clay Street on August 2, 1873. Other displays include an antique grip car and trailer that operated on Pacific Avenue until 1929 and dozens of exact-scale models of cars used on the various city lines. There's also a shop where you can buy a variety of cable-car gifts.

The literally shipshape **Maritime Museum** looks like a set for an old Hollywood movie. Shaped like an Art Deco ship, the museum is filled with sailing, whaling, and fishing lore. Nautical types will go nuts when they see all the intricate ship models and scrimshaw. The collection of shipwreck photographs and historic marine scenes includes an 1851 snapshot of hundreds of abandoned ships, deserted by crews dashing off to participate in the gold rush. Beautifully carved, brightly painted wooden figureheads from old windjammers line the walls.

DIVERSIONS

● ●

IF IT'S FREE, IT'S FOR ME

To beef up attendance, almost all of San Francisco's art galleries and museums are open free to the public 1 day of the week or month (or both), and several never charge admission.

> **First Tuesday:** *Asian Art Museum, California Palace of the Legion of Honor, Center for the Arts at Yerba Buena Gardens, San Francisco Museum of Modern Art*

> **First Wednesday:** *Exploratorium, California Academy of Sciences*
> **Always Free:** *Cable Car Museum, Maritime Museum (there's a fee to board ships), Musée Mécanique, Wells Fargo History Museum, Glide Memorial United Methodist Church*

● ●

Museums for special interests... When Pogo would make a more entertaining afternoon companion than Picasso, it's time to quit the cathedrals of culture and head for smaller houses of object worship, like the **Cartoon Art Museum.** It's the only museum in the United States dedicated to the preservation and exhibition of cartoon art in all its forms, housing thousands of pieces in its collection—from original Krazy Kat watercolors and Pogo comic strips to storyboards from the Disney classic, *Fantasia.* Some of the donors include *Peanuts* artist Charles Schulz and rock star Graham Nash.

If you can't resist penny arcades, you'll love the quirky little **Musée Mécanique** at Fisherman's Wharf. It's packed with the largest privately owned collections of antique coin-operated mechanical musical instruments in the world—160 machines dating back from the 1880s through the present (and they still work!)—from old carnival fortune tellers to marionette shows, antique movie machines, 19th-century music boxes, old-school strength testers, mechanical cranes, and player pianos. Admission is free, which is a good thing because you'll easily drop a small fortune in coins playing with all the doohickeys and thingamabobs. It's always amusing to watch little kids cower in fear as Laughing "Fat Lady" Sal gives her infamous cackle of a greeting. One really strange exhibit is a miniature amusement park made out of toothpicks. The fact that the piece was glued together by prisoners at San Quentin kind of makes you wonder.

To get a virtually private glimpse of the history of one of San Francisco's most intriguing neighborhoods, go to the **North Beach Museum,** tucked away on the mezzanine of the Bay View Street Bank. This little museum traces North Beach's past with photos and artifacts dating back to the turn of the 20th century. Hardly anybody knows the museum is there, so you may have it all to yourself, but you must go during banking hours.

Museums for really special interests... For flesh freaks, I have two recommendations: **Lyle Tuttle's Tattoo Museum** and **Good Vibrations** (also see the Shopping chapter). Lyle Tuttle, undisputed king of the San Francisco tattoo empire, moved his minimuseum from a seedy location at Seventh and Market streets long after he had already engraved Janis Joplin's flesh, but you can still see his collection of tattoo art—including candid shots of himself, covered head-to-toe with indelible designs—and classic tattoo instruments at his tiny shop in North Beach. More pleasurable pleasures of the flesh are explored at Good Vibrations, where the contraptions in the window display look like old-time hair dryers or permanent-wave doodads but are actually part of an eclectic collection of sex toys and vibratoriana, including the "Queen Victoria," a wooden hand-crank model from turn-of-the-century London. The museum/store—which tends to favor women's interests— is almost cheery; if it weren't for the dozens of plastic penises on the shelves, you'd expect a young Henry Fonda to appear from behind the counter and offer you an ice cream soda (well, maybe not).

DIVERSIONS

Outlandish out-of-town archives... Heading south from the city, US 101 is dotted with weird little wayside collections. The first stop is the **Burlingame Museum of Pez Memorabilia,** not far from the airport. Remember those little candies spit from the mouths of plastic cartoon characters? Since the first Pez dispenser hit the shelves in 1952, hundreds, if not thousands, of models have been issued, and the museum's collection is exhaustive. Moving right along to the Silicon Valley, you'll find the perfect antidote to Apple, Intel, and the rest of the area's high-tech cathedrals: the **Rosicrucian Egyptian Museum.** One of the mummies on display at this San Jose park was actually a postmortem hitchhiker discovered by the shippers at Neiman Marcus, who packaged up what was supposed to be a "vacant" case. The store graciously offered to dispose of the uninvited mummy, but the Rosicrucians were delighted to keep it as one of their many permanent guests. Last stop, Surf City. The **Santa Cruz Surfing Museum** is as close as you can get to a surfin' safari without climbing on a board and catching a wave. The museum itself overlooks Steamer Lane, time-honored haunt of inveterate Santa Cruz surfers and home to many championship surfing contests. Antique surfboards, videos, photographs, and other memorabilia depict the history and evolution of surfing around the world. The view is spectacular, and the exhibits inside are totally awesome, dude.

The bongo-rama beatnik tour... Bohemian-history buffs won't want to leave San Francisco without paying homage to some of the hallowed grounds that have made the city a capital of 20th-century counterculture. One might say the Beat movement, for instance, was born in 1953, when Allen Ginsberg moved to San Francisco and Lawrence Ferlinghetti opened City Lights Bookstore (see the Shopping chapter) at 261 Columbus Ave., even though Neal Cassady and Jack Kerouac already lived in the city at 29 Russell St. (a small alley off Hyde St. between Union and Grand sts.).

One weekend in 1955, stoned to the gills, Ginsberg wrote his magnum opus, "Howl," in his apartment at 1214 Polk St., between Bush and Sutter sts., and read it for the first time 2 weeks later to a spellbound audience at the tiny Six Gallery at 3119 Fillmore St., between Filbert and Greenwich sts. City Lights published the poem in 1956, and the police immediately declared it obscene, focusing national attention on North Beach. Chronicle columnist Herb Caen coined the term beatnik to describe the disheveled literati—Kerouac, Ferlinghetti, Ginsberg—who dug poetry and jazz at places like **Vesuvio,** 255 Columbus Ave., on the corner of what is now Jack Kerouac Alley; The Place, 1546 Grant Ave., which Jack Kerouac described in *The Dharma Bums* as "the favorite bar of the hepcats around the Beach"; the Cellar, 576 Green St.; and funky ol' **Specs' Adler Museum Cafe,** 12 Adler Place, my favorite North Beach dive.

In 1958, after Kerouac's *On the Road* became a bestseller and Hollywood producers came up with the watered-down TV series *Route 66* to exploit the theme, tour-bus gawkers descended on North Beach to stare at the beatniks, making popular hangouts like Caffe Trieste, 601 Vallejo St. (see the Dining chapter), the now defunct Co-Existence Bagel Shop, 1398 Grant Ave., and Enrico's, 504 Broadway (see the Dining chapter) feel like zoos for the caged poets. In 1960, The Place and the Co-Existence Bagel Shop closed, and the fuss over beatniks died down for a while.

Tune in, turn on, drop out... Just a few years later, the city was the center of a cultural convulsion of a more Day-Glo shade. By the time the infamous Summer of Love rolled around in 1967, San Francisco's psychedelic scene had actually been in full swing for more than two years, since

One Flew Over the Cuckoo's Nest author Ken Kesey [in]troduced Owsley acid (known as the "Cadillac of LSD") to the Grateful Dead, and acid rock was born. Another acid-powered band, the Jefferson Airplane, first played at a club called the Matrix, 3138 Fillmore St., near Union St., in August 1965, but the club got too loud for the neighbors, so the acidheads moved on and it evolved into a rowdy singles bar still doing business as Pierce Street Annex.

Examiner writer Michael Fallon coined the term *hippie* to distinguish the new hipsters from their beatnik predecessors shortly before the first big psychedelic concert was staged in October 1965 at Longshoreman's Hall in Fisherman's Wharf, 400 North Point, by Chet Helms and his production company, the Family Dog. The Family Dog later moved its gigs to the Avalon Ballroom at 1268 Sutter St., near Van Ness Avenue, now a multiplex movie theater. Meanwhile, Bill Graham entered the scene with a benefit for the San Francisco Mime Troupe (Dec 1965) at the Fillmore Auditorium, 1805 Geary Blvd., at the corner of Fillmore Street, (see the Nightlife chapter), which would become his virtual kingdom and the undisputed center of the psychedelic rock universe.

In January 1967, 20,000 people showed up for the first "Human Be-In" at the Polo Field, just off Middle Dr. between 30th and 36th avenues in Golden Gate Park, covered in luminous detail by the *Oracle,* a popular underground newspaper headquartered at 1371 Haight St. The Haight had become the center of hippie culture—Janis Joplin lived at 112 Lyon St., corner of Oak Street; the Grateful Dead around the corner at 710 Ashbury St., near Haight Street; and the Jefferson Airplane at 2400 Fulton St., closer to the park. By the summer of 1967, the whole world was watching the Haight, especially when Rudolf Nureyev and Margot Fonteyn were arrested at a pot party at 42 Belvedere St., near Haight Street. Drug busts became a priority—if not a sport—for San Francisco's Finest, and the October 1967 raid of the Dead house was the top feature of the premiere issue of *Rolling Stone,* which was produced in a small loft at 746 Brannan St., South of Market. Drug busts and a massive influx of unenlightened strangers were ruining the scene; that same month, the Psychedelic Shop, 1535 Haight St., closed its doors and a march through the neighborhood declared the death of the true hippie movement. The party was over.

The last-call saloon crawl... The party is never over at some good old watering holes—these historic saloons are still full of characters and stories. There are at least a half-dozen classic joints in North Beach, from beatnik haunts that orbit City Lights—**Specs' Adler Museum Cafe, Tosca Cafe,** and **Vesuvio**—to beloved neighborhood dives like **Gino & Carlo** and literary hangouts like **Washington Square Bar & Grill.** Many of the best old downtown retreats, like the Templebar, 1 Tillman Place, (now a popular bar and lounge called Azul), have given way to more stylish ventures, but a few remnants of Old San Francisco remain, the best of which is **Harrington's Bar & Grill,** a landmark Irish bar that has never been tamed by the genteel Financial District that surrounds it.

Painted ladies... Some 14,000 Victorian buildings—mostly private homes—are scattered throughout San Francisco, but the ones you usually see on the postcards (the 700 block of Steiner St.) are lined up around Alamo Square, the center of a small, wealthy neighborhood bordered by Golden Gate Avenue on the north, Fell Street on the south, Webster Street on the east, and Divisadero Street on the west. These ornate wooden homes range from gracious to almost garish, depending upon how much gingerbread is involved and who has been choosing the color scheme, but most of them have been meticulously restored. For a famous view, with the painted ladies in the foreground and the city and bay in the background, find a high spot anywhere in Alamo Square and face due east (toward Steiner St.), or stand on the corner of Hayes and Steiner streets. The Archbishop's Mansion, 1000 Fell St. (see the Accommodations chapter), now an exclusive bed-and-breakfast inn, is a huge blue Victorian mansion right at the northern edge of the Painted Ladies postcard block. (A word of caution: This affluent area is the southwestern neighbor of the Western Addition, which can be dangerous near the public housing projects, especially at night. If you're not familiar with the area, you may prefer to take a bus or a cab instead of walking.)

If picture-pretty private residences are less intriguing to you than time-worn structures in a working-class neighborhood, head over to the inner Mission District, where several types of the city's oldest Victorians—stick, Italianate, and Queen Anne—can be found on or near Liberty Street, a small side street between 20th and 21st streets. These structures survived the 1906 earthquake because the fires stopped at 20th Street. An 1878 stick-style building, characterized by square bay windows with flat wooden "sticks" that have carved scrolls, leaves, and flowers, stands at 956 Valencia St., on the corner of Liberty. Head north on Liberty, and you'll see rows of Victorians built between 1870 and 1894. At least five of them (19, 23, 35, 43, and 77) are Italianate style, distinguished by ornate porticos, facades above the rooflines, and slanted bay windows designed to bring in more light on foggy San Francisco days. The house at 27 Liberty is a local adaptation of a Queen Anne, identifiable primarily because of the shingled walls (most Queen Annes have rounded corner towers, but there are many variations on this theme). Some of the most interesting houses in the Mission District combined several architectural styles to get just the right amount of gewgaw and curlicues—the house at 827 Guerrero St., corner of Liberty Street, has a Queen Anne tower, a Gothic front window, and a Moorish doorway. The Mission is full of wonderful houses; walk around and explore for yourself.

Mural, mural on the wall... The 200 or so brilliant murals painted on the walls, fences, and sides of buildings in the Mission District are famous around the world, but they're often overlooked by visitors and locals alike. There are at least 250 more murals in other neighborhoods around the city—including the stunning Depression-era murals that cover the interior walls of the base of **Coit Tower.** Keep your eyes open wherever you venture, but here's a tip for quick total immersion in the art of the streets: Take BART to the 24th Street station and head up 24th toward Potrero Hill—you'll see it looming in front of you—until you come to Balmy Alley, nestled between Treat Avenue and Harrison Street. This one-block lane is inundated with murals: practically every inch of every fence, wall, and garage door is covered with color. Many of the alley's most cherished murals were defaced or destroyed by vandals in the past, but local muralists have painted new images and restored old ones. After you've perused Balmy Alley, go back out to 24th Street and head farther toward the hill until you reach York Street, about four blocks away. Again you will be treated to a marvelous assortment of brilliantly colored murals. **Precita Eyes Mural Center,** a community resource center, hosts a tour of this area that will show you at least 60 Mission District murals in one eight-block stretch.

Are we there yet?... The top family attractions besides **Fisherman's Wharf** and **PIER 39** (sorry) are the **Exploratorium, Alcatraz** (see the Getting Outside chapter), and the **San Francisco Zoo & Children's Zoo.** You simply cannot escape these places if your kids are even slightly persuasive. The current hot spot for kids is a place called **Zeum.** Its official tag is "art and technology center for ages 8 to 18," but that title doesn't do it justice. The events calendar features everything from live hip-hop concerts (free with admission) to interactive art studios where teen-artists-in-residence get visitors to help create projects like Megalopolis 3000, "a futuristic cityscape" that teaches kids how to make their own miniature film sets at home. There is also an animator's studio and a film production lab. This is hot, hot stuff for kids. One look at the website (www.zeum.org) will have your kids begging to go. It's a much better way to spend your time—and money— than big-hype **The Metreon,**

> **Bay Area BART Tour**
> One of the world's most complex commuter systems, Bay Area Rapid Transit (BART) links San Francisco with other cities and communities throughout the East and South bays. The air-conditioned train cars run along more than 100 miles of mostly elevated rail, including one of the longest underwater transit tubes in the world (don't let those earthquakes make you nervous). If you have some time and want to take a tour of the Bay Area, BART sells a $4.40 "Excursion Ticket," which allows you, in effect, to "sightsee" the entire BART system, but you must exit at the station where you entered (if you get out anywhere along the line, the gate instantly computes the normal fare). Call or visit their website for more information (Tel 415/989-BART; www.bart.gov).

Sony's huge, slick South of Market entertainment center that is a glorified shopping mall/video arcade/multiplex. The only good thing about The Metreon is that you can drop your teenagers off there for a few hours while you walk around the corner to SFMoMA, a museum they're almost certain to hate. But there are other places they're likely to enjoy, depending on their ages. Youngsters love the Children's Playground in Golden Gate Park, off Waller

Street, opposite Arguello Boulevard, with all the requisite paraphernalia, plus wheelchair-accessible equipment. If they get bored with the slides/swings/sandbox routine, there is a restored 1912 carousel next door. The last thing most teenagers want to do is go anywhere with their parents, but if you promise to hide across the room and pretend not to know them, they might just love you for taking them to the **Hard Rock Cafe,** where you'll need earplugs and they'll need enough money to buy expensive souvenir T-shirts.

Fabulous footsteps... Hills, schmills. Don't let a few slopes deter you from one of San Francisco's greatest pleasures—walking around the neighborhoods and exploring the city for yourself. Before you set out on your own, however, pick up some free walking-tour guides from the Visitor Information Center, Hallidie Plaza, 900 Market St. (Tel 415/391-2000; Powell St. BART/MUNI Metro stop).

The public library also offers about 20 free walking tours led by **City Guides,** volunteers who have completed an exhaustive training program in San Franciscan history, art, and architecture. Tours range from hidden rooftop gardens to brothels and boardinghouses. You can also download free walking tours from the San Francisco Convention & Visitors Bureau website. Guided walking tours of North Beach, Union Square, Pacific Heights, Fisherman's Wharf, and Chinatown are available online (www.sfvisitor.org/visitorinfo/html/walkpdfs.html). (*Note:* These walking tours are in a portable document format; Acrobat Reader is required to access and print PDF files.)

Local individuals who love to show off their favorite parts of San Francisco organize some of the city's most unusual tours. Stroll through cosmic history on the **Haight-Ashbury Flower Power Walking Tour,** with stops at erstwhile crash pads of famous hippies (Janis Joplin and the Grateful Dead) and other lost psychedelic ports of call, such as the Straight Theater, where Bill Graham first staged his dance concerts. Host Trevor Hailey, a beloved—and very friendly—local historian, will take you **Cruisin' the Castro,** where you'll visit only-in-San Francisco businesses, chat with the shopkeepers, enjoy brunch in a local hot spot, and discover why gay men have been migrating to San Francisco since the gold rush.

Television chef and cookbook author Shirley Fong-Torres is the mastermind of the **Wok Wiz Chinatown Walking Tours,** which treats walkers to a private tea ceremony, snacks, a visit to a rice noodle factory, more snacks, visits with local food merchants, another snack, and a full Chinese luncheon. Most guides are Chinese, speak fluent Cantonese or Mandarin, and are intimately acquainted with the neighborhood's alleys and small enterprises, as well as Chinatown's history, folklore, culture, and food.

There are no steep hills to climb in Elaine Sosa's **Javawalk,** a 2-hour jaunt through Union Square, Chinatown, Jackson Square, and North Beach, with pit stops along the way for—what else?—cups of joe. A multicourse lunch is the highlight of Chronicle food writer GraceAnn Walden's **Mangia! North Beach Tour,** a history, food, and culture walking tour that goes behind the scenes at brick-oven bakeries, delis, and sausage makers to show what life is like for serious Italian foodies in San Francisco's favorite neighborhood.

Jay Gifford hosts the **Victorian Homes Historical Walking Tour,** a leisurely 2½-hour tour that incorporates a wealth of knowledge about San Francisco's Victorian architecture and the city's history. You'll stroll through Japantown, the Western Addition (where you can take a break to cruise the trendy shops on Fillmore St.), and onward to Pacific Heights and Cow Hollow. In the process, you'll see more than 200 meticulously restored Victorians. The tour ends with a trolley bus ride back to Union Square, passing through North Beach and Chinatown.

The Index

City Guides (p. 115) Free walking tours offered by the public library range from Mission murals, hidden rooftop gardens, and Pacific Heights mansions to brothels, boardinghouses, and bawds.... *Tel 415/557-4266. www.sfcityguides.org.*

Coit Tower (p. 98) TELEGRAPH HILL Depression-era murals cover the interior walls at the base of the tower, while the top offers a 360-degree view.... *Tel 415/362-0808. www.coittower.org. MUNI bus 39. Daily 10am–6:30pm. Base admission free, elevator $3.75.*
See Map 7 on p. 94.

Cruisin' the Castro (p. 115) CASTRO Walk through the city's gay mecca with a local historian who knows every nook and cranny. Brunch at a popular cafe included. Host: Trevor Hailey.... *Tel 415/255-1821. www.webcastro.com/castrotour. Tour and lunch $45 for adults, $40 seniors over 62, price for children is flexible depending on their age.*

Exploratorium (p. 106) MARINA Kids love this wacky, blow-your-mind science circus—especially the dark and often creepy crawl-through Tactile Dome. The gift shop is probably the best you'll ever encounter at a museum. (Don't miss the Einstein relativity theory wristwatches.)... *Tel 415/561-0360. www.exploratorium.edu. Palace of Fine Arts, 3601 Lyon St. MUNI bus 30. Tues–Sun 10am–5pm. Admission $12 adults; $9.50 seniors, youth 13–17, visitors with disabilities, and college students with ID; $8 children 4–12; free for children under 4.*
See Map 7 on p. 94.

Fisherman's Wharf (p. 104) It's a tacky tourist trap, but if you have to go, try to save your sanity by feasting on some fresh crab from a sidewalk stall and remembering that it used to be a real fishing port. Your kids may want to hit the Wax Museum and the Ripley's Believe It or Not Museum.... *Tel 415/956-3493. www.fishermans wharf.org Any Powell St. cable car; MUNI buses 15, 30, or 42. Free admission.*
See Map 7 on p. 94.

Gino & Carlo (p. 112) NORTH BEACH No bar in North Beach has more loyal regulars than this classic neighborhood dive almost invariably free of tourists. Venture through the double doors, and be prepared for spirited arguments (mostly about sports) and patrons who will retell at least one episode from the bar's long history.... *Tel 415/421-0896. 548 Green St. MUNI bus 15. Daily 6am–2am. Free admission.*
See Map 7 on p. 94.

Glide Memorial United Methodist Church (p. 107) TENDERLOIN Charismatic civic leader Reverend Cecil Williams and his gospel choir host services every Sunday morning that seem to lift the spirits of the whole city.... *Tel 415/674-6000. www.glide.org. 330 Ellis St., west of Union Sq. Services Sun at 9 and 11am. Free admission.*
See Map 7 on p. 94.

Golden Gate Ferry (p. 104) EMBARCADERO Join the locals who ride from San Francisco's Ferry Building at the foot of Market Street to downtown Sausalito, a scenic seaside village with lots of expensive stores, restaurants, real estate, boats—and gorgeous sunsets. The ride takes about a half-hour. Fare is $6.45 each way for adults, $4.85 for children, and $3.80 for seniors. Call for schedule.... *Tel 415/923-2000. www.goldengateferry. org. Embarcadero BART/MUNI Metro stop.*

See Map 7 on p. 94.

Good Vibrations (p. 108) MISSION DISTRICT/NOB HILL This is a comfortable, clean, airy, healthy place to shop for sex toys, sex books, and videos.... *Mission: Tel 415/522-5460; www. goodvibes.com; 603 Valencia St.; 24th St. BART station. Nob Hill: Tel 415/345-0400; 1620 Polk St., at Sacramento St.; Sun–Thurs 11am–7pm, Fri–Sat 11am–8pm.*

See Map 7 on p. 94.

Grizzly Peak (p. 102) BERKELEY A popular Berkeley Hills perch for a great sunset vista of the entire bay. From San Francisco: Drive across the Oakland–San Francisco Bay Bridge, follow the signs to Highway 24 toward Walnut Creek (via Interstate 580), go through the Caldecott Tunnel (stay to the far right), and exit immediately after the tunnel at Fish Ranch Road. (The exit turns sharply right, then right again over the freeway.) Drive up to the top of the hill on Fish Ranch Road, turn right at the stop sign onto Grizzly Peak Boulevard, and drive about a half mile or so until you find a turnout that appeals to you (the view parking spots will be on your left).... *Free admission.*

Haight-Ashbury Flower Power Walking Tour (p. 115) UPPER HAIGHT Take a walking tour through Haight-Ashbury, and check out the crash pads, concert halls, and psychedelic shops that gave birth to the hippie era.... *Tel 415/863-1621. www.hippy gourmet.com. $15 per person. Reservations required.*

Hard Rock Cafe (p. 115) FISHERMAN'S WHARF Teenagers love the super-loud rock music, juicy hamburgers, and T-shirts that prove they've been there.... *Tel 415/956-2013. www.hardrock. com. PIER 39, Fisherman's Wharf. Powell–Hyde cable car; MUNI buses 15, 30, 42, or 69. Sun–Thurs 11am–11pm, Fri–Sat 11am–midnight.*

See Map 7 on p. 94.

Harrington's Bar & Grill (p. 112) DOWNTOWN When original owner Leo Harrington died in 1959, a procession of motorcycle police led a mile-long cortege in his honor—that's how beloved this Irish bar is. The old building is wonderfully creaky, and the floors have been known to get ankle-deep in green beer on St. Patrick's Day.... *Tel 415/392-7595. 245 Front St. California St. cable car. Mon–Sat 11:30am–9:30pm. Closed Sun. Free admission.*

See Map 7 on p. 94.

Javawalk (p. 116) NORTH BEACH Walk the coffee trail in Chinatown, Jackson Square, and North Beach with Elaine Sosa.... *Tel 415/673-9255. www.javawalk.com. Sat 10am. $20 per person, $10 for kids under 12.*

Lyle Tuttle's Tattoo Museum (p. 108) NORTH BEACH Lyle Tuttle is the undisputed king of the San Francisco tattoo empire. His list of satisfied clients includes Gregg Allman, Cher, Joan Baez, and Peter Fonda.... *Tel 415/775-4991. www.lyletuttle.com. 841 Columbus Ave. MUNI buses 15 or 30. Daily noon–9pm. Free admission.*

See Map 7 on p. 94.

Mangia! North Beach Tour (p. 116) NORTH BEACH This 5-hour tour is worth taking just for the full, multicourse lunch. Host: GraceAnn Walden.... *Tel 415/925-9013. Sat only; during the week by prior arrangement. $60 per person.*

Maritime Museum (p. 107) FISHERMAN'S WHARF Kids like it because it looks like a life-size plaster model of a ship. Inside, the nautical exhibits—models, relics, and other inanimate sailor stuff—might bore the youngsters, but the macramé knots are kind of fun for parents with a twinge of '70s arts-and-crafts nostalgia.... *Tel 415/556-3002. www.nps.gov/safr. Fisherman's Wharf, 900 Beach St. Powell–Hyde cable car; MUNI buses 15, 30, 42, or 69. Open daily 10am–5pm. Free admission.*

See Map 7 on p. 94.

The Metreon (p. 114) SOMA Sony's four-story, 350,000-square-foot entertainment arcade is a real money-sucker, from high-tech arcade games changing $1 to $2 a pop and 15 movie theaters at $10 (adult) a go to the overdose of gift and theme stores. Sony has several stores here selling various electronic gadgets, with all items at full retail. It's crowded, it's commercial, and the only real reason to go there is to park your kids while you visit nearby SFMoMA.... *Tel 415/369-6000. www.metreon.com. 101 Fourth St., at Market St. Powell–Hyde or Powell–Mason cable car; Powell St. or Montgomery St. BART/MUNI Metro station; any Market St. MUNI bus. Open 10am–9pm Mon–Thurs, Fri–Sat until 10pm. Free admission.*

See Map 7 on p. 94.

Musée Mécanique (p. 108) FISHERMAN'S WHARF This ingenious little museum is full of mechanical gadgets you can actually play with, from player pianos and old carnival fortune-tellers to an entire miniature amusement park. Bring your own quarters.... *Tel 415/346-2000. Pier 45. Powell–Hyde cable car; MUNI buses 15, 30, 42, or 69. Open Mon–Fri 11am–7pm, weekends 10am–8pm. Free admission.*

See Map 7 on p. 94.

Nick's Lighthouse (p. 104) FISHERMAN'S WHARF Nick's funky sidewalk seafood stall recalls the way things used to be when the area was still a bustling wharf.... *Tel 415/929-1300. www.nickslighthouse.com. Fisherman's Wharf, at Jefferson St. MUNI bus 32. Sun–Thurs 11am–10:30pm, Fri–Sat 11am–11pm.*

See Map 7 on p. 94.

No Name Bar (p. 105) SAUSALITO The music is live (blues and jazz), and the rowdy baby boomers are always in the mood to dance 7 nights a week.... *Tel 415/332-1392. 757 Bridgeway, Sausalito. Daily 10am–2am.*

North Beach Museum (p. 108) NORTH BEACH Tucked away on the mezzanine of the U.S. Bank, this entertaining little museum traces North Beach's history with photographs and artifacts dating back to the turn of the century. Call for schedule.... *Tel 415/391-6210. 1429 Stockton St., at Columbus Ave. MUNI buses 15, 30, or 45. Mon–Fri 10am–5pm. Free admission.*

See Map 7 on p. 94.

Palace of Fine Arts (p. 106) MARINA This wonderful old building resembling a Roman ruin is home to the Exploratorium (see above) and the sole surviving structure from the 1915 Panama Pacific Exposition.... *Tel 415/567-6642. www.palaceoffinearts.org. 3601 Lyon St. MUNI bus 30. Open Tues–Sun 10am–5pm, Wed until 9. Free admission.*

See Map 7 on p. 94.

Pier 23 Cafe (p. 104) EMBARCADERO Great views of the bay and live jazz, R&B, salsa, and reggae. There's even free salsa lessons on Wednesday nights.... *Tel 415/362-5125. www.pier23cafe.com. Pier 23. MUNI bus 32. Daily 10am–2am.*

See Map 7 on p. 94.

PIER 39 (p. 104, 114) FISHERMAN'S WHARF Basically a glorified shopping mall/carnival, but not so bad if you steer toward the sea lions (K-dock).... *Tel 415/705-5500. www.pier39.com. MUNI buses 15, 30, or 42. Open daily 10:30am–8:30pm, restaurants until 11:30. Free admission.*

See Map 7 on p. 94.

Precita Eyes Mural Center (p. 114) MISSION DISTRICT This community resource center for murals and muralists offers information, tours, and workshops.... *Tel 415/285-2287. www.precitaeyes.org. 2981 24th St., near Harrison St. 24th St. BART/MUNI Metro Station. Sat & Sun 11am tour $10 adults, $8 students with ID, $5 seniors, and $2 children under 18; the 1:30pm tour, which is a half hour longer and includes a slide show, costs $12 adults, $8 students with ID, $5 seniors and children under 18.*

See Map 7 on p. 94.

DIVERSIONS

THE INDEX

DIVERSIONS

THE INDEX

Rosicrucian Egyptian Museum (p. 109) SAN JOSE The West Coast's largest collection of Egyptian, Babylonian, and Assyrian antiquities: jewelry, pottery, tools, textiles, mummies, and funerary exotica.... *Tel 408/947-3636. www.egyptianmuseum.org. 1342 Naglee Ave., at Park Ave. Mon–Fri 10am–5pm, Sat–Sun 11am–6pm. Admission $9 adults, $7 seniors and students with ID, $5 children 5–10, free for children under 5.*

San Francisco Museum of Modern Art (p. 106) SOMA Opened in 1995, this ultramodern skylit structure set in the middle of the city's art center, South of Market, features major modern and postmodern artists, but the best part is its huge collection of art photography.... *Tel 415/357-4000. 151 Third St. Montgomery St. BART/MUNI Metro station; MUNI buses 15, 30, or 45. Open daily 11am–5:45pm, Thurs until 8:45pm, closed Wed. Admission $10 adults, $7 seniors, $6 students over 12 with ID, free for children 12 and under; half-price for all Thurs 6–9pm.*

See Map 7 on p. 94.

San Francisco Zoo & Children's Zoo (p. 114) SUNSET DISTRICT At this 125-acre zoo, nothing can top Gorilla World, one of the world's largest assortments of the big guys. Other delights include the Children's Zoo, adjacent to the main park, where kids can pet baby animals in the zoo nursery or visit the Insect Zoo (more than 6,000 specimens).... *Tel 415/753-7080. www.sf zoo.org. Sloat Blvd. and 45th Ave. L Taraval MUNI Metro to the end of the line. Daily 10am–5pm; children's zoo 11am–4pm, weekends and summer 10:30am–4:30pm. Admission to main zoo and children's zoo: adults $9 residents, $11 nonresidents; seniors 65 and over and youth 12–17 $4.50 residents, $8 nonresidents; for children 3–11 $2.50 residents, $5 nonresidents; free for children under 3 accompanied by an adult; $1 discount with valid Muni transfer.*

See Map 7 on p. 94.

Santa Cruz Surfing Museum (p. 109) SANTA CRUZ Cowabunga! This beachside museum features surfboards (from the old redwood "planks" to today's high-tech designs), ancient wetsuits, photos, and other artifacts from 100 years of surfing.... *Tel 831/420-6289. www.santacruzsurfingmuseum.org. Mark Abbott Memorial Lighthouse, West Cliff Dr. Wed–Mon noon–4pm. Donation suggested ($1).*

Specs' Adler Museum Cafe (p. 110) NORTH BEACH This tiny brick-walled bar, a beatnik landmark, is cluttered with mementos including a whale's penis bone that hangs over the bar.... *Tel 415/421-4112. 12 Adler Place, off Columbus Ave. near Broadway. Mon–Fri 4:30pm–2am, Sat–Sun 5:30pm–2am. Free admission.*

See Map 7 on p. 94.

Tosca Cafe (p. 112) NORTH BEACH Everyone who stays in San Francisco long enough eventually ends up at Tosca, where the jukebox plays Pavarotti and the cappuccino automatically comes with a shot of booze.... *Tel 415/986-9651. 242 Columbus Ave. at Broadway. MUNI buses 15 or 30. Daily 5pm–2am. Free admission.*
See Map 7 on p. 94.

Vesuvio (p. 110) NORTH BEACH The list of poets who have spent hours at Vesuvio's getting anywhere from pleasantly buzzed to totally soused stretches from Dylan Thomas (soused) and his namesake Bob Dylan (buzzed) to Jack Kerouac (soused) and Allen Ginsberg (soused and buzzed).... *Tel 415/362-3370. www. vesuvio.com. 255 Columbus Ave., at Broadway. MUNI buses 15 or 30. Free admission.*
See Map 7 on p. 94.

Victorian Homes Historical Walking Tour (p. 116) CITYWIDE See more than 200 meticulously restored Victorians, including the one where *Mrs. Doubtfire* was filmed.... *Tel 415/252-9485. www.victorianwalk.com. $20 per person (including transportation from Union Square).*

Washington Square Bar & Grill (p. 112) NORTH BEACH Whatever it is, it's already been done at the "Washbag"—weddings, wakes, funerals, deals, scandals—during the past quarter-century.... *Tel 415/982-8123. www.wsbg.citysearch.com. 1707 Powell St., at Union St. MUNI buses 15, 30. Lunch Mon–Fri 11:30am–3pm; brunch Sat–Sun 10:30am–3pm; dinner Sun–Tues 5–10pm, Wed–Sat 5–11:30pm, Sun 5:30–11pm. Free admission.*
See Map 7 on p. 94.

Wok Wiz Chinatown Walking Tours (p. 116) CHINATOWN Shirley Fong-Torres lets you in on a private tea ceremony, among other gustatory delights, before you reach your final destination: a huge Chinese luncheon.... *Tel 650/355-9657. www.wokwiz.com. With lunch, $40 adults and $35 children under 11; without lunch, $28 and $23, respectively.*

Yerba Buena Center for the Arts (p. 106) SOMA This dynamic multigallery center focuses on emerging local and regional artists.... *Tel 415/978-ARTS. www.ybca.org. 701 Mission St., at Third St. Montgomery St. BART/MUNI Metro station; MUNI buses 14, 15, 30, or 45. Open Tues, Wed, Sun noon–5pm; Thurs–Sat noon–8pm. Admission for gallery $6 adults, $3 seniors, teachers, and students. Free for seniors and students with ID every Thurs.*
See Map 7 on p. 94.

DIVERSIONS

THE INDEX

Zeum (p. 114) SOMA This is a cutting-edge funhouse where kids not only can see art, film, and computer exhibits, they can help make them. The events calendar includes everything from live hip-hop concerts to workshops with Australian Aboriginal didgeridoo masters. You can't miss the vintage Playland at the Beach carousel at the entrance atop Yerba Buena Gardens.... *Tel 415/ 777-2800. www.zeum.org. 221 Fourth St., at Mission St., Yerba Buena Gardens, Moscone Center. Powell St. BART/Metro MUNI station. Open Wed–Sun 11am–5pm. Admission $7 adults, $6 students and seniors, $5 youths 4–18, free for children under 4.*

See Map 7 on p. 94.

GETTING

OUTSIDE

4

The Bay Area's public greenbelt—more than 860,000 acres of open land and watershed—is the largest of any major metropolitan area in the country. Add undeveloped private land, and there is easily more than a million acres of open space in and around the city, with almost a third of it set aside as public park and recreation areas, including such huge, inviting parks as Golden Gate Park and the Presidio. There's a lot of great stuff to explore offshore, too—the islands that inhabit San Francisco Bay are just a short ferry ride from the heart of the city and a great escape from the hubbub. And, of course, there's the Golden Gate Bridge, which you must walk across before you can truly claim to have seen San Francisco. So get off thy buttocks and go play.

GETTING OUTSIDE

The Lowdown

Parks... Two dozen neighborhood parks within the city limits include facilities for baseball, basketball, barbecues, boating, bird-watching, bocce, bicycling, cricket, jogging, football, fishing, picnics, swimming, tennis, golf, soccer, volleyball, windsurfing, handball, and lawn bowling. Some even have gyms. **Golden Gate Park** covers 1,000 acres stretching from the Panhandle to the beach. Besides various major attractions covered in the Diversions chapter, it has 11 lakes, 2 waterfalls, 21 tennis courts, horseshoe pits (off Conservatory Way near Grove St.; bring your own horseshoes), a nine-hole golf course, fly-casting pools, a miniature yacht club, a 5-acre Japanese Tea Garden, a primitive garden featuring plants from the dinosaur era, and the very same polo grounds where Allen Ginsberg and Timothy Leary ushered in the Summer of Love at the first "Human Be-In" in 1967.

There's even a resident herd of bison at the **Buffalo Paddock** on John F. Kennedy Drive (parallel to 38th Ave.), adjacent to the Chain of Lakes (the bison are particularly fond of stale bread tossed to them by passersby). The animals are the progeny of two cows, Sarah Bernhardt and Princess, and a bull named Ben Harrison, purchased by the city in 1890 and brought down from the Montana plains. Not far from the paddock is the **Model Yacht Club Boat House,** where miniature yachts are prepared for racing on Spreckels Lake by the second-oldest miniature yacht club in America, founded in 1901. Another goofy little wonder is near the M. H. de Young Memorial Museum, off Tenth Avenue and Fulton Street. Called the **Forgotten Works,** it's a field of carved rocks (some hidden beneath the grass) which are actually part of the ruins of El Monasterio de Santa Maria de Avila, a monastery near Madrid, Spain, part of which was reassembled in the museum nearby.

Another fun spot is **Marina Green,** a bayshore strip of park where you can listen to the **Wave Organ,** a bizarre contrivance made of different lengths of pipes that extend into the bay and resonate to the motion of the waves. Sometimes it's so quiet you can barely hear it; other times it's like a soothing liquid mantra. Just west of Marina Green, the **Presidio**—where the city was originally founded as Yerba Buena in 1776—is now a national park, with spectacular views of the Golden Gate Bridge, hiking and biking trails, a fishing stream, and other diversions, not the least of which is the city's pet cemetery. At **Crissy Field,** at the west end of the Golden Gate Promenade in the Presidio, you can watch expert windsurfers carving around on the bay. **Mountain Lake Park,** at the edge of the Presidio, has great running trails, four tennis courts, and fishing; **Lake Merced Park,** near the zoo and Fort Funston, has all the watersports you can imagine, plus two golf courses and lots of jogging trails. It's also the city's best park for bird-watching.

Stretching your legs... Some of the most beautiful—and least hilly—places to jog or walk in San Francisco are its promenades, which trace the shoreline of the bay from the Embarcadero's South Beach area to the foot of the Golden Gate Bridge at Fort Point. MUNI bus 42 will drop you off near China Basin, a block from King Street and the Embarcadero, which is a good place to start your trek along the **South Promenade.** Heading north, you'll experience a stunning perspective change as you approach and then pass directly under the Oakland–San Francisco Bay Bridge. On your left, across the street, you'll see sidewalk cafes and lush palm trees. On your right, nothing but a railing separates you from the bay. It's the most spectacular sea-level view in the city. On Saturdays, you may want to stop at the outdoor farmer's market at the **Ferry Building,** on the Embarcadero at the foot of Market Street. It takes place year-round, rain or shine, every Saturday and Sunday from 8am to 2pm, Tuesdays from 10am to 2pm, and Thursdays from

GETTING OUTSIDE

3 to 7pm at the Ferry Building, on the Embarcadero at the foot of Market Street (about a 15-minute walk from Fisherman's Wharf). If you continue along the Embarcadero, you'll pass PIER 39 on your right and end up at **Fisherman's Wharf.**

The **Golden Gate Promenade** starts at Aquatic Park/Fort Mason at the western edge of Fisherman's Wharf—the MUNI bus 28 route runs near the trail, so you can go one-way or round-trip or stop anywhere along the way. The Promenade, which is marked by blue-and-white signs, ends at **Fort Point,** where steps lead up to the Golden Gate Bridge's pedestrian walkway; the entire route is less than 4 miles long (not counting the walk across the bridge), and it is popular with cyclists because of the beautiful views, varied terrain, and decided lack of automobile traffic. Heading west, there's a 2.5-mile Parcourse loop (a system that includes stations with additional strengthening or conditioning exercises) for fitness buffs who aren't satisfied with a simple walk or jog, as the trail follows the seawall along the Marina Green. Look north and you'll see the Marin Headlands, Mount Tamalpais, Angel Island, and Alcatraz. When you get to the **Palace of Fine Arts,** you will have gone a bit more than 1.5 miles. Continue along the promenade to the **St. Francis Yacht Club,** where, if you want to distract yourself for a quiet moment, you can go east past the lighthouse and the Golden Gate Yacht Club to find the Wave Organ (see "Parks," above). Head back out to the promenade, pass Crissy Field, and you'll have another mile to your credit. From there, it's about one more mile to Fort Point; on a windy day, the ocean may spray its mist onto your face as you pass.

On Sundays and holidays, **Golden Gate Park** is great for jogging; John F. Kennedy Drive is closed to vehicular traffic from 19th Avenue to Kezar Stadium—about 2.5 to 3 miles. To get there, take the N Judah MUNI Metro streetcar or MUNI bus 7 to Kezar, or take MUNI bus 5 to Park Presidio and Fulton Street, then walk into the park to John F. Kennedy Drive. Neighborhood parks with running trails include the 700-acre **Lake Merced** at Harding Road off Skyline Boulevard, and the 15-acre **Mountain Lake Park** at Lake Street and 12th Avenue. Slightly wacky joggers and walkers—two-, four-, or many-legged—are always welcome to join the **Bay to Breakers** in May, one of

America's favorite footraces, when more than 100,000 revelers in goofy costumes make their way from the Embarcadero to the ocean. If you aren't in shape to run the distance ($7^1/_2$ miles), you'll have plenty of company—most people walk, trot, dance, or just sort of drift along with the crowd. It's a popular race; register well in advance (Tel 415/359-2800; www.baytobreakers.com for info) to ensure getting your T-shirt at the finish line.

There is no more intimate view of the city than the fantastic scenery along the route of the **San Francisco Marathon,** run in early July (register by June; Tel 800/698-8699; www.runsfm.com), a time of year when the oddball weather here is generally pleasantly cool. The 26.2-mile race takes runners through some of the city's most scenic areas—the Presidio, the Marina, Ghirardelli Square, PacBell Park, downtown's "Wall Street West"—and the vibrant neighborhoods of North Beach, Chinatown, the Mission District, and Haight-Ashbury. For more information, visit the website.

Pedal pushing... It's no accident that mountain bikes were invented in the Bay Area. There are two basic ways to ride a bicycle in San Francisco—laboring up the hills and zooming back down. Fortunately, however, there are exceptions—most notably Golden Gate Park, the Great Highway, the Golden Gate

---

Bicycles, Bridges, Beers, and Bay Cruises

*One of my all-time favorite things to do on my day off is ride my bike from Fisherman's Wharf to Sam's Anchor Café in Tiburon (that small peninsula just north of Alcatraz Island). It's a beautiful and exhilarating ride that takes you over the Golden Gate Bridge, through the heart of Sausalito, along the scenic North Bay bike path, and ends with a frosty beer and lunch at the best outdoor cafe in the Bay Area. And here's the best part: You don't have to ride back. After lunch, you can take the passenger ferry across the bay to Fisherman's Wharf—right back to where you started. Brilliant. You can rent a single or tandem bike for a full day from **Blazing Saddles** bicycle rental shop at 2715 Hyde St., between Beach and North Point streets near Ghirardelli Square (Tel 415/202-8888; www.blazingsaddles.com). A map pointing out the route to Sam's in Tiburon is free, as is a bike lock and helmet, but be sure to purchase return ferry tickets and a bottle of water from the bike shop. Lastly, bring sunscreen, a hat (for the deck at Sam's), and a light jacket—no matter how warm it seems to be.*

Promenade, and the Golden Gate Bridge—which are relatively easy to ride and absolutely gorgeous to behold. The best time to ride in **Golden Gate Park** is ostensibly on Sunday, when John F. Kennedy Drive ($7^1/_2$ miles) is closed to automobile traffic, but since that fact is well known to every cyclist, in-line skater, jogger, and baby stroller in the city, congestion can be a bit of a nuisance for cyclists, even without cars. A good alternative is to use the park during the week and steer clear of the area between Arguello Street and 19th Avenue, where most of the museums and other popular attractions are located.

The **Great Highway,** from Ocean Beach (at the end of Golden Gate Park) to Lake Merced (turn right on Sloat Blvd.), is an easy 3-mile ride along the ocean on a flat sidewalk with three bike lanes. Add-ons: a 5-mile ride around Lake Merced or a 200-foot ascent on Point Lobos Avenue (near the Cliff House) on your return trip to the park. You can rent a bike for these rides at **Avenue Cyclery,** 756 Stanyan St., at Waller Street (Tel 415/387-3155), but if you're more interested in riding across the Golden Gate Bridge or into the village of Sausalito, you'd be better off picking up your wheels at **Blazing Saddles,** 1095 Columbus Ave., Pier 41, or Pier $43^1/_2$ (Tel 415/202-8888; www. blazingsaddles.com), or the **Adventure Bicycle Company,** 734 Lombard St., North Beach (Tel 415/771-8735; www. adventurebike.com). As their names imply, they rent the latest mountain bikes, as well as cool kids' bikes and tandems. They throw in everything from maps, handlebar bags, water bottles, and cycling computers to windbreakers for the chilly 1.5-mile ride across the bridge.

When you do get to the other side of the bridge—if you're still going for thighs of steel—take the bike lane (parallel to Hwy. 101) from the Vista Point parking lot and turn off onto Alexander Avenue for a downhill jaunt to Sausalito, another 2 miles. Just remember: What goes down, must come up, way up, if you make the 2,500-foot climb to the top of **Mount Tamalpais,** birthplace of the mountain bike. This ride is not for wimps. Nor is it for wannabes. In fact, it's pretty much for maniacs and iron-men, so make sure somebody takes your picture at the summit to prove you actually did it. The rest of us can enjoy the view from a convertible with the top down. **Angel Island** is also a great place to explore on two wheels. Take a ferry (see "Islands with a past," on p. 138) to the state park, and then rent a mountain bike at Ayala Cove (helmet included). There are about 8 miles of beginning and intermediate trails and many steeper advanced trails. Finally, keep in mind that BART allows cyclists to board on off-peak hours. Bike route maps and information are available from the **San Francisco Recreation and Park Department** (Tel 415/831-2700) and the **East Bay Regional Park District** (Tel 510/635-0135).

Working up a sweat... If you get the urge to pump iron in the middle of the night, there's always **24 Hour Fitness,** with several facilities in the city. You won't find many gym rats there, nor will you find many women in the middle of the night, but at other hours there's a fairly even mix of men and women, varied according to the neighborhood. A day pass costs $10 (1200 Van Ness Ave., Tel 415/776-2200; 350 Bay St., Tel 415/395-9595; 303 Second St., Tel 415/543-7808; 2145 Market St., Tel 415/864-0822; and 100 California St., Tel 415/434-5080). Of the city's four YMCA health clubs, the cream of the crop is the **Embarcadero YMCA,** 169 Steuart St. (Tel 415/957-9622; $15 a day), with a sparkling pool, state-of-the-art exercise equipment, and a spectacular view of the bay from the Lifecycle machines. During the week, the club is filled with Financial District types—especially at lunchtime—but on weekends, you're likely to see locals just in from their morning espresso at a North Beach cafe.

Hitting the beach... Here's a newsflash: Northern California ain't anything like Malibu. The water is usually as cold as ice, the wind can be fierce enough to blow your tuna sandwich into the next person's picnic basket, and the summer sky is generally overcast—though it will still give you dreadful sunburn if you don't wear sunblock. So don't look for swaying palms and white-sand beaches. That's a different California. The rugged, cliffside beaches here are some of the most spectacular in the world. Huge waves crash against sheer walls of rock, but a treacherous undertow and unpredictable surf conditions make them dangerous for swimming.

    Ocean Beach (at the end of Golden Gate Park, near the Cliff House) is the most dramatic seaside vista in the city—at least the sea lions that gather on Seal Rocks seem to think so—but it is absolutely forbidden to swim there.

GoCar Tours of San Francisco

If the thought of walking up and down San Francisco's brutally steep streets has you sweating already, consider renting a talking **GoCar** *instead. The tiny yellow three-wheeled convertible cars are easy and fun to drive—every time I see one of these things the people riding in them are grinning from ear to ear—and they're cleverly guided by a talking GPS (Global Positioning System), which means that the car always knows where you are, even if you don't. The most popular computer-guided tour is a 2-hour loop around the Fisherman's Wharf area, out to the Marina District, through Golden Gate Park, and down Lombard Street. As you drive, the talking car tells you where to turn and what landmarks you're passing. Even if you stop to check something out, as soon as you turn your GoCar back on, the tour picks up where it left off. Or you can just cruise around wherever you want (but not across the Golden Gate Bridge). There's a lockable trunk for your things, and the small size makes parking a breeze. You can rent a GoCar from 1 hour (about $40) to a full day. You'll have to wear a helmet, and you must be a licensed driver at least 18 years of age. The GoCar rental shop is at 2715 Hyde St, between Beach and North Point streets at Fisherman's Wharf, (Tel 800/91-GoCar or 415/441-5695; www.gocarsf.com.)*

You can enjoy sunbathing, beachcombing, hiking, and sipping a drink at the **Cliff House,** 1090 Point Lobos Ave. (Tel 415/386-3330), but don't even think about dipping your little toe in the water. Swimming is also prohibited at **Land's End Beach** (north of the Cliff House), **Kirby Beach** (below the northern end of the Golden Gate Bridge), **Rodeo Beach** (at Fort Cronkite, Marin Headlands), and **Tennessee Beach** (north of Rodeo Beach), though beachcombing can be fun if you stay a safe distance from the water. There are safe swimming beaches in the city, if you can stand the cold water: **China Beach,** 28th Avenue and Sea Cliff Drive, and **Aquatic Park,** end of Hyde Street. Both are sandy coves where lifeguards are on duty during the summer; they're open April 15 to October 15 from 7am to dusk. More popular with adventurous locals is **Baker Beach,** where nude sunbathing is fashionable for gay and straight sunbathers. Officially designated clothing-optional by the city, it's easily reached by public transportation. The truly gay men's section is beyond the large rock formations, which are most easily navigated at low tide. That part of the beach is definitely a cruise scene. The rest of the beach, however, has a predominant atmosphere of comfortable indifference to the fact that many people are not wearing clothes. Swimming is not prohibited but is definitely very dangerous and should be avoided. No lifeguards are on duty; there are changing rooms, which seem rather pointless when no one's wearing clothes anyway. The beach is open April 15 to October 15 from 7am to 9pm.

If you want to meet some real-live local maniacs, get out the wetsuit and join in the **Alcatraz Shark Fest** each September, a 1.5-mile swim from the Rock to the city shore. Believe it or not, it's a pretty popular event, so pre-register (Tel 415/868-1829; www.envirosports.com). For beachcombing, tide-pool exploring, hiking, camping, or bed-and-breakfast getaways, a trip to **Point Reyes National Seashore** is without equal. At 65,000 acres, it's the largest and wildest section of the Bay Area's green-belt—32,000 acres of designated wilderness. You may even be lucky enough to spot a great white shark out in the water. Point Reyes' beaches and tiny villages are accessible by **Golden Gate Transit** public transportation (Tel 415/923-2000) but are much easier to reach by car, less than an hour from the city.

Bathing in the buff beyond Baker Beach... While Baker Beach (see "Hitting the beach," above) is the most popular, three other city beaches are also clothing-optional—**Land's End, Fort Funston Beach,** and **Golden Gate Bridge Beach**—and bare-butt bathing is allowed at all **Golden Gate National Recreation Area beaches** as long as nobody complains (which they rarely do). To get the skinny on any—or all—of California's nude beaches, check out the *Bay Guardian*'s online guide at www.sfbg.com.

Poolside plunges... Okay, the beaches weren't made for swimming, and not many of the hotels have pools, but if you really want to take off your summer cold-weather gear and dive in, the best poolside scene in the city is at **The Phoenix,** 601 Eddy St. (Tel 415/776-1380; see the Accommodations chapter), where rock stars and their groupies lounge, socialize, sip cocktails, and sometimes even swim—but you must be a hotel guest (or invited by one) to join in. The abstract mural on the bottom of the pool—painted by New York City artist Francis Forienza—was almost outlawed by state inspectors, who insisted it was a hazard and claimed, "People have been hurt by art before." Ultimately the governor of California enacted a bill exempting the mural from an antiquated law that requires all pool bottoms to be painted white.

Watersports... You won't have to worry about dangerous murals lurking at the bottom of the bay when you go sea kayaking, windsurfing, sailing, or fishing. Watching the windsurfers on the bay just off Crissy Field, it's easy to forget there are skyscrapers a few minutes away. On an ideal day, the waves are high and the wind is strong enough to give advanced windsurfers a ride that would make anyone forget the stress of urban life; beginners should definitely stick with calmer waters.

The **San Francisco School of Windsurfing** (Tel 415/753-3235) offers lessons and rentals. All-day kayaking trips offered by **Sea Trek Ocean Kayaking Center** are definitely the up-close-and-personal way to enjoy the dramatic cliffs, secluded beaches, and unbelievable views on Angel Island—and you don't even have to know how to paddle. All trips are led by expert naturalists and require specific advance reservations; the $110 to $135 fee includes lunch. Paddlers may rent single kayaks for $15 the first hour, and doubles rent for $25 the first hour (Tel 415/488-1000; www.seatrekkayak.com).

Sailing is kind of a misnomer for what one does in a rented boat on **Stow Lake** in Golden Gate Park (Tel 415/752-0347), but few things in life are more fun than getting in a pedal boat with someone else and simply pretending to pedal while your friend does all the work. At Stow Lake, you can also rent rowboats, which are especially suitable for afternoon trysts or for dressing up fancy and pretending you're in an Impressionist painting. If you're feeling sort of Hemingway-esque and you just have to get out on the bay in a real boat, **Spinnaker Sailing,** Pier 40, South Beach Harbor (Tel 415/543-7333), offers sailing instruction and rentals. If you'd rather sip cocktails and let the captain sail the ship, there are dozens of charters, from dinner cruises to overnighters aboard yachts (see the Diversions chapter). **Cass Marina,** 1702 Bridgeway, Sausalito (Tel 800/472-4595 or 415/332-6789; www.cassmarina.com), is a sailing school that also rents sailboats measuring 22 to 35 feet. You can sail under the Golden Gate Bridge on your own or with a licensed skipper.

Reeling them in... If that Hemingway thing just won't go away, you could always pay your money and take your chances on a fishing boat. There are dozens of charters, but only one is owned and operated by a woman: **Wacky Jacky** (Tel 415/586-9800). Skipper Jacky has been having a great time on the bay for more than 30 years, and her sense of humor makes even the most inexperienced angler have fun—and catch fish. A day on Jacky's sleek, fast 50-footer (board at Fisherman's Wharf at 5:30am, depart 6am, return 3pm) will cost around $85, including license, rod, tackle, and anything else you'll need to land a big fish. The **Berkeley Marina Sports Center** (Tel 510/849-2727; www.berkeleysportfishing.com), also makes daily trips for ling cod, rock fish, and many other types of game fish year-round, and trips for salmon runs April through October. And if the swoosh-swoosh-plop of a perfect fly-cast is your cup of tea, bring your own rod to the **Golden Gate Park Fly Casting Pools,** opposite the Buffalo Paddock off John F. Kennedy Dr. (Tel 415/386-2630), where tournament-level fly-casters can be found practicing (ask them for pointers). Tuesday, Saturday, and Sunday are the best days; there's no fee, but then there are no fish here either—it's strictly for practice.

Par for the course... If you suddenly get the urge to sink one but you didn't bring your clubs, don't worry. The **Lincoln Park Golf Course,** 34th Ave. and Clement St., near the California Palace of the Legion of Honor (Tel 415/221-9911), will rent you a set of clubs for $25 and send you out to try your luck on this 18-hole, par-68 course, where you may get distracted by the vista of the Pacific Ocean and the Golden Gate Bridge. Greens fees are $31 weekdays, $35 weekends; golf carts are $25.

The magnificent **Presidio Golf Course,** 300 Finley Rd. (Tel 415/561-4664)—where Teddy Roosevelt, Dwight Eisenhower, and even Babe Ruth used to play—was opened to the public in 1995 when the Presidio became a national park. The 18-hole, par-72 course—San Francisco's oldest—overlooks the Pacific Ocean, San Francisco Bay, and the city itself. It is spectacular, immensely popular, and expensive: Greens fees are $50 until 12:30pm for residents Monday through Thursday and $96 for nonresidents; rates drop to $40 until 2pm and then $26 for the rest

GETTING OUTSIDE

of the day for residents and nonresidents. Friday though Sunday rates are $96 for residents and $108 for nonresidents from 8am to 11am; from 11am to 12:30pm, the cost is $60 for residents, and after that it's $50 for everyone until 2pm, and for the rest of the day $26 (got all that?). You can book a tee time, preferably well in advance, online at www.presidiogolf.com (click on "Reservations").

The **Golden Gate Golf Course,** 47th Avenue and Fulton Street (Tel 415/751-8987; www.goldengatepark golf.com) is less challenging—9 holes, par 27, and 1,357 yards—but it's three blocks from the Pacific Ocean and is a great place to practice your swing and stay in shape without spending a fortune. Greens fees are just $13 weekdays, $18 weekends. A good place to tune up your game is the **Mission Bay Golf Center,** Sixth Street at Channel Street (Tel 415/431-7888). San Francisco's most popular driving range is an impeccably maintained 7-acre facility that consists of a double-decker steel and concrete arc containing 66 covered practice bays. The grass landing area extends 300 yards, has nine target greens, and is lit for evening use. There's a putting green and a chipping and bunker practice area. The center is open Monday from 11:30am to 11pm, and Tuesday through Sunday from 7am to 11pm. A bucket of balls costs $8, and the last bucket is sold at 10pm. To get there from downtown San Francisco, take Fourth Street south to Channel Street and turn right.

If you need golfing info, call the **Automated Tee Time and Golf Information Line** (Tel 415/750-4653), with a menu of information on San Francisco's five public courses—tee times, fees, directions, and more. You can reserve a tee time, get directions to the courses, and obtain information on the hours of operation, greens fees, cart and club rentals, and lessons.

Lawn bowling... At the opposite end of the park, you'll find another rather peculiar sport—lawn bowling. Free lessons are offered by the **San Francisco Lawn Bowling Club** at the Golden Gate Park Bowling Green (Tel 415/753-9298). The three greens are located just south of the tennis courts on Bowling Green Drive between Middle Drive East and MLK Jr. Drive.

Islands with a past... Alcatraz is certainly the most commemorated of the San Francisco Bay's 14 islands—virtually every souvenir stand in the city sells a variety of tacky T-shirts proclaiming the wearer to be an inmate, escapee, or survivor of the notorious island prison, once home to folks like Al Capone and Machine Gun Kelly. But far from being a tourist trap, it's more like a set for a nightmarish Fellini movie co-authored by Stephen King—part bucolic Mediterranean island, part claustrophobic cellblock nightmare. After the prison was closed down, fitness guru Jack LaLanne once swam from Alcatraz to the city's shore handcuffed or blindfolded or both (who can remember?), perhaps inspiring today's **Escape from Alcatraz triathlon,** which originally included a bicycle ride to Marin County and a brutal Double Dipsea run over a twisted, mountainous course—better designed for billy goats—from Stinson Beach to Mill Valley and back. The race now finishes with a 12-mile run through the Golden Gate National Recreation Area and has 500 competitors. Aside from morbid and/or historical fascination, however, the jagged island, 135 feet above the bay, is a surprisingly nice spot for walking, with views of the city's skyline and the Golden Gate Bridge that are worth every penny of the $16 round-trip ferry ride (children $11, seniors $15; ferries operated by Blue & Gold Fleet; Tel 415/773-1188). Ferry reservations are suggested at least two weeks in advance during the summer. Also, wear comfortable shoes and take a heavy sweater or windbreaker because even when the sun's out, it's cold.

   Angel Island—a 640-acre state park with a 360-degree view of the bay from atop Mount Livermore (781 ft.)—is a favorite with locals for cycling, hiking, sea-kayaking, and overnight camping. Besides being a quarantine station and a Nike missile base, it was once a detention center for more than 175,000 Chinese and other Pacific Rim immigrants (1910–40). It used to be nearly impossible to explore that immigration station, but now the park offers an open-air **TramTour** (Tel 415/897-0715; www.angelisland.com) through the area, with a narrated history and aerial views that evoke audible sighs from passengers. Fare is $13, $7.50 for children 6 to 12, $11 for seniors. Ferries to Angel Island, operated by Blue & Gold Fleet (Tel 415/705-5555; www.blueandgoldfleet.com), cost $12 round-trip, $6.50 for children 6 to 11. For cycling information, see "Pedal pushing," earlier in this chapter; for kayaking, see "Watersports," above.

Skates at the Haight... Always good for a laugh is a day spent skating through **Golden Gate Park** (particularly if your skating skills are rusty). Although people skate in Golden Gate Park all week long, Sunday is best because on Sundays, John F. Kennedy Drive between Kezar Drive and Transverse Road is closed to automobiles. Another hot skating, biking, and walking spot is the **Embarcadero promenade,** which stretches from SBC Park (Townsend St. and Embarcadero) to Fisherman's Wharf. **Skates on Haight,** 1818 Haight St. (Tel 415/752-8375; www.skatesonhaight.com), located a block from the park, is the best place to rent in-line or conventional skates. The cost of $9 per hour includes protective wrist guards and kneepads.

GETTING OUTSIDE

> ### San Francisco Segway Tours
>
> *So new on the San Francisco scene that even the locals haven't figured out where they're coming from, Segway Human Transporters are those weird-looking upright scooters you've probably seen on TV. The two-wheeled transporter is an ingenious electric-powered transportation device that uses gyroscopes to emulate human balance. After the free 40-minute lesson, riding a Segway becomes intuitive: lean forward, go forward; lean back, go back; stand up, stop. Simple. The **San Francisco Electric Tour Company** offers Segway-powered tours of the San Francisco waterfront daily, starting from Fisherman's Wharf and heading out all the way to the Marina Green. It's the closest you'll come to being a celebrity (everyone checks you out) and very fun. **Note:** You have be at least 12 years old to join the tour. For more information log onto their website or give them a call (Tel 415/474-3130; www.sfelectrictour.com).*

The wine country... Most people, including locals, don't realize that California's famous Napa Valley wine country is less than an hour and a half from downtown San Francisco by car. If you leave the city around 10am, you'll miss the morning traffic and be in the heart of vineyard-and-spa land in time for lunch. Take the Golden Gate Bridge out of town and stay on Highway 101 North about 15 miles and take Highway 37 East (toward Napa). After about 8 miles, turn left onto 121 North, then right on Highway 12, which eventually takes you to Highway 29, the main road through the Napa Valley. As you drive along it, you'll see dozens of NO WINERY HERE signs on side roads and driveways, a testament to the hundreds of wineries—and millions of visitors—in the area.

It's possible to check out a few choice wineries in an afternoon without straying far from Highway 29. Be sure to stop in at the first winery you see when you leave the town of Napa: **Trefethen,** 1160 Oak Knoll Ave., Napa (Tel 707/255-7700; www.trefethen.com). Built in 1886 and meticulously restored, it is the only existing wooden "gravity-flow" winery in Napa County and is on the National Register of Historic Places. A bit farther up the highway, one of the largest modern art collections in California is housed at what was once the Christian Brothers' first Napa Valley winery.

The **Hess Collection,** 4411 Redwood Rd., Napa (Tel 707/255-1144; www.hesscollection.com), is a working winery, but its biggest draw is beautiful ivy-covered stone buildings (ca. 1903) and a permanent exhibit of paintings and sculptures by contemporary artists such as Francis Bacon, Robert Motherwell, Frank Stella, Magdalena Abakanowicz, and Gerhard Richter. The collection is open to the public daily 10am to 4pm. The next must-stop is **Niebaum-Coppola,** 1991 St. Helena Hwy., Rutherford (Tel 707/968-1100; www.niebaum-coppola.com), a magnificent 19th-century chateau that had been chopped up and sold to a huge vintner's conglomerate before Francis Ford Coppola and his family bought it in 1995. A big draw here is the two-floor display of Coppola's personal movie memorabilia collection, including his Oscars, handwritten scripts and storyboards, and Don Corleone's desk from *The Godfather*.

Continuing to Calistoga, treat yourself to a bottle of bubbly at **Schramsberg,** 1400 Schramsberg Rd., Calistoga (Tel 707/942-2414; www.schramsberg.com). Immortalized by Robert Louis Stevenson, who called wine "bottled poetry," Schramsberg's sparkling wine was served as the "Toast to Peace" between President Nixon and Premier Chou En-lai in Beijing in 1972 and has been poured in the White House ever since. Ironically, it was Chinese "coolie" laborers who built most of the two miles of caves in which the wine is aged. Built in 1862, Schramsberg is an historical landmark and one of the most interesting tours in the Wine Country.

Dozens of books, websites, and tours are devoted to California's wine country. The most comprehensive Napa Valley website, **www.napavalleyonline.com**, offers as many options on its home page as Yahoo! plus detailed maps and a webcam stationed in a St. Helena vineyard that updates photos hourly.

Insider's tip: Most small, family-owned wineries allow visitors only by appointment. It's worth a call to arrange a tour, where you will likely get to meet and talk with the winemaker instead of a tour guide.

Soothing spas and marvelous massages... The spa that's most recommended by locals to their out-of-town guests is **Kabuki Springs & Spa,** 1750 Geary Blvd. (Tel 415/ 922-6000; www.kabukisprings.com), in Japantown. There are few, if any, misfortunes that a soak in the Kabuki's communal hot pool can't cure. The ultimate city indulgence has separate days for men and women except co-ed Tuesdays (women's days are Sun, Wed, and Fri; men are welcome Mon, Thurs, and Sat) and costs a mere $16 to $20. The service menu also includes massage ($55–$125), facials, seaweed wraps, and an 80-minute Javanese Lulur body treatment that involves flower oil massage, a jasmine scrub, a yogurt massage, and an exotic flower bath ($115).

If you want all of these spa services and one of the most beautiful urban resort settings in America, take BART just four stops across the bay to Rockridge and have a cab drop you off at the **Claremont Resort & Spa,** Ashby and Domingo avenues, Oakland (Tel 800/551-7266; www.claremontresort.com). This spectacular Victorian landmark hotel, nestled in 22 lush acres at the foot of the Oakland/Berkeley hills, is especially lovely during the summer—when San Francisco is foggy and cold, the Claremont is sunny and warm. The full-service European spa here offers nine different types of massage, seven body-care treatment packages, and many varieties of facials and salon treatments. Reservations are a must—1 to 2 weeks in advance for weekend visits—but midweek visits can often be arranged on the same day.

PING

5

Map 8: San Francisco Shopping

Aardvark's Odd Ark **27**
African Safari **2**
American Rag CIE **10**
Amoeba Music **20**
The Anonymous Place **9**
Basic Brown Bear **30**
The Bead Store **41**
The Booksmith **23**
The Buddhist Bookstore **6**
Buffalo Exchange **28**
Carol Doda's Champagne and Lace Lingerie Boutique **8**
Citizen **44**
City Lights Bookstore **17**
A Clean Well-Lighted Place For Books **36**
Cronan Artefact **31**
Crystal Way **42**
D&M Wine and Liquor Co. **5**
Dal Jeets **21**
Danilo Bakery **14**
A Different Light **43**
Dottie Doolittle **3**
Forever After Books **26**
Gargoyle Beads **25**
General Bead **34**
Gimme Shoes **38**
Good Vibrations **11**
House of Cashmere **7**
Italian French Baking Co. **12**
Lady Luck Candle Shop **39**
Let It Be **19**
Medium Rare Records **40**
Minis By Profili **4**
Molinari's **16**
Open Mind Music **1**
Patrick James **8**
Piedmont Boutique **24**
PlaNetweavers Treasure Store **29**
Rolo SF **35**
Stella Pastry & Caffe **15**
Stormy Leather **33**
A Taste of Leather **32**
Wasteland **22**
Worldware **37**
Yone of San Francisco **13**

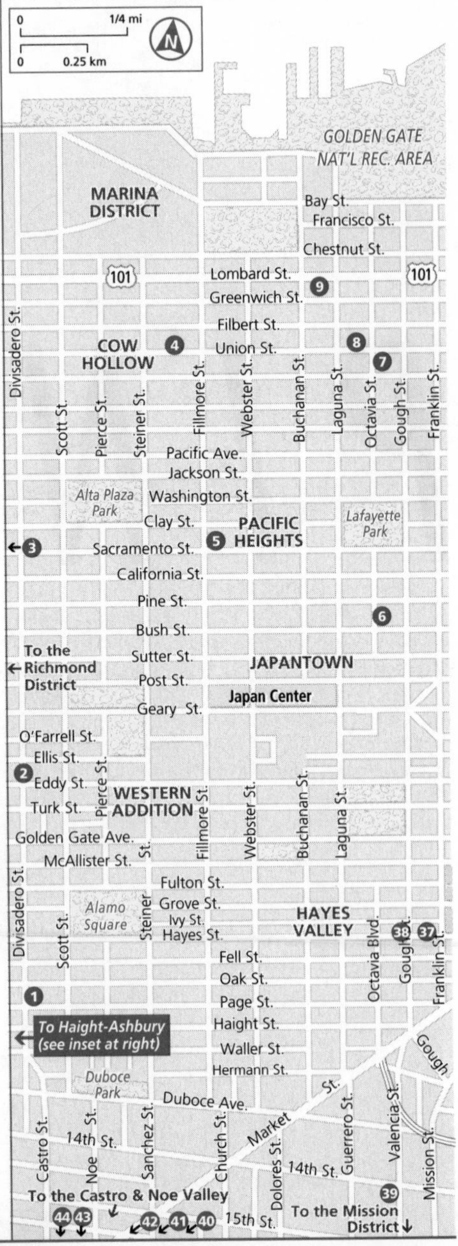
0 1/4 mi
0 0.25 km
N
GOLDEN GATE NAT'L REC. AREA
MARINA DISTRICT
Bay St.
Francisco St.
Chestnut St.
101
Lombard St.
Greenwich St.
Filbert St.
Union St.
COW HOLLOW
Divisadero St.
Scott St.
Pierce St.
Steiner St.
Fillmore St.
Webster St.
Buchanan St.
Laguna St.
Octavia St.
Gough St.
Franklin St.
Pacific Ave.
Jackson St.
Washington St.
Alta Plaza Park
Clay St.
PACIFIC HEIGHTS
Lafayette Park
Sacramento St.
California St.
Pine St.
Bush St.
To the Richmond District
Sutter St.
JAPANTOWN
Post St.
Japan Center
Geary St.
O'Farrell St.
Ellis St.
Eddy St.
Turk St.
WESTERN ADDITION
Golden Gate Ave.
McAllister St.
Fulton St.
Grove St.
Alamo Square
Ivy St.
Hayes St.
HAYES VALLEY
Octavia Blvd.
Fell St.
Oak St.
Page St.
Haight St.
To Haight-Ashbury (see inset at right)
Waller St.
Hermann St.
Duboce Park
Duboce Ave.
Market St.
Gough
Castro St.
Noe St.
Sanchez St.
Church St.
Dolores St.
Guerrero St.
Valencia St.
Mission St.
14th St.
15th St.
To the Castro & Noe Valley
To the Mission District

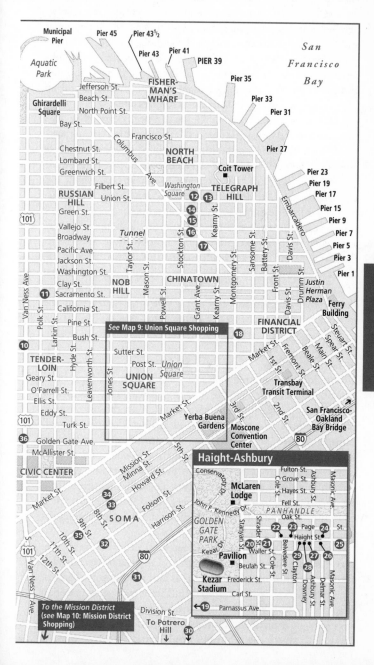

Like its population, San Francisco's shopping scene is incredibly diverse. Every style, era, fetish, and financial status is represented here—not in huge shopping malls, but in hundreds of boutiques and secondhand stores scattered throughout the city. Whether it's a Chanel knockoff or Chinese herbal medicine you're looking for, San Francisco's got it. Just pick a shopping neighborhood and give yourself a spending budget, and you're sure to end up with at least a few affordable take-home treasures.

Then, of course, there's Union Square, where the city's conservative and classic side asserts itself with high-end department stores and designer boutiques. Refined dowagers in white gloves still bemoan the loss of the landmark City of Paris building, on the corner of Stockton and Geary streets, which has been replaced by the modern Neiman-Marcus store. But tradition is hardly threatened in this neighborhood.

Not much can be said for San Francisco's shopping centers and malls. With few exceptions, an afternoon at the Anchorage, the Cannery, the Crocker Galleria, or PIER 39 isn't all that different from an afternoon in any other well-groomed mall. Some of the stores are in historic buildings—just as they are in Denver, Seattle, Sacramento, and dozens of other cities—but the intrigue tends to end with the architecture.

Target Zones

Union Square (bordered by Kearny and Mason sts., from Market St. to Bush St.) is the stop for department stores and designer shops that rival the world's best. Even the larger stores offer courteous personal service and at least a couple of small cafes; Saks and Neiman Marcus still provide elegant lounges where female shoppers can freshen their lipstick and rest on comfy chairs when a quick trip to the toilet just isn't enough. Nearby **Maiden Lane,** a hidden two-block alley that runs from Kearny Street to Stockton Street (between Geary and Post sts.), continues to count Brooks Brothers and Chanel among its many upscale tenants.

Oh-so-prettified **Union Street** (between Van Ness Ave. and Fillmore St.) has become rather old-hat and overpriced, a favorite haunt of well-heeled tourists and visiting suburbanites. Union Street's shops seem to sell stuff from everywhere but San Francisco—New York bagels, Seattle coffee, European clothes. It's also a great place to find top-quality children's clothing and toys or just watch the beautiful people parade by.

Fillmore Street (between Sutter and Jackson sts.) is on the verge of becoming the next Union Street. A few short years ago, when there were just a handful of interesting shops and cafes— and D & M Wine and Liquor Co., the best wine store in the city—some of the merchants tried to establish this small patch of real estate as part of wealthy Pacific Heights rather than the notoriously slummy Fillmore District. They succeeded. Now you have to wait in line to get a cup of coffee on a Sunday morning, the bars are jammed with *GQ*-model look-alikes, and the sidewalks are congested with yuppie baby strollers. Locals looking for something truly interesting to do look elsewhere.

Chinatown is one of the most popular neighborhoods among tourists, though the bounty to be found here is often of dubious value—souvenirs made in Taiwan, jade jewelry at a discount, or XXX-rated fortune cookies. Hand-painted signs swear that everybody is going out of business and must sell everything at incredibly low prices *right now*. Sidewalk stalls are stuffed with every plastic and rubber item ever sold for less than $5. Herbalists sell dragon's blood and other exotic ingredients next to vegetable stands, jewelry stores, banks, and dim sum parlors. There are some fun bazaars, though, and the smells alone are worth the visit. Grant Avenue is the area's main thoroughfare, and the side streets between Bush Street and Columbus Avenue are full of restaurants, markets, and eclectic shops. Stockton Street is best for grocery shopping (including live fowl and fish). Walking is best, since traffic through this area is slow at best and parking is next to impossible. Most stores in Chinatown are open daily from 10am to 10pm.

The **Hayes Valley** (Hayes St. between Franklin and Buchanan sts.) is a happy byproduct of the 1989 earthquake, which brought down a nearby freeway and let the sunshine in. It's fun, hip, eclectic, friendly, and not yet full of itself, mainly because it's not the prettiest area in town, with some of the shadier housing projects a few blocks away. But while most neighborhoods cater to more conservative or trendy shoppers, lower Hayes Street, between Octavia and Gough, celebrates anything vintage, artistic, or downright funky. Still in its developmental stage, it's definitely the most interesting newer shopping area in town, with furniture and glass stores, thrift shops, trendy shoe stores, and men's and women's clothiers. You can find lots of great antiques shops south on Octavia and on nearby Market Street.

San Francisco is loaded with thrift stores and secondhand clothing stores, a prime source of cool couture for local hipsters (though prices on quasi-vintage clothing, which can be very hip, can also be steep). Haight, Valencia, and Mission streets are the best spots for super scores. (Also see "Recycled regalia" and "Cheap thrills," below.) For discounts on all kinds of new merchandise, there are more than 40 factory outlets South of Market—you really need a guide to hit them all, especially since the city's only version of an outlet mall, Yerba Buena Square, is now defunct. All you'll find there now is a multilevel Burlington Coat Factory, and who would go all the way to San Francisco for that?

SHOPPING

Haight Street ain't what it used to be, but it's still quasi-psychedelic and filled with people and things you certainly won't see in Kansas. Vintage clothing stores are a big thing, but the value ranges from great deals on retro-fashions to ridiculously overpriced castoffs. Don't get caught paying $75 for a used Levi's jacket just because some guy with a mohawk cut the sleeves off it. If you're looking for avant-garde new clothing and shoes, this is the place. And if you're a man looking for a pair of shimmering red cha-cha heels in a perfect size 12, this may be the only place. Most of the shops are between Central and Stanyan streets.

North Beach will never leave you bored, with everything from beatnik bookstores and hippie poster shops to tattoo parlors and record stores. You can buy postcards, wigs, shoestrings, old clothes, new clothes, incense, bells, beads, crystals, jewelry, pasta machines, furniture, focaccia, and anything else you can imagine—even a new set of bocce balls.

The **Mission District** (between 16th and 24th sts.) is a weird and wonderful place to shop, if you can handle being on two planets at once. Mission Street has the tightest cocktail dresses and shiniest spiked-heel shoes in town, alongside pure white confirmation and wedding dresses. Valencia Street sells used books and new vibrators, candles for Catholic and other rituals, expensive clothes that look like they've already been through the wringer, antiques, and thrift-shop treasures.

Trading with the Natives

San Francisco's merchants are by and large well disposed toward out-of-towners. All major department stores will hold merchandise for a reasonable amount of time and will ship your packages home for you. (If you live out of state, you won't have to pay sales tax.) Most will accept your personal check if you have proper identification, such as a driver's license with photo; it is illegal to ask for a credit card as a form of identification. Some small stores may not accept out-of-state checks, but as a rule, paying by check is not a problem in the Bay Area. It's not common practice to negotiate prices unless you're at a flea market, garage sale, or used-car lot, but it's always acceptable to point out a flaw or defect and ask for a reduction. (Whether you get it is up to the sales staff.) Most department stores will usually give you 10% to 20% off for a broken zipper, missing button, or similar problem; smaller stores vary in their policies. Stores are not required to give refunds if you're not satisfied with your purchase—many stores will, though some will offer it only in the form of exchange credit. Stores cannot charge an extra fee for credit card purchases but may offer a discount for cash payment.

Hours of Business

Most stores tend to open around 10 or 11am (noon on Sun) and close up at times that suit the neighborhood and clientele— usually around 6pm. Department stores usually stay open through early evening, while many neighborhood boutiques and bookstores don't close until 10 or 11 at night.

Sales Tax

A sales tax of 8.5% is added to every purchase unless the store ships it out of state for you. This is a state tax, with a .25% surcharge for rapid-transit subsidy; some outlying areas don't include this surcharge, leaving the tax at 8.25%. To make matters more confusing, some items—including just about anything edible—are not taxable.

The Lowdown

Shopping bags to show off... When shopping in Union Square's exclusive stores, it's always wise to carry a shopping bag that proves you're buying—not just looking—and therefore deserve deferential treatment. Post Street is heaven for bourgeois bags; you can start small, with a few pieces of candy from **Saks Fifth Avenue,** so long as you get a nice big bag to carry them. Then carry the bag with the logo in full view as you work your way down Post Street, visiting **Tiffany and Co., Cartier, Louis Vuitton, Burberry's, Brooks Brothers, Gump's,** or **The Polo Store/Ralph Lauren.**

Are you being served?... The best service in town is definitely proffered by **Nordstrom,** in the San Francisco Centre. While you relax in the fitting room, sales assistants will run up and down the store's five floors to locate a blouse in the exact shade of ivory that flatters your face and matches the navy skirt you're thinking about buying. They'll even keep a customer card on file if you have particular needs and intend to return to shop some other time. If that's not enough to make you feel pampered, Nordstrom also offers a full-service European spa and four restaurants.

One-stop shopping... Head for the department stores. There's no shame in shopping at **Macy's,** especially now that it's got an entire building devoted to men's clothing and accessories. Plus, there are almost always sales and clearance racks in every department. The other big department stores are **Neiman Marcus,** the super-upscale Texas implant that's sometimes bigger on price than on taste (it does offer a fur salon for those who aren't afraid of being pelted by animal-rights activists); **Saks Fifth Avenue,** where the sales staff can be a bit too uppity for the rather pedestrian merchandise on display; and, as mentioned above, **Nordstrom,** which is the most fun of any of them.

No business like shoe business... Nordstrom probably has the largest selection of women's and men's shoes in the city, in prices ranging from reasonable to check-your-credit-limit. If expensive isn't a scary concept to you, head to **Kenneth Cole** (in the San Francisco Centre, the same mall that houses Nordstrom) for trendy, high-fashion numbers. **Gimme Shoes** on Hayes Street sells funky new designs from Belgium and France. And don't forget those sensible shoes: Get 'em at **Ria's, Birkenstock Natural Footwear,** and **First Step.**

If it's July, you're going to need a sweater... Tse Cashmere features rich colors and luxurious 10-ply handknits; **House of Cashmere** is just what its name implies; and **Irish Castle Shop** has fisherman-knit sweaters and the claim to fame of having served Sinéad O'Connor in the past.

For men who want to look like Cary Grant... It's tough to go wrong at **Wilkes-Bashford,** whose small line of impeccably tailored clothing has served as a mark of distinction in San Francisco for more than 30 years. **Cour-toué** features both classic and avant-garde Italian designers and made-to-measure tailoring. If the tailoring idea appeals to you but you're in a rush, try **David Stephen,** a mostly sportswear store that offers same-day alterations.

For men who'd rather look like Lou Reed... Rolo SF and **Dal Jeets** will outfit you in off-the-rack alternative styles suitable for clubs, cafes, or taking a little walk on the wild side. **Citizen** is a bit more elegant but still a good bet for hip men's clothes that you won't find in department stores, including a small selection of shoes. For specially designed clothes from Michael Cronan, stop by **Cronan Artefact** (South of Market), which features what it calls "threshold attire." A less pretentious description might be clothing for both work and play, but you're talking capital-D designer here.

If you can't make it to Hong Kong, but you're into custom-made shirts... The California Gentleman by **Astanboos** makes dress and casual shirts right there on the premises; a staff person will come to your hotel if you prefer. They also make suits and ties, and blouses for women. **Patrick James** also does custom shirts and clothing and offers tailoring and alterations for the lifetime of the garment.

If you simply can't live without a feather boa and a new tiara... Go right to **Piedmont Boutique** in the Haight, where drag queens, strippers, and ultra-hip high school girls buy their velvet-and-feather bell-bottoms, sequined micro-miniskirts, and long chartreuse gloves. When you see Piedmont's wall of earrings (more than 18,000 pairs) starting at a mere $2 and racks of fishnets and other outlandish tights, you'll know why Sister Dana van Iniquity, one of the drag nuns in the Sisters of Perpetual Indulgence, prays, "Please, God, let only my seams be straight."

Recycled regalia... We're not talking flannel shirts and dirty hair—grunge is, y'know, so 1994—we're talking the hottest street couture around. Haight Street is the used-clothing mecca of San Francisco. The best prices are at **Buffalo Exchange,** where you can also sell your clothes for cash or trade. **Aardvark's Odd Ark** has a huge and fairly boring collection, but it's good for simple items like jeans and vests. **Wasteland** is staffed by inattentive young hipsters who seem truly impressed with the loud music, high prices, and each other. You can occasionally find something great, but most of the ordinary stuff here is overpriced. Meanwhile, in other parts of the city, **American Rag CIE** has already sorted through the maybe rack and trimmed its stock down to the most desirable items, while **Clothes Contact** sells clothing by the pound, which sounds terrific until you put an old leather jacket on the scale and see how much it weighs. **Guys and Dolls** is the place to buy a used tuxedo and all the accessories to go with it.

Cheap thrills: nonprofit thrift shops... The trouble with thrift shops is that you could spend your entire vacation combing them and never turn up a thing, or you could spend an hour in one place and come out with the outfit of the century for a couple of dollars. There's no way to predict, but if a scavenger hunt appeals to you, try these favorites: **Goodwill Stores** (eight locations), **Community Thrift Store,** and **Thrift Town.**

Ethical splurges... If you're ambling along Hayes Street and you come across a store that looks like Martha Stewart's ecologically correct attic, you've probably arrived at **Worldware,** where you can purchase sheets and towels made from organically grown cotton and linen, as well as housewares made of exotic hardwoods from sustainable forests. The goods are actually very nice, but they're rather expensive, and the atmosphere is a bit contrived. **Global Exchange** is part of a national network that buys crafts from third-world countries and pays the artisans roughly 40% of the retail price—far more than most importers share. Pick up that voodoo wall hanging you've always wanted, and you can sleep well knowing you've helped a Haitian artist pay the rent. **PlaNetweavers Treasure Store,** a UNICEF store located in the Haight, also sells crafts made by indigenous people around the world and doesn't rip them off in the process. The prices for these goods can be higher than some of the large import chains, but proceeds directly benefit UNICEF's programs to fight hunger and disease among the world's children.

Crystals and other assorted New Age hoodoo...

What else would you expect from a city with a gigantic pyramid in the middle of its financial district? **Crystal Way** specializes in crystals and will arrange psychic or tarot card readings for you by appointment. **Lady Luck Candle Shop** will supply you with candles and other ritual objects you might need. If you're really, truly sick and tired of watching the Yankees and the Braves in October, **Botanica Yoruba** is the place to do something about it. You can curse your enemies—and bring winning Lotto tickets to your friends and family—with the supercharged Santeria candles and charms in this Mission District shop. If you speak Spanish and are duly respectful, the owners may tell you how.

Baubles, bangles, and beads...

Be an artist for a day, or at least a wild-and-crazy jewelry maker. In true San Francisco style, local bead stores reflect the grab bag of artists and hangers-on who live and work in the city—hippie holdouts (and their kids and grandkids), European exiles, African Americans keeping their heritage alive, and, of course, assorted opportunists out to make a buck off unsuspecting tourists. So if you're truly a bead freak, you'll love this town, but choose your shops carefully. And if you're just looking, wander into any shop you see. No matter where you go, you'll find loads of beads, as well as a staff of artisans willing to help you make your own necklaces and earrings. **The Bead Store** is worth a visit to check out the sacred statues and ethnic jewelry; **African Safari** has beads to use in hair braiding; **Gargoyle Beads** specializes in Czech beads; **General Bead** is huge—3,000 square feet—and offers many closeouts at bargain prices; and **Yone of San Francisco** in North Beach is hailed by locals for its unusual beads.

Goofatoriums...

San Franciscans pride themselves on being a bit off-center, and many of the city's small stores go out of their way to milk that image. At first, **Paxton Gate,** at the hub of the hip Mission District, seems to be a high-end gardening store—until you spot the mounted insects and glass eyes used for taxidermy. Then comes the kicker, the collection that recently made the store a huge favorite among avant-garde gift-givers: stuffed mice (real, dead mice) dressed up in costumes. You'll find Hamlet, the Pope, and many other "seasonal favorites." After you've spent $100 on stuffed mice, you'll probably need some **Therapy,** not for analysis but for odd little knickknacks that were clutter in someone else's dream but are now incredibly cool home accessories in your reality. There's also some mighty tempting new and used retro-contemporary furniture, but it won't fit in your suitcase, so you might want to stick with the doodads.

Richie Rich grows up... Comics for adults are a booming business, and San Francisco sells more than its share. Union Square's **Kar'ikter** offers a complete library of beautifully illustrated books about the popular European comic-book adventurers Tin Tin and Asterix; it's the only official Tin Tin store in the United States. Kar'ikter stocks the books in a variety of languages, along with watches, luggage, clocks, and other collectibles. The store's staff is helpful and friendly, and there are even beanbag chairs up front to curl up in as you read.

If you've got an itch for leather... North Beach **Leather** is probably the city's most famous manufacturer of stylish leather clothing for men and women. The quality and prices are high, but the workmanship is unbeatable, and jackets can be custom-made. If, however, your interests tend toward leather in its more exotic sense, head for **Stormy Leather,** which bills itself as San Francisco's premier erotic-fetish boutique. It never disappoints the whip-and-chain crowd. **A Taste of Leather** deals in adult items including leather toys and body jewelry.

Everything you ever wanted to know about sex... Don't be afraid to ask at **Good Vibrations,** an airy, comfortable bookstore/sex-toy shop owned and run by women. Their mail-order business is one of the most successful in the country, but this flagship store in the Mission District is still small, personal, and as far from sleazy as you could possibly get. The clientele is primarily women, but the books and toys are for both sexes. They've opened a second retail branch on Polk Street as well.

Or sexy underwear... Now that the Wonder Bra has almost single-handedly taken the term "flat-chested" out of the popular American lexicon, you can walk into any Kmart and buy the kind of seductive lingerie that once would've been found only at Frederick's of Hollywood. Still, there's something delicious about a small underwear boutique. Carol Doda, for years queen of the city's premier strip joint, the Condor, now sells all the expected sexy stuff for women at **Carol Doda's Champagne and Lace Lingerie Boutique,** along with some racier inducements for both sexes, including see-through underwear and G-strings for men, stripper's accouterments, and other fun little *objets d'amour.* Yeah, yeah, yeah, there's all the rubber and latex stuff, but the basic mode is Cher, all the way.

Uncommon scents... **Jacqueline Perfumery** has the best selection of scents in San Francisco, including some French perfumes that aren't available anywhere else in the U.S. If you don't know what you want, simply ask her for a suggestion or two; her olfactory intuition is uncanny. Check your shopping bag when you get back to your hotel; Jacqueline has been known to tuck in samples of expensive and exotic perfumes with customers' purchases.

Sweets for the sweet... At **Joseph Schmidt Confections,** feast your senses on the most delectable chocolate sculptures in the Western world. Buy at least a truffle or two (your taste buds will worship you for it), and do not miss the ever-changing, elaborate window displays. While you're there, step across 16th Street and peek at the outdoor mural entitled *La Madre Tonantsin,* to get in the mood for a trip to the **Pacitas Salvadorian Bakery** for *pan dulce,* sugary pastries in the Central American tradition, and *bolillos,* yummy little torpedo-shaped rolls that are especially wonderful dunked in Mexican hot chocolate. **Just Desserts** is full of fabulous, fattening goodies at all of its six locations, including an award-winning chocolate fudge cake that will put you on a sugar-high for hours (especially if you down it with a double cappuccino, as many locals do).

Italian treats to go... Just about any cafe in North Beach has great pastries, but **Stella Pastry & Caffe** has all that and La Sacripantina, too. Owner Frank Santucci will be happy to tell you about the patent he has on this puffy, sweet dessert that's one of Luciano Pavarotti's favorite confections. **Dianda's Italian American Pastry** has the best Italian cakes; **Danilo Bakery** bakes breads, panettone, tortes, and cookies for many of the top local restaurants; and **Italian French Baking Co.** still uses a brick oven and makes the best hand-rolled bread sticks you'll ever taste. While you're visiting North Beach, stop by the landmark deli **Molinari's** for a classic selection of Italian grocery and deli items; the old Italian locals shop there daily. Oddly enough, another great Italian deli is in the Mission District: **Lucca Ravioli Co.**, a traditional full-service deli with good-humored employees in white aprons. Their takeout sandwiches are superb and inexpensive.

The best deal on the best bubbly... Don't even bother shopping around; this is the place to buy champagne. The staff at **D & M Wine and Liquor Co.** is friendly, funny, and more knowledgeable about champagne than all the wine editors in the country combined. They offer the largest selection of champagne in the United States and will steer you away from overpriced status wines to lesser-known and cheaper labels that will make you think you've died and floated away to heaven. Every wine in the store has been personally tasted by the staff—all of whom are inveterate oenophiles—and you can be absolutely certain that any bottle they suggest will meet your expectations, and then some. They also carry the best selection of single-malt scotch in San Francisco.

Kid stuff... Terrific toy spots in San Francisco include **Jeffrey's Toys** and **Basic Brown Bear,** where you can watch teddy bears being made and even stuff your own, if you like. If you go in for designer clothing for kids, try **Dottie Doolittle** or **Minis By Profili.**

Words, words, words... As befits a place with a heralded literary heritage, the city of San Francisco has a wealth of independent booksellers. **A Clean Well-Lighted Place For Books** is a favorite of author Armistead Maupin (who immortalized 1960s San Francisco in *Tales of the City*); **The Booksmith** boasts more than 1,000 foreign and domestic magazines and newspapers; **City Lights Bookstore** is Lawrence Ferlinghetti's legendary 1950s beatnik haunt and offers one of the best poetry sections in the United States; **A Different Light** is the foremost gay and lesbian bookstore in San Francisco, as well as a resource center for gay information. **The Anonymous Place** carries 12-step recovery books (it's become quite a budding genre); **The Buddhist Bookstore** represents many Buddhist traditions and also offers altar supplies; **Forever After Books** sells used books on spirituality, psychology, health, history, true crime, and other assorted topics. **McDonald's Bookshop** has more than a million used books and can get you a copy of *Life* magazine published when you were born. **Dog Eared Books** is a wonderful place to pick up some choice reading material—check out the "Lust and Desire" section; **Argonaut Book Shop** is a rare-book shop that specializes in California history.

In search of 12-inch vinyl... If you're one of those people who understands the magic of a phonograph needle dropping softly into a groove, you're in luck. San Francisco has a couple of record stores that still sell records: **Streetlight Records** and **Medium Rare Records.**

Music meccas... Every city in America has plenty of generic music stores that sell CDs and tapes, but San Francisco's music stores boldly go into musical niches that the MTV nation barely dreams of. **Open Mind Music,** for instance, is a clothing/music emporium that features "cool collectibles and the esoteric." **Let It Be** carries (naturally) Beatles memorabilia, rare and out-of-print records, assorted music collectibles, and concert items.

For Latin and salsa selections, **Discolandia** is a good bet—you'll hear the music pounding long before you get within sight of the Latin/psychedelic/airbrush/jukebox storefront. **Amoeba Music** in the Haight (and Berkeley) offers more than 30,000 used CDs, plus original Fillmore and Avalon concert posters from the sixties; **Mod Lang,** located in Berkeley, features imports, indies, acid jazz, ambient, trance, and reissues; Oakland's **Saturn Records** offers an eclectic collection of music in one of the most fun walking neighborhoods (Rockridge) in the East Bay; and the **Groove Yard,** also in Oakland, specializes in jazz, blues, and soul selections.

Map 9: Union Square Shopping

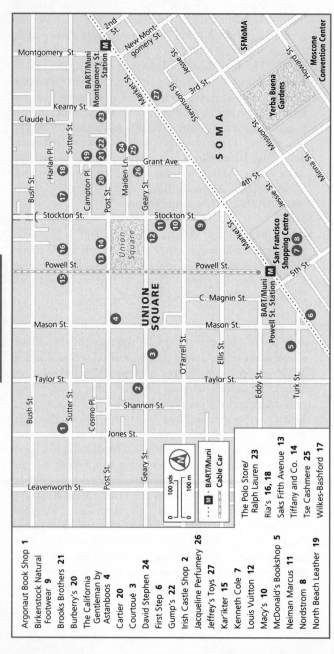

Argonaut Book Shop **1**
Birkenstock Natural
  Footwear **9**
Brooks Brothers **21**
Burberry's **20**
The California
  Gentleman by
  Astanboos **4**
Cartier **20**
Courtoué **3**
David Stephen **24**
First Step **6**
Gump's **22**
Irish Castle Shop **2**
Jacqueline Perfumery **26**
Jeffrey's Toys **27**
Kar'ikter **15**
Kenneth Cole **7**
Louis Vuitton **12**
Macy's **10**
McDonald's Bookshop **5**
Neiman Marcus **11**
Nordstrom **8**
North Beach Leather **19**

The Polo Store/
  Ralph Lauren **23**
Ria's **16, 18**
Saks Fifth Avenue **13**
Tiffany and Co. **14**
Tse Cashmere **25**
Wilkes-Bashford **17**

Map 10: Mission District Shopping

Botanica Yoruba **8**

Clothes Contact **2**

Community Thrift Store **5**

Dianda's Italian
American Pastry **14**

Discolandia **15**

Dog Eared Books **7**

Global Exchange **11**

Good Vibrations **10**

Guys and Dolls **13**

Joseph Schmidt
Confections **1**

Lucca Ravioli Co. **9**

Paxton Gate **6**

Streetlight Records **12**

Therapy **3**

Thrift Town **4**

The Index

Aardvark's Odd Ark (p. 153) UPPER HAIGHT This huge store sells used clothing in current styles. It's not as eccentric as some other Haight Street shops.... *Tel 415/621-3141. 1501 Haight St., at Ashbury St. MUNI bus 7.*

See Map 8 on p. 146.

African Safari (p. 155) WESTERN ADDITION Beads for use in hair braiding are sold in this shop, both to wholesale and retail customers.... *Tel 415/922-2899. 1221 Divisadero St., between Eddy and Ellis sts. MUNI buses 5 or 38.*

See Map 8 on p. 146.

American Rag CIE (p. 154) RUSSIAN HILL Stylish, contemporary secondhand and vintage clothing that's not cheap. The staff ranges from friendly to way-too-hip.... *Tel 415/441-0537. 1305 Van Ness St., between Sutter and Bush sts. California St. cable car; MUNI bus 42.*

See Map 8 on p. 146.

Amoeba Music (p. 159) BERKELEY This massive music store—voted best in the Bay Area by the *Guardian*—has a huge selection of used CDs.... *Haight: Tel 415/831-1200; www.amoebamusic.com; 1855 Haight St., at Stanyan St.; MUNI bus 7. Telegraph: Tel 510/549-1125; 2455 Telegraph Ave., at Haste St.; Berkeley BART station.*

See Map 8 on p. 146.

The Anonymous Place (p. 159) MARINA The specialties here are 12-step recovery books and gifts—sold to customers by a supportive staff, as one might well imagine.... *Tel 415/923-0248. 1885A Lombard St., at Laguna St. MUNI buses 28 or 30.*

See Map 8 on p. 146.

Argonaut Book Shop (p. 159) UNION SQUARE Fine and rare books and manuscripts are bought and sold here, especially volumes on California history. Established in 1941.... *Tel 415/474-9067. www.argonautbookshop.com. 786 Sutter St., at Jones St. Powell St. BART station.*

See Map 9 on p. 160.

Basic Brown Bear (p. 158) FISHERMAN'S WHARF Kids absolutely love this teddy-bear factory. Discount prices.... *Tel 415/626-0781. 2801 Leavenworth St., the Cannery. Powell–Hyde or Powell–Mason cable car; MUNI buses 30 or 42.*
See Map 8 on p. 146.

The Bead Store (p. 155) CASTRO Come here for beads, sacred statues, ethnic jewelry.... *Tel 415/861-7332. 417 Castro St., at Market St. Castro St. MUNI Metro Station.*
See Map 8 on p. 146.

Birkenstock Natural Footwear (p. 152) UNION SQUARE Comfort shoes, California-style.... *Tel 415/989-2475. 42 Stockton St. MUNI buses 38 or 30.*
See Map 9 on p. 160.

The Booksmith (p. 158) UPPER HAIGHT A source for lots of books and a huge selection of domestic and foreign magazines and newspapers. Knowledgeable staff.... *Tel 415/863-8688. 1644 Haight St., between Clayton and Cole sts. MUNI bus 7.*
See Map 8 on p. 146.

Botanica Yoruba (p. 155) MISSION DISTRICT This is a down-home, dead-serious, we-mean-business Santeria supply shop with some of the most potent candles and charms in the city.... *Tel 415/826-4967. 998 Valencia St. 16th St. BART station.*
See Map 10 on p. 161.

Brooks Brothers (p. 151) UNION SQUARE In any word association game, definitely traditional, but not as stodgy as you might think. Men's, women's, and boys' clothing.... *Tel 415/397-4500. 150 Post St. Powell St. BART station.*
See Map 9 on p. 160.

The Buddhist Bookstore (p. 159) JAPANTOWN As the name suggests—a source for Pure Land, Zen, and Tibetan literature. Altar supplies and gifts, too.... *Tel 415/776-7877. 1710 Octavia St., between Bush and Pine sts. MUNI bus 38.*
See Map 8 on p. 146.

Buffalo Exchange (p. 153) UPPER HAIGHT Come here for stylish used clothing in new condition—hip street fashions at very good prices.... *Haight: Tel 415/431-7733; 1555 Haight St., at Ashbury St.; MUNI bus 7. Polk: Tel 415/346-5726; 1800 Polk St.; MUNI buses 19, 47 or 49.*
See Map 8 on p. 146.

Burberry's (p. 151) UNION SQUARE The famous Burberry plaid, inside raincoats and all over clothing, luggage, and other wearables.... *Tel 415/392-2200. 225 Post St. Powell St. BART station.*
See Map 9 on p. 160.

The California Gentleman by Astanboos (p. 153) UNION SQUARE This custom clothier makes dress and casual shirts and suits for men and women. By appointment only.... *Tel 415/781-8989 (800/697-4478). 490 Post St., Room 336. Powell St. BART station.*

See Map 9 on p. 160.

Carol Doda's Champagne and Lace Lingerie Boutique (p. 157) MARINA DISTRICT San Francisco's No. 1 stripper sells some of the sexiest women's and men's underthings in town.... *Tel 415/776-6900. 1850 Union St. #1, the Courtyard. MUNI bus 45.*

See Map 8 on p. 146.

Cartier (p. 151) UNION SQUARE Exclusive timepieces and fine jewelry.... *Tel 415/397-3180. 231 Post St. Powell St. BART station.*

See Map 9 on p. 160.

Citizen (p. 153) CASTRO The racks here are full of urban contemporary clothing for men—pricey, but worth it.... *Tel 415/558-9429. 536 Castro St., at 18th St. Castro St. MUNI Metro station.*

See Map 8 on p. 146.

City Lights Bookstore (p. 158) NORTH BEACH The legendary beatnik hangout and bookstore.... *Tel 415/362-8193. 261 Columbus Ave. MUNI buses 15 or 30.*

See Map 8 on p. 146.

A Clean Well-Lighted Place For Books (p. 158) CIVIC CENTER This independent bookstore has a very helpful and informed staff, who will be happy to ship internationally.... *Tel 415/441-6670. 601 Van Ness Ave., Opera Plaza. Civic Center BART station.*

See Map 8 on p. 146.

Clothes Contact (p. 154) MISSION DISTRICT Used clothing is sold here for $8 per pound. Lots of leather jackets.... *Tel 415/621-3212. 473 Valencia St., at 16th St. 16th St. BART station.*

See Map 10 on p. 161.

Community Thrift Store (p. 154) MISSION DISTRICT It's sort of junky, but there's a great book and record section here.... *Tel 415/861-4910. 623 Valencia St., between 17th and 18th sts. 16th St. BART station.*

See Map 10 on p. 161.

Courtoué (p. 153) UNION SQUARE Beautiful Italian designer clothing for men, classic to avant-garde.... *Tel 415/775-2900. 459 Geary Blvd. Powell St. BART station.*

See Map 9 on p. 160.

Cronan Artefact (p. 153) SOMA This showroom is the home of Walking Man clothing by designer Michael Cronan.... *Tel 415/241-9111. 543 Eighth St. Powell St. BART station; MUNI buses 15, 30, or 45.*

See Map 8 on p. 146.

Crystal Way (p. 155) CASTRO Thousands of beautiful natural crystals and New Age books are sold here.... *Tel 415/861-6511. 2335 Market St., near Castro St. Castro St. MUNI Metro station.*

See Map 8 on p. 146.

D&M Wine and Liquor Co. (p. 158) PACIFIC HEIGHTS Simply the best selection of champagne in the country and discount prices to boot.... *Tel 415/346-1325. 2200 Fillmore St., at Sacramento St. six blocks from MUNI bus stop 38.*

See Map 8 on p. 146.

Dal Jeets (p. 153) UPPER HAIGHT These two stores, across the street from each other, sell super-hip men's clothing at not-totally-expensive prices.... *Location 1: Tel 415/752-5610; 1744 Haight St., at Cole St. Location 2: Tel 415/668-8500; 1773 Haight St., at Cole St. MUNI bus 7.*

See Map 8 on p. 146.

Danilo Bakery (p. 158) NORTH BEACH Wonderful breads and panettone.... *Tel 415/989-1806. 516 Green St., between Stockton and Grant sts. MUNI buses 15 or 30.*

See Map 8 on p. 146.

David Stephen (p. 153) UNION SQUARE Featuring European clothing for men, this store has an experienced staff and offers same-day tailoring.... *Tel 415/982-1611. 50 Maiden Lane. Powell St. or Montgomery St. BART station.*

See Map 9 on p. 160.

Dianda's Italian American Pastry (p. 158) MISSION DISTRICT Prize-winning Italian cakes have made this store's reputation.... *Tel 415/647-5469. 2883 Mission St., at 25th St. 24th St. BART station.*

See Map 10 on p. 161.

A Different Light (p. 159) CASTRO Gay and lesbian literature, magazines, and community resource information are sold here by a friendly staff.... *Tel 415/431-0891. 489 Castro St. Castro St. MUNI Metro station (K, L, M).*

See Map 8 on p. 146.

Discolandia (p. 159) MISSION DISTRICT The selection of Latin music is enormous, so it helps to have an idea of what you're looking for.... *Tel 415/826-9446. 2964 24th St., at Alabama St. 24th St. BART station.*

See Map 10 on p. 161.

Dog Eared Books (p. 159) MISSION DISTRICT A fun place for browsing and buying.... *Tel 415/282-1901. 900 Valencia St., at 20th St. 24th St. BART station.*

See Map 10 on p. 161.

Dottie Doolittle (p. 158) PACIFIC HEIGHTS Look here for designer clothes for infants, toddlers, girls 7 to 14, and boys 4 to 7.... *Tel 415/563-3244. 3680 Sacramento St., between Spruce and Locust sts. MUNI buses 1, 3, or 4.*

See Map 8 on p. 146.

First Step (p. 152) UNION SQUARE Comfortable footwear: Nike, Reebok, Rockport, and so on. Great shoes, great prices, great location.... *Tel 415/989-9989. 939 Market St. Powell St. BART station.*

See Map 9 on p. 160.

Forever After Books (p. 159) UPPER HAIGHT Here you'll find used books on many esoteric and mainstream subjects.... *Tel 415/431-8299. 1475 Haight St., at Ashbury St. MUNI bus 7.*

See Map 8 on p. 146.

Gargoyle Beads (p. 155) UPPER HAIGHT This store sells zillions of beads and offers ear piercing and jewelry-making classes.... *Tel 415/552-4274. 1310 Haight St., between Central and Masonic sts. MUNI bus 7.*

See Map 8 on p. 146.

General Bead (p. 155) SOMA The biggest bead store anywhere.... *Tel 415/621-8187. 637 Minna St., between Seventh and Eighth and Mission and Howard sts. Montgomery St. BART station; MUNI buses 15, 39, or 45.*

See Map 8 on p. 146.

Gimme Shoes (p. 152) HAYES VALLEY An eclectic, chic mix of footwear merchandise.... *Tel 415/864-0691. 416 Hayes St., at Gough St. Civic Center BART station.*

See Map 8 on p. 146.

Global Exchange (p. 154) NOE VALLEY Handcrafted items from international artisans are sold at this Fair Trade Network store.... *Tel 415/648-8068. 4018 24th St., between Noe and Castro sts. J Church MUNI Metro.*

See Map 10 on p. 161.

Good Vibrations (p. 156) MISSION DISTRICT/NOB HILL This is a comfortable, clean, airy, healthy place to shop for sex toys, sex books, and videos.... *Mission: Tel 415/522-5460; www. goodvibes.com; 603 Valencia St., at 17th St. Nob Hill: Tel 415/ 345-0400; 1620 Polk St., at Sacramento St.*

See Map 8 on p. 146
and Map 10 on p. 161.

Goodwill Stores (p. 154) CITYWIDE Hit-or-miss secondhand shopping, but when you hit, the price is definitely right.... *Mission: Tel 415/575-2240. 1580 Mission St. Call for other locations.*

Groove Yard (p. 159) OAKLAND If you're into jazz, blues, and soul, you'll be thrilled with this store, where they buy, sell, and trade new, used, and rare records and CDs.... *Tel 510/655-8400. 4770 Telegraph Ave., at 48th St. Ashby BART station.*

Gump's (p. 151) UNION SQUARE What used to be a grand San Francisco department store is now scaled down but still a local classic. Orientalia is a particular specialty.... *Tel 415/982-1616. 135 Post St., between Grant and Kearny sts. Powell St. BART station.*
See Map 9 on p. 160.

Guys and Dolls (p. 154) NOE VALLEY This vintage-clothing store for men and women specializes in tuxedos and formal accessories from the 1930s to the '50s. Hats, ties, jewelry.... *Tel 415/285-7174. 3789 24th St., between Church and Delores sts. J Church MUNI Metro.*
See Map 10 on p. 161.

House of Cashmere (p. 152) MARINA Cashmere, wool, and angora sweaters are the specialties of this men's and women's clothing store.... *Tel 415/441-6925. 2764 Octavia St., off Union St. MUNI bus 45.*
See Map 8 on p. 146.

Irish Castle Shop (p. 152) UNION SQUARE Expect everything Irish, from claddagh rings to fishermen's sweaters.... *Tel 415/474-7432. 537 Geary St., at Taylor St. Powell St. BART station.*
See Map 9 on p. 160.

Italian French Baking Co. (p. 158) NORTH BEACH Don't miss the delectable breads baked in brick ovens and the hand-rolled bread sticks.... *Tel 415/421-3796. 1501 Grant Ave., at Union St. MUNI buses 15 or 30.*
See Map 8 on p. 146.

Jacqueline Perfumery (p. 157) UNION SQUARE The best selection of perfumes in the city.... *Tel 415/981-0858. 103 Geary Blvd. Powell St. BART station.*
See Map 9 on p. 160.

Jeffrey's Toys (p. 158) SOMA Along with toys of all kinds, you can buy books and antique toys here.... *Tel 415/546-6551. 685 Market St., between Third and New Montgomery. Montgomery St. BART station.*
See Map 9 on p. 160.

THE INDEX

SHOPPING

Joseph Schmidt Confections (p. 157) MISSION DISTRICT A local treasure, this shop sells the most beautiful edible sculptures you'll ever see or taste.... *Tel 415/861-8682. 3489 16th St., between Sanchez and Church sts. J Church MUNI Metro line.*
See Map 10 on p. 161.

Just Desserts (p. 157) CITYWIDE This minichain is famous for its decadent desserts.... *Financial District: Tel 415/421-1609. 3 Embarcadero Center (Sacramento St.), between Drumm and Davis sts. Call for other locations.*

Kar'ikter (p. 156) UNION SQUARE The largest U.S. source for Tin Tin and Asterix fans.... *Tel 415/434-1120. www.karikter.com. 418 Sutter St., at Powell St. Powell St. BART station.*
See Map 9 on p. 160.

Kenneth Cole (p. 152) SOMA Footwear for the fashion-conscious.... *Market: Tel 415/227-4536; 865 Market St., at Fifth St. San Francisco Shopping Centre; Powell St. BART station. Union: Tel 415/346-2161; 2078 Union St.; MUNI bus 45.*
See Map 9 on p. 160.

Lady Luck Candle Shop (p. 155) MISSION DISTRICT Your basic Latino Catholic-voodoo-ritual botanica.... *Tel 415/621-0358. 311 Valencia St. 16th St. BART station.*
See Map 8 on p. 146.

Let It Be (p. 159) SUNSET DISTRICT If there is a heaven for Beatlemaniacs, this may be where you buy your tickets to get there. Besides rare and out-of-print records, it has a variety of memorabilia.... *Tel 415/681-2113. 2434 Judah St. N Judah MUNI Metro.*
See Map 8 on p. 146.

Louis Vuitton (p. 151) UNION SQUARE This is the place to get that fancy luggage with the monogram that opens doors around the world.... *Tel 415/391-6200. 233 Geary St., at Stockton St. Powell St. BART station.*
See Map 9 on p. 160.

Lucca Ravioli Co. (p. 158) MISSION DISTRICT Seemingly out-of-place in this Latino neighborhood, this wonderful Italian deli is always full of locals.... *Tel 415/647-5581. 1100 Valencia St. 24th St. BART station.*
See Map 10 on p. 161.

Macy's (p. 152) UNION SQUARE This huge store occupies two full buildings and has always been a reliable favorite for locals and visitors alike.... *Tel 415/397-3333. 170 O'Farrell St., at Stockton St. Powell St. BART station.*
See Map 9 on p. 160.

McDonald's Bookshop (p. 159) UNION SQUARE More than a million used books in stock.... *Tel 415/673-2235. 48 Turk St. Powell St. BART station.*
See Map 9 on p. 160.

Medium Rare Records (p. 159) CASTRO This is the place to find those old vinyl LPs you haven't heard for ages, as well as all the great jazz and Latin vocalists.... *Tel 415/255-7273. 2310 Market St., between Noe and Castro sts. Castro St. MUNI Metro K, L, M to Castro.*
See Map 8 on p. 146.

Minis By Profili (p. 158) MARINA DISTRICT Local designer Christina Profili left Gap to open her own business here. All the racks feature coordinating kids' sportswear separates.... *Tel 415/567-9537. 2042 Union St., between Steiner and Fillmore sts. MUNI bus 45.*
See Map 8 on p. 146.

Mod Lang (p. 159) BERKELEY This English modern-rock music store caters to serious collectors as well as curious onlookers. It's got a 24-hour fax line (510/486-1860).... *Tel 510/486-1850. 2136 University Ave., at Shattuck Ave. Berkeley BART station.*

Molinari's (p. 158) NORTH BEACH The traditional North Beach deli.... *Tel 415/421-2337. 373 Columbus Ave. MUNI buses 15 or 30.*
See Map 8 on p. 146.

Neiman Marcus (p. 152) UNION SQUARE This branch of the Texas-based luxury-goods store offers a high-class shopping experience. The cafe on the top floor is a real hoot.... *Tel 415/362-3900. 150 Stockton St. Powell St. BART station.*
See Map 9 on p. 160.

Nordstrom (p. 152) UNION SQUARE Get pampered with attentive, personal service on all five floors. Don't forget the store's eateries and full-service European spa.... *Tel 415/243-8500. San Francisco Shopping Centre, 865 Market St., at Fifth St. Powell St. BART station.*
See Map 9 on p. 160.

North Beach Leather (p. 156) UNION SQUARE This store sells the latest fashions—some custom-made—at prices to match.... *Tel 415/362-8300. 224 Grant St., between Post and Sutter sts. MUNI buses 15 or 30.*
See Map 9 on p. 160.

Open Mind Music (p. 159) LOWER HAIGHT New and used records and CDs, in addition to assorted esoterica and an in-store vintage-clothing shop.... *Tel 415/621-2244. 342 Divisadero St., at Oak St. MUNI bus 7.*
See Map 8 on p. 146.

Pacitas Salvadorian Bakery (p. 157) MISSION DISTRICT One of dozens of bakeries in the Mission District; this is in the newly Bohemian part.... *Tel 415/452-8442. 10 Persia St., near Mission St. 16th St. BART station.*

Patrick James (p. 153) FINANCIAL DISTRICT This store refers to itself as a "Purveyor to Gentlemen," if that gives you any idea.... *Tel 415/986-1043. 216 Montgomery St. Montgomery St. BART station.*
See Map 8 on p. 146.

Paxton Gate (p. 155) MISSION DISTRICT Truly a bizarre bazaar, this natural science/garden store is best known for its stuffed mice dressed in costumes.... *Tel 415/824-1872. 824 Valencia St., at 19th St. 16th St. BART station.*
See Map 10 on p. 161.

Piedmont Boutique (p. 153) UPPER HAIGHT Absolutely outrageous women's garments and accessories—sold mostly to men. If in your heart of hearts you've ever coveted any of the gaudy get-ups you've seen on drag queens, this is the place to find them.... *Tel 415/864-8075. 1452 Haight St., between Masonic and Ashbury sts. MUNI bus 7.*
See Map 8 on p. 146.

PlaNetweavers Treasure Store (p. 154) UPPER HAIGHT The official UNICEF store is full of international trinkets and works of art.... *Tel 415/864-4415. 1573 Haight St., at Clayton St. MUNI bus 7.*
See Map 8 on p. 146.

The Polo Store/Ralph Lauren (p. 151) UNION SQUARE For folks who affect the country-squire look. Tallyho.... *Tel 415/788-7656. 90 Post St., at Kearny St. Powell St. BART station.*
See Map 9 on p. 160.

Ria's (p. 152) UNION SQUARE Birkenstocks, Timberland, Rockports, and so on.... *Sutter: Tel 415/398-0895; 437 Sutter St., between Stockton and Powell sts. Grant: Tel 415/834-1420; 301 Grant Ave., at Sutter St. Powell St. BART station.*
See Map 9 on p. 160.

Rolo SF (p. 153) SOMA These two stores sell clothes for the modern urban guy, at modern urban prices (big).... *Howard: Tel 415/861-1999; 1301 Howard St.; Civic Center BART station. Market: Tel 415/431-4545; 2351 Market St.; Church St. MUNI Metro station.*
See Map 8 on p. 146.

Saks Fifth Avenue (p. 151) UNION SQUARE Not as glitzy as Neiman Marcus or as fun as Nordstrom's.... *Tel 415/986-4300. 384 Post St. Powell St. BART station.*
See Map 9 on p. 160.

Saturn Records (p. 159) OAKLAND An eclectic collection of records, tapes, CDs, and 45s makes this music store a really fun place to stop.... *Tel 510/654-0335. 5488 College Ave., at Lawton St. Rockridge BART station.*

Stella Pastry & Caffe (p. 157) NORTH BEACH The specialty at Stella's is Franco's La Sacripantina, a puffy slice of confectionery heaven.... *Tel 415/986-2914. 446 Columbus Ave., at Green and Vallejo sts. MUNI buses 15 or 30.*

See Map 8 on p. 146.

Stormy Leather (p. 156) SOMA Kinky leather goods.... *Tel 415/626-1672. 1158 Howard St., between Seventh and Eighth sts. Civic Center BART station.*

See Map 8 on p. 146.

Streetlight Records (p. 159) NOE VALLEY A major source for new and used vinyl, CDs, tapes, videos, and laserdiscs.... *24th: Tel 888/682-3550; 3979 24th St., near Castro St. Market: Tel 888/396-2350; 2350 Market St., near Castro St. Castro St. MUNI Metro station.*

See Map 10 on p. 161.

A Taste of Leather (p. 156) SOMA Adult and custom-leather items...*Tel 415/252-9166. 1285 Folsom, near Eighth St. MUNI bus 42.*

See Map 8 on p. 146.

Therapy (p. 156) MISSION DISTRICT A little retail indulgence can do more for your mood than months of analysis, so step inside for retro-contemporary knickknacks, home accessories, clothing, and new and used furniture.... *Tel 415/861-6213. 545 Valencia St., at 16th St. 16th St. BART station.*

See Map 10 on p. 161.

Thrift Town (p. 154) MISSION DISTRICT The unique thing about this thrift store is its grab-bag section in the rear, with items stuffed into sealed plastic bags to be sold for a dollar or two.... *Tel 415/861-1132. 2101 Mission St., at 17th St. 16th St. BART station.*

See Map 10 on p. 161.

Tiffany and Co. (p. 151) UNION SQUARE Jewelry and gifts, classic and very, very expensive.... *Tel 415/781-7000. 350 Post St. Powell St. BART station.*

See Map 9 on p. 160.

Tse Cashmere (p. 152) UNION SQUARE This stuff is soft—really soft. Great colors, too.... *Tel 415/391-1112. 60 Maiden Lane. Powell St. BART station.*

See Map 9 on p. 160.

THE INDEX

SHOPPING

Wasteland (p. 154) UPPER HAIGHT Trendy secondhand clothing, for sure, but sometimes it's a little bit, you know, expensive. Especially, like, the denim, you know?... *Tel 415/863-3150. 1660 Haight St., between Clayton and Cole sts. MUNI bus 7.*

See Map 8 on p. 146.

Wilkes-Bashford (p. 152) UNION SQUARE The ultimate classic men's store. The local designers are literally top drawer.... *Tel 415/986-4380. 375 Sutter St. Powell St. BART station.*

See Map 9 on p. 160.

Worldware (p. 154) HAYES VALLEY Eco-elegant housewares and personal items.... *Tel 415/487-9030. 336 Hayes St., between Franklin and Gough sts. Civic Center BART station.*

See Map 8 on p. 146.

Yone of San Francisco (p. 155) NORTH BEACH They call themselves a beehive of beads. Locals love 'em, but they're only open a few hours a week.... *Tel 415/986-1424. 478 Union St., at Grant Ave. MUNI buses 15 or 30.*

See Map 8 on p. 146.

THE INDEX

SHOPPING

NIGH

TLIFE

6

Map 11: San Francisco Nightlife

Abbey Tavern **2**

Amnesia **20**

asia sf **50**

Bambuddha Lounge **38**

Bimbo's **27**

The Bliss Bar **7**

Biscuits and Blues **39**

Boom Boom Room **3**

Bottom of the Hill **53**

Buddha Lounge **33**

Cafe du Nord **11**

Casanova Lounge **18**

City Nights **46**

Club Malibu **26**

Dalva **15**

Edinburgh Castle **36**

El Rio **25**

The EndUp **49**

Enrico's Sidewalk Cafe **31**

Esta Noche **17**

Factory 525 **45**

Fillmore Auditorium **4**

Gino & Carlo **28**

Gordon Biersch **43**

Grant and Green **29**

Great American
  Music Hall **37**

Harry Denton's
  Starlight Room **41**

Harvey's **10**

Hemlock Tavern **35**

Jazz at Pearl's **32**

Kilowatt **16**

Latin American Club **22**

Levende Lounge **14**

Lexington Club **19**

Make-Out Room **23**

Martuni's **13**

The Mint Karaoke
  Lounge **12**

Monkey Club **24**

Nickie's **5**

Noc Noc **6**

111 Minna **42**

Oxygen Bar **21**

Paradise Lounge **51**

The Pendulum **9**

The Plough and
  the Stars **1**

Plush Room **34**

Ruby Skye **40**

The Saloon **30**

Slim's **52**

1015 Folsom **48**

Thirsty Bear Brewing
  Company **44**

330 Ritch **47**

Toronado Pub **6**

Twin Peaks **8**

Wish Bar **53**

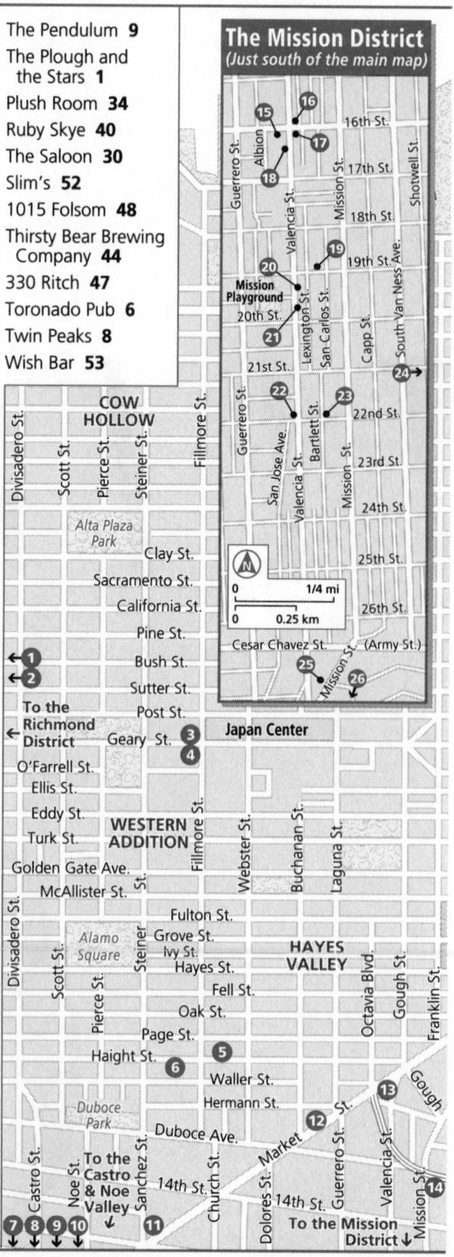

The Mission District
(Just south of the main map)

16th St.
17th St.
18th St.
19th St.
Mission Playground
20th St.
21st St.
22nd St.
23rd St.
24th St.
25th St.
26th St.
Cesar Chavez St. (Army St.)

Guerrero St.
Albion
Valencia St.
Mission St.
Shotwell St.
San Jose Ave.
San Carlos St.
Lexington St.
Bartlett St.
Capp St.
South-Van-Ness Ave.

0   1/4 mi
0   0.25 km

COW HOLLOW

Divisadero St.
Scott St.
Pierce St.
Steiner St.
Fillmore St.

Alta Plaza Park

Clay St.
Sacramento St.
California St.
Pine St.
Bush St.
Sutter St.

To the
Richmond
District

Post St.
Geary St.

Japan Center

O'Farrell St.
Ellis St.
Eddy St.
Turk St.

WESTERN
ADDITION

Golden Gate Ave.
McAllister St.

Webster St.
Buchanan St.
Laguna St.

Fulton St.

Alamo
Square

Grove St.
Ivy St.
Hayes St.
Fell St.
Oak St.
Page St.
Haight St.

HAYES
VALLEY

Octavia Blvd.
Gough St.
Franklin St.

Divisadero St.
Scott St.
Steiner St.
Pierce St.

Waller St.
Hermann St.

Duboce Park

Duboce Ave.

To the
Castro
& Noe
Valley

Castro St.
Noe St.
Sanchez St.
14th St.
Church St.
Dolores St.

Market St.
Guerrero St.
14th St.
Valencia St.
Mission St.

To the Mission
District

NIGHTLIFE

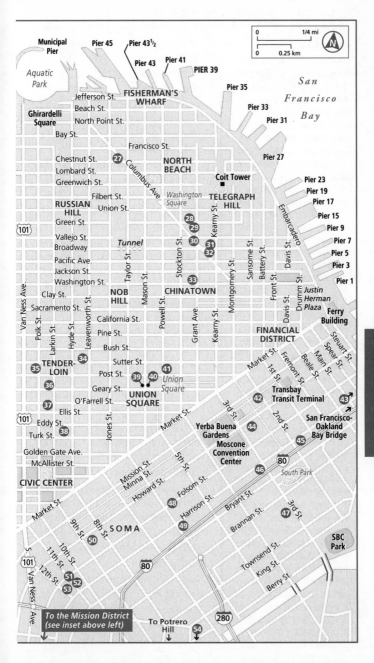

San Francisco's nightlife scene is phenomenal. Dozens of uber-hip lounges are augmented by one of the best dance-club cultures this side of New York, and skyscraper lounges offer some of the most dazzling city views in the world. In short, there's always something going on in the city, and, unlike in Los Angeles or New York, you don't have to pay outrageous cover charges or be "chosen" to be a part of the scene.

The biggest problem a visiting partyer might encounter is actually finding the party. Movable clubs that host theme parties—gay, lesbian, techno, salsa, rave, house—are a huge part of the night scene in San Francisco, and both the addresses and the crowds can change. What doesn't change is that the club scene in San Francisco always has been dominated by three things: neighborhoods, music, and people in their twenties who have the stamina and cash to buy lots of drinks and other mood enhancers. Every neighborhood has its own bar scene, and some are so packed with worthy joints that you can usually barhop on foot.

Though several old-standby clubs have closed or are up for sale in the **South of Market** neighborhood near 10th and Folsom streets, you'll still find a pack of blues, rock, and contemporary music haunts as well as the "Miracle Mile" of gay sex clubs; stop off at 16th and Valencia streets in the **Mission District** for the city's

---

Liquor & Smoking Laws

The drinking age is 21 in California, and bartenders can ask for a valid photo ID, no matter how old (or young) you look. Some clubs demand identification at the door, so it's a good idea to carry one at all times. Once you get through the door, however, forget about cigarettes. On January 1, 1998, smoking was officially banned in all California bars. The law is generally enforced and though San Francisco's police department has not made bar raids a priority, people caught smoking in bars can be—and occasionally are—ticketed and fined. Music clubs strictly enforce the law and will ask you to leave if you light up. There are mandatory NO SMOKING signs everywhere and no ashtrays anywhere; bartenders are required to tell anyone who asks that smoking is strictly forbidden. If you must smoke, do it outside. Meanwhile, the dreaded last call for alcohol usually rings out at around 1:30am, since state laws prohibit the sale of alcohol from 2 to 6am every morning. A very important word of warning: Driving under the influence of alcohol is a serious crime in California, with jail time for the first offense. You are likely to be legally intoxicated (.08% blood alcohol) if you have had as little as one alcoholic drink an hour. When in doubt, take a taxi.

NIGHTLIFE

hippest bar-hopping scene; head to Castro and Market streets to enter **the Castro,** gay capital of the world; the Haight is divided into two worlds—the **Upper Haight** (between Masonic and Stanyan sts.), a former hippie holdout with a young bar scene that appeals mostly to neighborhood bands, and the **Lower Haight** (between Pierce and Divisadero sts.), where you'll find a more alternative, head-banging crowd; Broadway and Columbus streets form the axis from which **North Beach** jazz clubs, late-night cafes, and strip joints flow.

What has gone away is the cocktail fad. Cosmopolitans and other party-girl cocktails went the way of the hula hoop several years ago. Then it was mandatory to drink nothing but the classics: martinis, scotch and soda, gin and tonic. That died too. Now you can drink whatever you want as long as you can pay for it, and considering how many dot-com high rollers are still living with their parents (are you reading this, Tad?), Pabst Blue Ribbon is more popular than ever.

The Lowdown

Destination bars with DJs... There's a new breed of bars emerging throughout the city, sort of a cross between a dance club and a bar lounge where the young and the trendy meet for a drink while listening to DJs spin vinyl. The **Monkey Club,** for example, is a casual, hip locals bar (think 20s through 30s) that's tucked away in a quiet section of the Mission. It's an ever fun and rather red spot to kick it on plush and comfy couches backed by giant picture windows; nibble on decent and inexpensive appetizers; and down stiff drinks while a DJ spins house, jazz, and world music Wednesday through Sunday. **The Bliss Bar** is a surprisingly trendy addition to sleepy, family-oriented Noe Valley. This small, stylish, and friendly bar is a great place to stop for a varied mix of locals, colorful cocktail concoctions, and a DJ spinning at the front window from 9pm to 2am every night except Monday (if it's open, take your cocktail into the too-cool back Blue Room). And if you're on a budget, stop by from 4:30 to 7pm when martinis, lemon drops, cosmos, watermelon cosmos, and apple martinis are $4. Flirtation, fun, and a very attractive staff await you at **Wish Bar,** an uber-cool bar in the popular night-crawler area around 11th and Folsom streets. Swathed in burgundy and black with exposed cinderblock walls and cement floors, all's aglow in candlelight and red-shaded sconces. With a bar in the front, a DJ spinning upbeat lounge music in the back, and seating—including cushy leather couches—in between, it's often packed with a surprisingly diverse (albeit youthful) crowd and always filled with eye candy.

Funky-cool grooves and great food... If you want to combine dancing and drinking with quality noshing, the two top places in the city for a fusion of fine dining and cocktails are **Bambuddha Lounge** and **Levende Lounge.** Bambuddha, a restaurant/bar adjoining the funky-cool Phoenix Hotel, is the place to feast and flirt. With a 20-foot reclining Buddha on the roof, ultramodern San Francisco–meets–Southeast Asian decor (including waterfalls in the dining room and outdoor poolside cocktail lounge and *salas,* Balinese-style outdoor lounge areas by a pool), very affordable and above-average Southeast Asian cuisine served late into the evening and topping out at $22, and a state-of-the-art sound system streaming ambient, downtempo, soul, funk, and house music, this is the "it" joint of the moment. Levende is the hottest addition to the Mission, recently voted best bar for singles, romance, bar food, and a slew of other accolades by CitySearch.com, while its chef Jamie Lauren was chosen as one of the city's Rising Star Chefs of 2005 by the *San Francisco Chronicle.* Drop in early for a meal of California-style tapas until the tables are traded for lounge furnishings for late-night noshing and grooving.

It's only rock 'n' roll... Rock, in its various forms, still dominates the live music scene in San Francisco. Any night of the week you can hit a number of clubs and hear garage bands, ska, post-punk, rockabilly, thrash, metal—in other words, just about every rock style except that acidy Jefferson Airplane/Grateful Dead stuff they once called the San Francisco sound. One of the most popular spots in town is **Bottom of the Hill** (South of Market), where most of the acts are locals who have landed recording contracts, but touring bands perform as well. Musicians like the cozy atmosphere and great acoustics; when U2 is in town, they hang out there. **Slim's** is the house that Boz built. In the

NIGHTLIFE

1980s, Boz Scaggs put South of Market on the map w
his first-class music club, voted best nightclub in America
by *Pollstar* magazine and best in the city by *Chronicle* readers. It originally leaned heavily toward blues but now features top names and new local faces in all popular genres,
from Jimmy Vaughan and Eek-A-Mouse to the Breeders
and the Paperboys. Actor Danny Glover stops by here to
see his favorite blues bands, but when the joint is
jammed—as it often is—he has to stand in the crowd with
everyone else.

The **Paradise Lounge** (South of Market) is less a club
and more a rock saloon, where four separate performance
rooms feature two or three acts playing simultaneously.
Modern rock is the main attraction, but rockabilly, funk,
acid jazz, gospel, and the spoken word are also on the bill.
The **Fillmore Auditorium** has been synonymous with San
Francisco's rock scene since Bill Graham put on his first
psychedelic concert there in 1965. Shuttered for years, the
Fillmore reopened in the early '90s to immense popularity
with both fans and musicians. Tom Petty wanted to play
there so badly that he appeared every night for a couple of
weeks in order to make enough money to pay his band
(which usually plays only in huge arenas for massive
amounts of money). Though it's technically a concert hall,
the **Great American Music Hall** is similar to the Fillmore
in terms of popularity, intimacy, and the feeling of being in
a club rather than an auditorium. It will never get too old
to be hip. Ditto **Bimbo's 365** (North Beach), where acts
like Sparklehorse, Tommy Castro, the Cheeseballs, and
Gregg Allman have replaced the swanky dinner shows and
swing dancing that have made the club famous since the
days when Rita Hayworth was part of the chorus line. The
lineup is eclectic, so check the schedule in advance, but
don't miss a chance to hang out in this lush San Francisco
classic.

All that jazz... The best jazz club in the Bay Area, if not the
entire West Coast, is across the bay. **Yoshi's** outgrew its former home in a small sushi restaurant near the Claremont
Hotel and moved to Oakland's Jack London Square, but
the setting is still so intimate that club owners insist you
can be stuck in the back row and still see McCoy Tyner's

EVEN COWGIRLS HIT THE BOOZE

Country music is far from hip in San Francisco, but nevertheless there are plenty of cowgirls—of both genders—who still like to put on their silver spurs and really kick it every once in a while. The best place in town—the only place, actually—is the **Sundance Saloon,** *550 Barneveld Ave., off Industrial Avenue (www.sundancesaloon.org). You can get lessons (5:30–7:15pm) and then dance your little pea-pickin' heart out until 10:30pm every Sunday night. Where else but in a fabulous gay-lesbian-bisexual-transgender blender dance hall could you learn line dances like the Tush Push, Backstreet Attitude, Circle Jerk, and Dog Bone Boogie? On a good night, you might just hook up with a cowpoke wearing nothing but chaps.*

fingers playing the piano. Some of the top jazz musicians in the world play at Yoshi's, which welcomes children and presents special shows and clinics for kids. Otherwise, jazz gigs are spread around town, but there's always something going on in North Beach, for free. **Enrico's Sidewalk Cafe** has live jazz 7 nights a week with no cover, and **Jazz at Pearl's** consistently presents such good music that players head over there to jam after their paying gigs are over. Another favorite is the **Plush Room,** one swank little boutique establishment that lures national talent to step on stage. Check out their schedule and perhaps you'll get to catch Paula West, Wesla Whitfield, Faith Winthrop, Jacqui Naylor, or other big talents doing their classic and under-celebrated thing.

Blues joints... Until a few years ago, all of the real blues joints were in Oakland. Then clubs started to appear in San Francisco, and though some purists might argue that these are a bit too sanitized to qualify as "joints," they do book topnotch talent and you don't need a bodyguard to get to the door. One of the most popular spots is the **Boom Boom Room** (Fillmore District), opened by the late, legendary John Lee Hooker, "the boogieman." With his credentials, he could've served nothing but tap water and it would've been a bona fide blues joint. But acts like the Ten Ton Chicken and John Cleary keep this down-home juke joint hopping 7 nights a week. Everybody who loves the blues loves this place, which the management proudly calls "the hippest, low-light, straight-up funky club on the West Coast." They won't get any argument from me. **Biscuits**

and Blues is a nationally recognized venue, despite its unlikely location in touristy Union Square. The down-home food is high in fat and good flavor, and the headliners are the best in the business—from venerable stars like James Cotton to local hotshots like Paris Slim. North Beach has two dives—**The Saloon** and **Grant and Green**—that have survived more than two decades and have produced a signature house-band sound dubbed "North Beach blues," most often identified with the hard-rocking, rowdy, Southern-style blues played by Johnny Nitro and the Doorslammers.

Move with the groove... Some of the best clubs in the city are actually hosts to a number of parties—sort of sub-clubs with distinct names and crowds—on different nights (for the latest listings, check out www.sfstation.com/clubs or www.sfclubs.com). **The EndUp,** a San Francisco institution immortalized in *Tales of the City,* is a prime example. It's a "mixed element" of music called WindUp on Thursdays, a total cruise scene on Fag Fridays, and a deep-house dance party (T-House) that has become such a part of club life on Sundays that many locals simply call it "church."

    Ruby Skye, a former 1890s Victorian playhouse, is downtown's most glamorous and gigantic nightspot, all gild and glimmer thanks to a dramatic renovation and the addition of killer light and sound systems. Inside, hundreds of partyers boogie on the ballroom floor, mingle on the mezzanine, and puff freely in the smoking room while DJs or live bands get the crowds dancing Thursdays through Saturdays. The crowd at **330 Ritch** varies by the night, from chic SoMa types to serious salsa freaks to hardcore hip-hoppers. Every Saturday is a new theme party. **111 Minna,** which changes almost every night, has a reputation for being truly "underground," free of parties sponsored by slick

NIGHTLIFE

• •

DIAL-A-CLUB

*The local newspapers won't direct you to the city's underground club scene, nor will they advise you which of the dozens of clubs are truly hot. To get dialed in, do what the locals do—call up the **Club Line** (Tel 415/339-8686) for its daily recorded update on the town's most hoppin' hip-hop, acid-jazz, and house clubs.*

• •

promoters. Walk through the doors and you could find a live band, performance art, a movie, or a hip-hop DJ. **City Nights** is a popular 18-and-over hangout every Saturday night, with three bars, 1,000 feet of dance space, and DJs spinning house, old-school, and hip-hop all night. All of these clubs have one thing in common—they don't really start to groove until at least 11pm, if not midnight.

Disco infernal... There's no longer a huge '70s-style disco scene in San Francisco—the theme parties mentioned above seem to satisfy most serious dance cravings. **Factory 525** (formerly Sound Factory) is one old standby that still attracts high-energy Gen-X crowds to its massive dance floors with elevated go-go cages and voyeur verandas: a glassed-in "SkyLounge" overlooking the club below and a catwalk that surrounds the entire building. Management tries to eliminate the riffraff by enforcing a dress code (no sneakers, hooded sweatshirts, or sports caps).

Another enormous party warehouse is **1015 Folsom**—three levels, a full-color laser system, and a gigantic dance floor make for an extensive variety of dancing venues, complete with a 20- and 30-something gyrating mass who live for the DJs' pounding house, disco, and acid-jazz music. Each night is a different club that attracts its own crowd, ranging from yuppie to hip-hop. Or cab out to 30th and Mission streets—beyond the reach of the gentrification district—and squeeze onto the dance floor at **Club Malibu,** where the largely Hispanic crowd grooves to terrific live salsa bands and DJs spinning Latin rhythms.

Cool cocktail lounges... The lounge scene in the Mission District has made it one of the hippest neighborhoods in America, according to the *Utne Reader*. The six-block stretch between 16th and 22nd streets is door-to-door cocktail world, on Valencia Street and almost every cross street that connects Valencia with Mission Street. At ground zero (16th and Valencia sts.), step into the **Casanova Lounge** and mingle with the young and the restless while you ponder the source of the poly-resin grapes that serve as hanging light fixtures over the bar. Don't stay too long there—remember, the Mission scene is all about barhopping—or you could get too comfy in the living-room furniture to move on. Resist that temptation, and head up 16th Street to **Dalva,** a narrow drinking hole next to the Roxie Theatre. A neighborhood favorite, perhaps because everybody looks so debonair in the rosy candlelight, Dalva offers addictive sangria along with the usual menu of cocktails. Try one, then cross the street and check out **Kilowatt,** an old fire station that has been reincarnated as many bars over the years. Have a beer, shoot some pool, dance a bit, then turn around and head back down to Valencia Street. Walk back up to Valencia Street, walk left past the Casanova Lounge and take your pick of the many bars and cafes along the next few blocks.

Get your groove thang on at **Amnesia,** a dance club between 19th and 20th streets that hosts nightly parties with names like Forget About It, Bubble & Squeak, Soulful Strut, and Hella Tight. They also specialize in tasty Belgian beers. Or stop in at **Oxygen Bar,** a sleek lounge that serves hits of oh-two and exotic herbal elixirs along with sushi and sake. Down a double shot of SuperNova (an energy blast with gobs of ginseng), then move right along to 22nd Street. Hang a left and you'll see two neighborhood favorites: the **Latin American Club** and the **Make-Out Room.** Both are crowded, hip, friendly, funky, eclectic, and always fun. These are essential stops if you want to hang with locals. The really cool thing about all these Mission District bars is that you can truly "hop" between them on foot—everybody does. But you really do need to watch your step outside of the hip zone or you could find yourself on the very wrong side of the barrio. The two BART stations at either end of the neighborhood—16th and 24th streets—are convenient during the day but can be serious danger zones at night. Don't even think about it; just take a cab.

Hangin' in the Haight... When the terminally hip Mission scene gets old, do as the locals do: Escape to the Lower Haight, where you don't have to walk more than a block in any direction from the corner of Haight and Fillmore streets to find a great little bar. Start with **Nickie's** (between Webster and Fillmore), a super-friendly, unpretentious dance club that was started in the late '80s by an ex-hooker who sold barbecue during the week and had rockin' DJs on the weekends. Nickie died in 1990; while the current owners no longer sell half a chicken and a Bud for two bucks, they do maintain a hopping down-home atmosphere with a great crowd that is rarely ready to take it down a notch, even when last call rings out. And just to keep the place really, truly San Francisco, every Monday night is nothing but the Dead, with an extensive collection that includes tunes recorded directly from the Grateful Dead's soundboard.

Also check out these two great neighborhood bars tucked in the block between Fillmore and Steiner streets: For selection alone, the **Toronado Pub** is the best beer bar in town, hands down. It has dozens of imported beers and microbrews on tap, and it's in a lot of tourist guidebooks, so don't be surprised to find it packed with out-of-towners who pour in on Friday nights to suck up brewskies and take home souvenir hats and T-shirts. **Noc-Noc** is more like a cozy Irish snug than a bar. The best seats in the house are the cushiony benches that line the wall, but you have to get there early to snag one. The happy hour is really popular and lasts later than any other bar in the neighborhood. They serve beer and sake—no hard stuff—and customers who are lucky enough to get a seat tend to burrow in for the night.

Kiss me, I'm Irish... Aside from O'Greenberg's, a former Fisherman's Wharf watering hole where the logo was Moshe Dayan with a shamrock for an eye-patch, San Francisco's Irish pubs for years have been clustered in the Clement Street neighborhood within a three-block radius of Third Avenue. The **Abbey Tavern** (Fifth Ave. and Geary Blvd.) is not as grungy or consistently lively as it was in the 1970s, when puddles of spilled beer and cigarette butts covered the floor and patrons stood three-deep around the huge bar, but it is still earthy enough to draw a flock of Irish regulars. Soccer posters are plastered on the walls, and the bathroom stalls are covered with partisan graffiti. It's a

UNDERGROUND ENTERTAINMENT

If you're really in the mood to participate in something irreverent on your vacation, log on to www.LaughingSquid.com. Since 1995 Laughing Squid has been the Bay Area's sine qua non online resource for underground art, culture, and technology. Along with links to local art and culture events, the Laughing Squid also hosts the Squid List, a daily event announcements list. There's some really freaky fringe stuff on this website, with plenty of garbage-level entertainment amongst several gems. Either way it makes for entertaining surfing.

bit too authentic to appeal to Americans who saw *River-dance* and are now dying to share a pint with a "real" Irish person. (Not recommended for conservative Brits.) **The Plough and the Stars** is a good middle-of-the-road bet for Celtophiles who love traditional Irish music but would prefer to steer clear of football hooligans or political arguments. There's live music on weekends for a minimal cover charge (usually $3), but get there early to nab a good seat.

Just your basic, friendly neighborhood bar... When you get sick of looking for a scene or a theme or a fancy cocktail, what you need is a good old neighborhood tavern, where the bartender will strike up a conversation and welcome you to the fold. **Gino & Carlo** has been serving cocktails to North Beach natives for as long as anyone can remember. Just pay your money, drink up, and get ready to hear some good stories from the local barflies. The **Edinburgh Castle** is a special treat, a Scottish dive in the no-man's land between Civic Center and the Tenderloin. Grab a pint of John Courage, and then drop a few quarters in the jukebox and get blasted by bagpipes. The crowd ranges from sodden old lushes to luscious young bar-hoppers. If that place is too crowded, try the nearby **Hemlock Tavern;** the owners of the popular Casanova Lounge transformed a defunct gay dance club (the Giraffe Lounge) into a hip-yet-comfy neighborhood bar with lots of dark wood, warm colors, and a back room that sometimes features live music. The crowd is a bit younger than the Edinburgh Castle crew, but there's a similar mix of locals, hipsters, musicians, and visitors who would never think of themselves as tourists. The jukebox is great, and you can chow down on warm peanuts (toss the shells on the floor) and wash 'em down with a really good selection of beers.

For a study in Chinatown culture, it's tough to beat **Buddha Lounge.** Most tourists shy away from what appears to be a solemn atmosphere there, but if you listen closely (and you speak Chinese), you'll find that it's really just a neighborhood bar like any other. Be brave. Step inside, order a drink, and pretend you're in a Charlie Chan movie. The best part is when the Chinese woman behind the bar answers the phone: "HELLO BUDDHA!!!"

Bustling brewpubs... The backlash against microbreweries was in full force a few years ago. Even **Gordon Biersch,** the king of the city's microbreweries, put up a billboard that complained about wheat beers and apple beers, asking: "How about beer-flavored beer?" Now the city has settled into a comfortable old friendship with its many brewpubs, and you just don't hear the word "microbrew" anymore. Gordon Biersch's loud, yuppie-infested brewpub is generally avoided by non-upwardly-mobile locals, but the beers are well crafted and it can be a lot of fun if you don't mind yelling to be heard by the person next to you. **Thirsty Bear Brewing Company** was named after an escaped circus bear who, in 1991, bit the hand of a Ukrainian pub patron and ran off with his beer (or at least that's the story). This popular brewpub near the Museum of Modern Art is famous for its tapas and paella, as well as the ales and beers brewed on the premises. Try the Lorca Ruby Ale, named after Spanish poet and playwright Federico García Lorca. Both brew pubs mentioned here are located South of Market.

Snazzy supper clubs... There are supper clubs per se, where the meal is as important as the entertainment (see the Dining chapter), and there are supper clubs perchance, where the crowd often arrives long after dinner, and the only thing that makes it a supper club is that it looks like the ones in old movies. The swing thing is basically dead, but some clubs are still fun to go to. Among those are **Cafe du Nord** (Upper Market), a former speakeasy that features live dance music and still looks enough like a bordello to bring out the party spirit in its eclectic clientele, and **Harry Denton's Starlight Room** (atop the Sir Francis Drake Hotel), where a slightly

The Great American Music Hall

In New York, blues singer Billie Holiday had to fight to perform at uppity Carnegie Hall. That never would have happened in San Francisco, where the closest thing to Carnegie Hall is an ornate, turn-of-the-20th-century concert hall that spent its first 30 years as a bordello and gambling hall. After the **Great American Music Hall** was taken over by a fan-dancer in the '30s, it had many lives—a swank dance hall, a jazz club, a Moose Lodge. Saved from a wrecking ball in 1972, it was impeccably restored and has thrived as a concert hall/night club ever since, hosting jazz greats from Duke Ellington to Count Basie, rock legends from the Grateful Dead to Van Morrison, and comedians from Robin Williams to Roseanne. It's located at 859 O'Farrell St., between Polk and Larking streets. For concert schedule, directions, and ordering information, call or log on to the hall's website (Tel 415/885-0750; www.musichallsf.com).

older crowd gets tanked on premium scotch and kicks up its heels on the dance floor. **Bimbo's 365** (North Beach), a swanky, landmark nightclub, is no longer a supper club but a popular rock venue (see "It's only rock 'n' roll," above).

Drag bars... Drag clubs did not survive the city's skyrocketing rent increases, so the drag scene shifted primarily to the long-standing neighborhood drag bars. The one exception is the hugely popular **asia sf** restaurant, where gorgeous "gender illusionists" serve some of the best Cal-Asian food in town and perform continuously. A local critic described the South of Market restaurant/club as "somewhere between Stepford and Wigstock." One of the most interesting neighborhood drag bars is **Esta Noche,** a small, Latino-oriented club in the Mission District where the drag queens are more likely to be at the bar or on the dance floor than on stage. (Esta Noche does host drag shows, but not on a regular basis.) The DJs play mostly salsa music—with some disco thrown in—and the dance floor is always jammed. The bartenders are friendly, as are most of the customers, but this is definitely a gay club and not recommended for curious heteros wondering what drag queens do in their spare time. It is also in a kind of seedy section of 16th Street, where there have been a few isolated gay-bashing incidents in the past, so take a cab to the door.

Gender blenders... You don't have to be totally gay to enjoy the free-spirited atmosphere of a primarily gay bar. San Francisco has a long tradition of gender-blender bars, where gay, straight, male, and female revelers mix it up on the dance floor, at the bar, and wherever else they choose. These places are not for peepers who want to see what queers look like up close; they're for fun-loving, non-judgmental partyers looking to get down with their bad selves. When it's karaoke time at **The Mint Karaoke Lounge** (see "Where the boys are," below), no one knows or cares what your gender or sexual preferences are, as long as you clap really loud for anyone who has the guts to get up on stage. And who could resist a piano bar called **Martuni's** (Valencia at Market St.)? It has everything you want and expect: a neon martini glass on the sign, a huge bar in the front room, and a cozy little piano bar in the back room, where you can sing along or listen in awe as I-coulda-been-a-star types belt out every show tune known to man.

NIGHTLIFE

Where the boys are... In practically any San Francisco neighborhood there are too many gay bars to name, so I'll just mention a few "musts." If you are a gay man, you must go to **Twin Peaks** (Castro at Market St.), simply because it is the gateway to the Castro and is the first thing you see when you get out of the Castro Street MUNI/Metro station. The huge picture windows, the wonderful old burgundy-colored sign that beckons from a block away, and the antique wooden bar make it feel like a neighborhood cafe. Much of the crowd is over 40—it's not the top cruising spot in town—but it is a wonderful place to stop by for an afternoon pick-me-up, whether you are male or female. Around the corner is another historic Castro bar, **Harvey's** (Castro at 18th St.), where in 1979 police stormed in, dragged out gay men, and beat them. The bar won a famous lawsuit against the police department and has been a landmark in gay history ever since. It is cozy and candlelit—a great place for a date for gay men and lesbians alike.

The Pendulum (around the corner on 18th St.) is frequented primarily by African-American men and those who can't resist them. Weekends are totally jammed—and jammin'. **The Mint** (upper Market St. near Guerrero) is one of the oldest gay bars in the city—open since World War II—and can be quite a hot spot during karaoke hours (Mon–Sat 9pm–2am, Sun 4pm–2am). If you think you may be Bette Midler trapped in a shy man's body, this is the place for you. The crowd applauds everyone who gives it a try, especially if it knows it's your first time at the mic.

For a full rundown on the gay scene in the city, stop by **A Different Light,** 489 Castro St. (Tel 415/431-0891; see the Shopping chapter), where you can pick up any number of free gay publications that include entertainment listings. Recommended: *Bay Times, Odyssey,* and *The Sentinel.*

Where the girls are... Until the late '80s, the Bay Area's homosexual population was pretty much divided into two territories—gay men in San Francisco and lesbians in Oakland. Now there is a much more active lesbian community in San Francisco—particularly in the Mission District and nearby Bernal Heights—and there are a lot of fun lesbian hangouts, including a number of gay bars with special nights for women. The place to be on any night is the

Lexington Club, just off Valencia Street (at 19th). It has everything a girl could want: cheap drinks, a pool table, loads of lesbians, and a killer jukebox with everything from the Replacements to Edith Piaf. This bar is really fun, and it's friendly to men and straight women as well. Another popular semi-lesbian bar is **El Rio** (Mission District; Mission and Army sts.), with a mixed crowd and most definitely a mixed motif. It's predominantly Latin, but it also has a big backyard that would give it that Doris Day/Rock Hudson patio party kind of feel if it weren't for the bigger-than-life Carmen Miranda paper doll out there. The music schedule varies, but there is often good live salsa. Sunday afternoons are the best. Go kind of late and stay for the transition from a mellow afternoon to a wild night.

The Index

THE INDEX

NIGHTLIFE

Boom Boom Room (p. 182) FILLMORE DISTRICT The late John Lee Hooker's Fillmore blues joint.... *Tel 415/673-8000. www.boom boomblues.com. 1601 Fillmore St., near Geary Blvd. MUNI bus 38. Cover varies.*
See Map 11 on p. 176.

Bottom of the Hill (p. 180) POTRERO HILL This Potrero Hill club is way off the beaten path but worth the effort.... *Tel 415/ 621-4455. www.bottomofthehill.com. 1233 17th St. Take a cab. Cover varies.*
See Map 11 on p. 176.

Buddha Lounge (p. 187) CHINATOWN It's dark. It's quiet. Not many people are speaking English. This heart-of-Chinatown bar is a great glimpse into neighborhood culture.... *Tel 415/362-1792. 901 Grant Ave. MUNI buses 1, 15, 30, or 45. No cover.*
See Map 11 on p. 176.

Cafe du Nord (p. 188) MISSION DISTRICT One of the hippest clubs in town, located in a dark, ornate, former basement speakeasy. An artistic crowd comes for acid jazz, jive, salsa, and cabaret.... *Tel 415/861-5016. www.cafedunord.com. 2170 Market St. Church St. MUNI/Metro station. Cover varies.*
See Map 11 on p. 176.

Casanova Lounge (p. 184) MISSION DISTRICT Be sure to check out the high-kitsch retro light fixtures in this cozy, crowded Mission District cocktail lounge.... *Tel 415/863-9328. www.casa novasf.com. 527 Valencia St. 16th St. BART station. No cover.*
See Map 11 on p. 176.

City Nights (p. 184) SOMA A high-tech dance club with an outrageous sound system. The floating parties at this South of Market space are for a very young crowd.... *Tel 415/339-8686. 715 Harrison St. MUNI bus 42. Hours vary. Cover varies.*
See Map 11 on p. 176.

Club Malibu (p. 184) MISSION DISTRICT Don't go to this disco unless you love to dance to hot Latin grooves because it is definitely too crowded to find a place to sit.... *Tel 415/821-7395. 3395 Mission St., between 29th and 30th sts. Cover varies.*
See Map 11 on p. 176.

Dalva (p. 184) MISSION DISTRICT Cozy into this narrow, smoke-filled (ssssh!) bar and sip delicious sangria with the locals. Great jukebox.... *Tel 415/252-7740. 3121 16th St., at Valencia. 16th St. BART/MUNI Metro station. No cover.*
See Map 11 on p. 176.

Edinburgh Castle (p. 187) CIVIC CENTER Soak up the friendly atmosphere along with British Isles ale at this snug Civic Center/ Tenderloin bar.... *Tel 415/885-4074. www.castlenews.com. 950 Geary Blvd., at Polk. MUNI bus 38. No cover.*
See Map 11 on p. 176.

THE INDEX

NIGHTLIFE

El Rio (p. 191) MISSION DISTRICT This eccentric Mission District dive is supposedly a Latina lesbian haunt, but it is also a friendly neighborhood bar, comfortable for all.... *Tel 415/282-3325. www.elriosf.com. 3158 Mission St., at Army St. 24th St. BART station. No cover.*

See Map 11 on p. 176.

The EndUp (p. 183) SOMA John Waters, Grace Jones, Naomi Campbell, and Kate Moss "ended up" here—you should too. Check out Kit Kat and Club Dread during the week; Friday nights are a major gay cruise scene.... *Tel 415/357-0827. www.theendup.com. 401 Sixth St. MUNI buses 12, 27, or 42. Cover varies.*

See Map 11 on p. 176.

Enrico's Sidewalk Cafe (p. 182) (See also the Dining chapter) NORTH BEACH A North Beach sidewalk cafe with great food and great jazz.... *Tel 415/982-6223. www.enricossidewalkcafe.com. 504 Broadway St. MUNI buses 15 or 30. No cover.*

See Map 11 on p. 176.

Esta Noche (p. 189) MISSION DISTRICT This Mission District bar is a friendly neighborhood hangout for drag queens, with occassional preplanned shows.... *Tel 415/861-5757. 3079 16th St., at Valencia St. 16th St. BART station. Cover varies.*

See Map 11 on p. 176.

Factory 525 (p. 184) SOMA The biggest dance club in San Francisco, with six different rooms. The music is techno, with some funk, hip-hop, and disco thrown in. No athletic attire allowed.... *Tel 415/339-8686. 525 Harrison St. MUNI bus 42. Open Fri–Sat. Cover $10–$15.*

See Map 11 on p. 176.

Fillmore Auditorium (p. 181) FILLMORE DISTRICT The infamous concert hall that made psychedelic music a household staple during the 1960s is going strong again.... *Tel 415/346-6000 (show information). www.thefillmore.com. 1805 Geary Blvd. MUNI bus 38. Ticket prices vary.*

See Map 11 on p. 176.

Gino & Carlo (p. 187) NORTH BEACH North Beach locals have been drinking here for longer than most of them can remember.... *Tel 415/421-0896. 548 Green St. MUNI bus 15. No cover.*

See Map 11 on p. 176.

Gordon Biersch (p. 187) SOMA Probably the best microbrew in the city, but the South of Market pub is unbearably loud.... *Tel 415/243-8246. www.gordonbiersch.com. 2 Harrison St., at the Embarcadero. MUNI bus 42. No cover.*

See Map 11 on p. 176.

Grant and Green (p. 182) NORTH BEACH Crowded North Beach blues dive.... *Tel 415/693-9565. www.grantandgreen.com. 1371 Grant St. MUNI bus 15. Cover for live music varies.*

See Map 11 on p. 176.

Great American Music Hall (p. 181) TENDERLOIN Formerly a grand bordello, the Great American is now the city's grande dame of nightclubs, a wonderfully lush and civilized live music venue where you can get down wit' yo bad self in a place that looks like a scaled-down opera house. Plus there's a modern kitchen that serves pretty good food during all shows.... *Tel 415/885-0750. www.musichallsf.com. 859 O'Farrell St., between Ellis and Geary. Civic Center BART/Muni Metro station. MUNI bus 38. Ticket prices vary.*

See Map 11 on p. 176

Harry Denton's Starlight Room (p. 188) UNION SQUARE Big-band sound, elegant surroundings, and amazing views.... *Tel 415/395-8595. www.harrydenton.com. 450 Powell St. Powell St. BART/MUNI Metro station; Powell–Hyde or Powell–Mason cable car. Open nightly. Cover varies.*

See Map 11 on p. 176.

Harvey's (p. 190) CASTRO Made famous the night of the "White Night Riots" in 1979, this Castro bar is now a gay landmark. It's a quiet, romantic spot.... *Tel 415/431-4278. 500 Castro St., at 18th St. Castro St. MUNI Metro station. No cover.*

See Map 11 on p. 176.

Hemlock Tavern (p. 187) MISSION DISTRICT This friendly neighborhood bar is a lot like the hip haunts in the Mission District— comfy, stylish, but totally down to earth.... *Tel 415/923-0923. www.hemlocktavern.com. 1131 Polk St., at Hemlock. MUNI bus 38. No cover.*

See Map 11 on p. 176.

Jazz at Pearl's (p. 182) NORTH BEACH Straightforward jazz in an old-style jazz club in North Beach.... *Tel 415/291-8255. www.jazzatpearls.com. 256 Columbus Ave. Muni buses 15 or 30. No cover but two-drink minimum.*

See Map 11 on p. 176.

Kilowatt (p. 185) MISSION DISTRICT The latest watering hole to inhabit this former firehouse is pretty much like the last few: pool table, beer, a little bit of cruising, the usual.... *Tel 415/861-2595. 3160 16th St., at Valencia St. 16th St. BART station. No cover.*

See Map 11 on p. 176.

Latin American Club (p. 185) MISSION DISTRICT You don't have to be a fashion model to feel comfortable at this Mission District neighborhood bar.... *Tel 415/647-2732. 3286 22nd St., at Valencia St. 24th St. BART station. No cover.*

See Map 11 on p. 176.

Levende Lounge (p. 180) MISSION DISTRICT Voted best in the city for the killer combo of food, drinks, singles scene, and sex appeal.... *Tel 415/864-5585. www.levendesf.com. 1710 Mission St. Church St. MUNI/Metro station. No cover.*
See Map 11 on p. 176.

Lexington Club (p. 191) MISSION DISTRICT This is one of the first lesbian clubs that isn't just a theme night at another club, and it's so much fun that the crowd includes a considerable share of straight women and men of all persuasions.... *Tel 415/863-2052. www.lexingtonclub.com. 3464 19th St., between Valencia and Mission sts. 16th St. BART station. No cover.*
See Map 11 on p. 176.

Make-Out Room (p. 185) MISSION DISTRICT Yes, some people do. But this isn't a pick-up scene—any more than any other bar—just a pleasant, funky, casual neighborhood spot. Try it.... *Tel 415/647-2888. www.makeoutroom.com. 3225 22nd St., between Mission and Valencia sts. 16th or 24th St. BART station. No cover.*
See Map 11 on p. 176.

Martuni's (p. 189) MISSION DISTRICT Admit it, you've always wanted to walk right into a piano bar and sing show tunes until you're hoarse.... *Tel 415/241-0205. 4 Valencia St., at Market St. Castro St. MUNI metro station. No cover.*
See Map 11 on p. 176.

The Mint Karaoke Lounge (p. 189) MISSION DISTRICT If you haven't been to a gay karaoke bar, you haven't lived.... *Tel 415/626-4726. www.themint.net. 1942 Market St., near Guerrero St. Church St. MUNI metro station. No cover.*
See Map 11 on p. 176.

Monkey Club (p. 179) MISSION DISTRICT Comfy couches, cheap appetizers, DJ grooves, and stiff drinks combine to make this club one of the hottest bars in the city.... *Tel 415/647-6546. 2730 21st St. Church St. MUNI/Metro station. No cover.*
See Map 11 on p. 176.

Nickie's (p. 185) LOWER HAIGHT Originally opened by an ex-hooker with the heart of a chef, this down-home dance club remains a perennial favorite.... *Tel 415/621-6508. 460 Haight St., between Webster and Fillmore sts. MUNI buses 6, 7, 66, or 71. No cover.*
See Map 11 on p. 176.

Noc-Noc (p. 186) LOWER HAIGHT Everybody loves quirky little Noc Noc, with its cushy seating along the walls, zebra prints all over the place, and a lengthy happy hour.... *Tel 415/861-5811. 557 Haight St., between Steiner and Fillmore sts. MUNI buses 6, 7, 66, or 71. No cover.*
See Map 11 on p. 176.

111 Minna (p. 183) SOMA A back-alley art gallery that doubles as a dance club, this informal spot changes every night with live bands, movies, performance art, and DJs.... *Tel 415/974-1719. www.111minnagallery.com. 111 Minna St., at Second St. MUNI buses 14 or 15. Cover varies.*
See Map 11 on p. 176.

Oxygen Bar (p. 185) MISSION DISTRICT Partyers fuel up at this popular Mission District lounge on hits of oxygen and shots of sake.... *Tel 415/255-2102. www.oxygensf.com. 795 Valencia St., between 19th and 20th sts. Take a cab. No cover.*
See Map 11 on p. 176.

Paradise Lounge (p. 181) SOMA Up to five bands play in this unusual South of Market club every night, where modern rock, blues, funk, poetry, and occasionally even a lounge-lizard act can be heard. The crowd is unpretentious and diverse.... *Tel 415/621-1911. www.paradiseloungesf.com. 1501 Folsom St., near 11th St. MUNI bus 42. Open nightly. Cover varies.*
See Map 11 on p. 176.

The Pendulum (p. 190) CASTRO This is the city's only predominantly African-American gay bar, and it is absolutely packed on weekends.... *Tel 415/863-4441. 4146 18th St., at Collingwood St. Castro St. MUNI Metro station. No cover.*
See Map 11 on p. 176.

The Plough and the Stars (p. 187) RICHMOND DISTRICT The traditional Irish music played here can be heavenly as long as you don't mind the Birkenstock crowd.... *Tel 415/751-1122. 116 Clement St., at Second Ave. MUNI bus 38. Cover varies.*
See Map 11 on p. 176.

Plush Room (p. 182) UNION SQUARE One swank little boutique establishment that lures national talent.... *Tel 415/885-6800. www.plushroom.com. 940 Sutter St., between Hyde and Leavenworth sts. MUNI buses 2, 3, 4, 27, or 76. Ticket prices vary.*
See Map 11 on p. 176.

Ruby Skye (p. 183) DOWNTOWN This former 1890s Victorian playhouse is downtown's most glamorous and gigantic club where hundreds of partyers boogie on the ballroom floor.... *Tel 415/693-0777. www.rubyskye.com. 420 Mason St., between Geary and Post sts. MUNI buses 2, 3, 4, 30, 38, or 45. Cover varies.*
See Map 11 on p. 176.

The Saloon (p. 183) NORTH BEACH This rowdy North Beach blues dive has live music 7 nights a week. It's usually loud, local, and not well known.... *Tel 415/989-7666. 1232 Grant Ave., near Columbus Ave. MUNI bus 15. Cover varies.*
See Map 11 on p. 176.

THE INDEX

NIGHTLIFE

Slim's (p. 180) SOMA Get your tickets in advance for most shows at this South of Market music club. Go early or you'll be stuck in the suffocating crowd on the dance floor.... *Tel 415/522-0333. www.slims-sf.com. 333 11th St., near Folsom. MUNI bus 42 (cab recommended). Cover varies.*
See Map 11 on p. 176.

1015 Folsom (p. 184) SOMA A gigantic dance floor and DJs pounding house, disco, and acid-jazz music attract a 20- and 30-something gyrating mass.... *Tel 415/431-1200. 1015 Folsom St., at Sixth St. www.1015.com. MUNI bus 42. Cover varies.*
See Map 11 on p. 176.

Thirsty Bear Brewing Company (p. 188) SOMA Close to the Museum of Modern Art, this is the best of the South of Market brew pubs.... *Tel 415/974-0905. www.thirstybear.com. 661 Howard St., near Third St. MUNI buses 15, 30, or 45. No cover.*
See Map 11 on p. 176.

330 Ritch (p. 183) SOMA A cool, cool crowd gathers nightly in this industrial building, located on a little South of Market alleyway, for changing theme parties.... *Tel 415/541-9574. 330 Ritch St. MUNI buses 15, 30, or 45. Food 5–11pm or midnight, happy hour 5–8pm Tues–Fri, music in two sets: 6:30–8pm and 9pm–1:30am. Closed Mon. Cover varies.*
See Map 11 on p. 176.

Toronado Pub (p. 186) LOWER HAIGHT You'll have to go early to get a seat at the bar on a Friday night because this excellent beer bar (best on-tap variety in the city) is a hit with locals and tourists alike.... *Tel 415/863-2276. www.toronado.com. 547 Haight St., at Steiner. MUNI buses 6, 7, 66, or 71. No cover.*
See Map 11 on p. 176.

Twin Peaks (p. 190) CASTRO The crowd at this old-fashioned, picture-windowed bar is usually relatively quiet and 40-plus.... *Tel 415/864-9470. 401 Castro St. Castro St. MUNI Metro station. No cover.*
See Map 11 on p. 176.

Wish Bar (p. 179) SOMA Drinks in the front, DJs in the back, cushy leather couches, and eye candy all around.... *Tel 415/278-9474. www.wishsf.com. 1539 Folsom St. MUNI bus 42. No cover.*
See Map 11 on p. 176.

Yoshi's (p. 181) OAKLAND This is definitely the top jazz venue on the West Coast. Take the ferry or drive across the bridge to Jack London Square (Oakland).... *Tel 510/238-9200. www.yoshis. com. 510 Embarcadero West. Ticket prices vary.*

ENTERTA

INMENT

7

Map 12: San Francisco Entertainment

Alcazar Theater **10**

American Conservatory
Theater (ACT) **9**

BATS/Fort Mason Center **2**

Beach Blanket Babylon **3**

Castro Theatre **24**

Curran Theater **7**

Dance House **18**

Dancers Group
Studio Theater **17**

Exit Theater **11**

Golden Gate Theater **12**

Intersection for the Arts **23**

Lorraine Hansberry
Theater **6**

Magic Theater **1**

Marines Memorial
Theater **5**

The Marsh **22**

Mission Cultural Center
for Latino Arts **21**

Orpheum Theater **13**

Phoenix Theater **8**

Project Artaud Theatre **19**

The Punch Line **4**

San Francisco Ballet **14**

San Francisco Giants **16**

San Francisco Opera **14**

San Francisco Symphony **15**

SBC Park **16**

Theater Rhinoceros **20**

ENTERTAINMENT

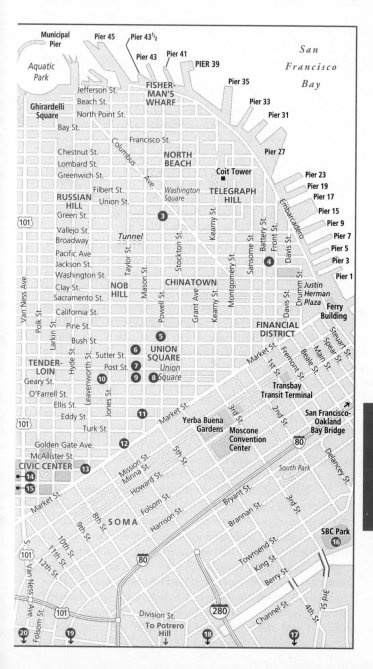

It's a fact: San Francisco sells more theater tickets per capita than any major city in America. Most people would be shocked to hear that little trivia gem, given the fact that so many of the high-profile productions in town are recycled Broadway musicals that appeal mostly to out-of-towners. Sure, you can spend your money on tickets to *The Phantom of the Opera* (yawn), but your hard-earned entertainment dollar would be more wisely spent on some of the most innovative, dynamic stage productions in the country—written, produced, directed, and performed by top local talent.

San Francisco leaves the monumental cost of producing mainstream shows to Broadway, concentrating its own money and effort on unconventional creations. The city's dozens of unusual options include the **Lorraine Hansberry Theater,** a small space in the downtown Theater District that focuses on new and experimental works by established African-American playwrights; **Theater Rhinoceros** in the Mission District, the oldest gay/lesbian theater group in the country; and **The Marsh,** another Mission District venue for avant-garde theater and dance. And by all means, don't leave town without going to North Beach to see San Francisco's trademark show, *Beach Blanket Babylon,* the longest-running musical revue in history.

Here's another surprising bit of trivia: The oldest professional ballet company in the United States is the **San Francisco Ballet.** And its glory is not at all in the past: the *New York Times* proclaimed the current troupe, led by artistic director Helgi Tomasson (formerly a principal dancer with the New York City Ballet), "one of the country's finest." If you're looking for more unorthodox dance performances, there are plenty of troupes to see, from the midsize companies that perform at **Project Artaud Theatre** (Potrero Hill) to the small, cutting-edge shows in the Mission District's **Dance House.**

The **San Francisco Opera** performs in the opulent 1932 War Memorial Opera House, which reopened in September 1997 after extensive renovations. The refurbished auditorium has all the requisite high-tech improvements—state-of-the-art lighting and computerized scenery-rigging equipment—plus bigger bathrooms for women. The **San Francisco Symphony** has its own digs—Davies Symphony Hall—and superstar maestro Michael Tilson Thomas, who left the London Symphony to become the toast of the Bay Area. Most other music—jazz, blues, folk, and rock—is performed primarily at the clubs you'll find in the Nightlife chapter.

There are also enough **spectator sports** in the Bay Area to balance out the high culture—two major league baseball teams, two NFL teams, an NBA team, an NHL team, and two major horseracing tracks. Just keep reading.

Sources

For theater and music listings, the best mainstream source is the "**Datebook**" insert in the Sunday *Chronicle*, known to locals as "the pink section" because it used to be printed on pink newsprint. The *Bay Guardian* and *SF Weekly*, free alternative weeklies that can be found at almost every coffee shop and street corner, are recommended for listings of more offbeat or intimate happenings. For the truly underground fringe events, log on to **www.LaughingSquid.com**, the Bay Area's online resource for underground art, culture, and technology. *Where*, a free tourist-oriented monthly, also lists information on programs and performance times; it's available in most of the city's upscale hotels. Three reliable online nightlife resources are **San Francisco CitySearch** (www.sf.citysearch.com), **SFGate.com**, and **SFStation** (www.sfstation.com). For information on local theater, check out **www.bayareatheatre.org**. Radio stations that offer diverse programming and information on local performances and concerts include **KPOO** 89.5 FM, **KQED** 88.5 FM, and **KPFA** 94.1 FM.

Getting Tickets

San Franciscans are an odd lot when it comes to performing arts. They adore the opera and ballet and snap up season tickets so fast you barely have time to read through the season's program if you hope to get a good seat, yet the major blockbuster shows that seem to be a priority to out-of-towners are not that big of a draw for locals. (They also dine before the theater, not afterward.) Here's the moral of that story: If you want to go to an opera, symphony, or ballet performance, make arrangements before you get to town. You can call Tickets.com (see below) for one-stop ticket shopping, but if you aren't familiar with the concert halls or don't want to pay the absurd surcharge, you may prefer to deal directly with each company's box office, where ticket representatives tend to have much more information about the best seats. If you want to see a major Broadway-type show that's probably sold out, mention it to your hotel concierge and be prepared to tip well if he or she locates some tickets. Tickets for smaller venues and more avant-garde productions are usually available on relatively short notice, but you should check out the *Bay Guardian* and *SF Weekly* as soon as you get to town to find out what's going on and to reserve your seats.

For half-price, day-of-performance tickets to major theater, dance, and music events at selected venues, go to the **TIX Bay Area** pavilion on Powell Street between Geary and Post Streets (Tel 415/433-7827; www.tixbayarea.org; Tues–Thurs 11am–6pm, Fri 11am–7pm, Sun 11am–3pm; cash only). Half-price tickets for Sunday will be sold on Saturday and Sunday. Even fairly popular shows sometimes need to fill seats with the steep discount. To find out which shows they are selling half-price tickets for, call their info line or check out their website. TIX Bay Area also sells advance full-price tickets for most performance halls, sporting events, concerts, and clubs. A service charge, ranging from $1.75 to $5, is levied on each ticket depending on its price.

You can also get tickets to most theater and dance events through **City Box Office,** located at 180 Redwood St., Suite 100, between Golden Gate and McAllister streets off Van Ness Avenue (Tel 415/392-4400; www.cityboxoffice.com; Mon–Fri 9:30am–5pm, Sat 10am–4pm). **Tickets.com** is the primary advance-sales outlet for all major Bay Area events, including sports, and you can purchase computer-generated tickets by telephone, but expect to pay a hefty surcharge (Tel 415/478-BASS, 510/762-BASS, 800/225-BASS outside California). **Ticketmaster** (Tel 415/421-TIXS; www.ticketmaster.com) also offers advance ticket purchases (also with a hefty service charge).

In every big city, there are **scalpers** on the street at sold-out events—even though it's against the law—but if you're not familiar with the seating chart, you can easily plunk down a bundle of cash for a "great seat" behind a pillar or up in nose-bleed territory. Counterfeit tickets are also a common scam, and they are very difficult to detect. If you're willing to pay more than face value for a good seat or a sold-out event, it's probably better to go through a **ticket broker.** They will charge a steep price for a premium ticket, but they usually have choice seats and impossible-to-get tickets. You can also check the local Yellow Pages for ticket brokers who specialize in finding premium seats at premium prices—there are more than two dozen agencies listed under "Ticket Sales."

The Lowdown

The best from Broadway... San Francisco's "Theater District" is just west of Union Square, but like its New York
counterpart, it brushes up against a less cultivated neighborhood—in this case, the Tenderloin. There is no particular danger during performance times, but you might want
to take a cab at night, especially if you're dressed up and
look like you might have a purse or wallet worth snatching.
All of the theaters that specialize in Broadway and Broadway-bound shows are within a few blocks of each other—
if Andrew Lloyd Webber turned the Michael Jackson trial
into a musical, it would eventually end up at the
Orpheum, Golden Gate, or **Curran** theaters. The
Orpheum's meticulously restored Spanish baroque building is every bit as glamorous as the productions it hosts—
The Lion King, Jesus Christ Superstar, and so on. The grand
old Golden Gate Theater—located a little deeper into the
Tenderloin than some overdressed theatergoers would prefer—stages lots of Broadway favorites and revivals, as does
the Curran.

    One of the less-publicized casualties of the 1989
Loma Prieta earthquake, the Geary Theater, is now fully
refurbished and modernized to such an extent that it's
regarded as one of America's finest performance spaces. It's
also the home of the **American Conservatory Theater
(ACT),** one of the most highly regarded repertory groups
in the country. ACT continues to be a company with great
range and is nationally recognized for its groundbreaking
productions of classical works and bold explorations of
contemporary playwriting. The **Marines Memorial Theater** presents both local and off-Broadway productions; it
was the San Francisco home of Tony Kushner's *Angels in
America* and August Wilson's pre-Broadway premiere of
Seven Guitars. The ornate **Alcazar Theater** often stages
long runs of its plays; you won't see anything out of the
ordinary, but classics like *The Lion in Winter* please drama
lovers who can't stand the idea of another tap-dancing chorus line.

On the fringes... Predictably, San Francisco concentrates a
great deal of its theatrical resources on gay and lesbian,

multicultural, and avant-garde productions. Many of the most experimental companies are housed in or near San Francisco's "New Bohemia"—the Mission District—but nonmainstream theater can be found throughout the city. The current *ne plus ultra* avant-garde venue is **The Marsh,** a Mission District performance space where you pay your money (usually $7–$17) and take your chances and often see remarkably talented artists right before they become trendy and famous. Aspiring actors, dancers, playwrights, and performance artists, take note: The Marsh is also the best place in town to network. Its predecessor—still among the most respected progressive art centers in the city—is another Mission District space called **Intersection for the Arts,** where Sam Shepard and Whoopi Goldberg tried out their acts before they got their 15 light-years of fame. The not-yet-discovered performers here are generally cutting edge.

Downtown, amid all the Broadway musicals and other big-money productions, the cozy little **Exit Theater** serves beer and wine and stages avant-garde "classics," from one-act comedies set in cafes to absurdist murder mysteries. You don't have to be a sullen existentialist to be experimental—this is a place to be a tad eccentric and have fun at the same time. It's always a pleasure to see a dance, theater, or multimedia production at **Project Artaud Theatre** (Mission District) because the space itself is so well run; this medium-size mainstay of the experimental-theater scene has been around long enough to know how to give impeccably professional stagings of the most avant-garde works.

The **Lorraine Hansberry Theater** (downtown) provides a showcase for some of the top African-American playwrights and artists in the country, presenting both experimental and well-known works. The **Mission Cultural Center for Latino Arts** (Mission District) emphasizes works written and produced by multinational Latino artists, much of it political in nature and aimed at the neighborhood's Mexican, Central American, and Chicano populations (many of the productions are in Spanish). **Theater Rhinoceros** (Mission District) was the first theater group in the United States to focus strictly on contemporary gay and lesbian issues; its productions range from bizarre, avant-garde performance pieces to traditional plays that feature gay characters. New works by local playwrights and artists are staged at the **Magic Theater,** a major West Coast company dedicated to presenting the works of new playwrights. Over the years it has nurtured the talents of such luminaries as Sam Shepard and Jon Robin Baitz. The progressive **Phoenix Theater** also features the work of local playwrights; the productions are often mounted on a shoestring budget, but they can be powerful.

Such a drag... Easily San Francisco's most beloved and lasting comedy performance is *Beach Blanket Babylon*, a comedic musical send-up that is best known for outrageous costumes, oversize headdresses, and hilarious lampoons of celebrities and politicians. It evolved from Steve Silver's Rent-a-Freak service, a group of party-givers extraordinaire who hired themselves out as a "cast of characters" to entertain guests by combining razor wit with fabulous costumes, sets, props, and gags. After their act caught on, it moved into the Savoy-Tivoli, a North Beach bar. By 1974, the audience had grown too large for the facility, and *Beach Blanket* has been at the 400-seat Club Fugazi ever since. The show has been running continuously for three decades, and almost every performance sells out. In fact, the show is updated often enough that even locals attend regularly. Those under 21 are welcome at Sunday matinees, when no alcohol is served; photo ID is required for evening performances. Write for weekend tickets at least 3 weeks in advance, or get them through TIX Bay Area (see "Getting Tickets," above). Performances are Wednesday and Thursday at 8pm, Friday and Saturday at 7 and 10pm, and Sunday at 1 and 4pm.

Mostly Mozart... Under the innovative direction of maestro Michael Tilson Thomas, who left the London Symphony to become the toast of the Bay Area in 1995, the **San Francisco**

• •

WHOSE BAT IS IT, ANYWAY?

*What happens when you combine improvisation with competition? You get BATS and lots of laughs. **Bay Area Theatresports** is a hilarious improvisational tournament in which four-actor teams compete against each other, taking on comical challenges from the audience. Judges flash scorecards and good-naturedly honk a horn for scenes that just aren't working. It's similar to the show* Whose Line is it Anyway? *but without the edits and G-rated language. Shows are on Fridays, Saturdays, and Sundays only; phone for reservations. Performances take place at the Center for Improvisational Theatre at the Fort Mason Center, Building B, 3rd floor (Tel 415/474-8935; www.improv.org). Tickets are $8 to $15.*

• •

Symphony grabbed national attention by winning both the 1997 Grammy award for Best Orchestral Performance and the American Society of Composers and Songwriters (ASCAP) award for Strongest Commitment to New American Music that same year. Davies Symphony Hall has had a slightly less direct route to public relations heaven. A huge, modern concert hall with what seems like acres of concrete and glass, it had a number of embarrassing acoustical glitches (echoes in the balcony, for example) when it opened in 1980. Since then it has undergone a complete renovation and is now considered one of the finest modern concert venues in the world, with amenities that include the Ruffatti Organ, one of the largest concert hall organs in North America (eight divisions of 163 ranks and 9,235 pipes). The season runs September through June.

Men in tights... One of the city's cultural treasures, the world-class **San Francisco Ballet** normally shares its home with the opera, performing regularly at the War Memorial Opera House. Artistic director Helgi Tomasson is a darling of dance critics, especially in New York, where he was considered a premiere danseur and worked closely with Balanchine. The ballet's primary seasons are spring and fall, but special Christmas performances include *The Nutcracker*. If you're inclined to take BART across the bay, you can see the **Oakland Ballet** perform at the gorgeous Paramount Theater, a perfectly restored landmark Art Deco movie palace that alone is worth the trip. This exuberant, multiracial company is not as developed as its San Francisco counterpart, but some of the pieces are actually more interesting, in part because they feature a number of brilliant, enthusiastic young dancers. The dancing isn't always perfect, but they are a lot of fun to watch.

Dancing with the avant-garde... The city's unconventional dance companies gather where the rest of the avant-garde performing artists do—in the Mission District. Small, funky groups and extreme, cutting-edge choreographers showcase their work at **Dancers Group Studio Theater,** a small Mission District studio where local choreographers are having a creative field day and neighborhood audiences are eating it up. The best part is that the "attitude factor" is minor. Some very innovative productions have been staged at **Dance House,** with local choreographers and ethnic traditions (a natural for the Mission

A BIG ORGAN IN THE CASTRO

If you are a sucker for those grand old theaters, then you absolutely have to see a film at the gorgeous 1922 Timothy Pflueger-designed **Castro Theatre,** *one of the finest examples of a 1920s movie palace in the nation. The theater screens everything from director's cuts to Hitchcock classics and touring art-house flicks. To get the full effect of this rare experience, arrive well before showtime to hear the organist pump out a rousing rendition of "San Francisco, Open Your Golden Gate" on the vintage Wurlitzer pipe organ (it emerges from the orchestra pit on a hydraulic lift—very cool). 429 Castro St., near Market St. (Tel 415/621-6120; www.castrotheatresf.com).*

District). It's worth checking for. A few blocks away, experimental, midsize touring and local companies perform at **Project Artaud Theatre.**

A night at the opera... The **San Francisco Opera** is an experience, not just for the thrilling performances by top international stars such as Frederica Von Stade and Plácido Domingo, but also for the little risks the company takes just because, after all, this is San Francisco. There were, for example, the nuns (played by "supernumeraries," opera's version of extras) who stripped totally naked and physically climbed the walls to illustrate their possession by the devil and an opera composed by jazz/pop vocalist Bobby McFerrin with progressive novelist Ishmael Reed as the librettist. Then there is the audience, half of which is dressed to the nines while the other half arrives in jeans and sneakers. Boxes at the grand old War Memorial Opera House are worth the steep price, with elegant brocade chairs and heavy velvet curtains. Don't worry if you don't speak the language—all productions have English supertitles. The opera season starts in September and runs through January. Tickets are not easy to come by, so plan in advance. Your only alternative may be one of the 200 standing-room tickets, available for every performance for $10, cash only, one per person. Line up at the box office at 10am on the morning of the performance and hope they don't sell out before you get to the window. *Insider tip:* Every year, the San Francisco Opera stages a number of free performances during the summer months that are open to the public as part of the Brown Bag Opera program. Schedule details can be found on the opera's website (www.sfopera.com).

ENTERTAINMENT

Humor me... You would think the city that brought you Robin Williams would be full of comedy clubs, but it seems San Franciscans are just too cool to spend their evenings doing something as pedestrian as seeing a comedy show ("How Sacramento!"). So it's mostly out-of-towners who'll be laughing it up at San Francisco's best comedy club: **The Punch Line.** Ellen DeGeneres, Rosie O'Donnell, Drew Carey, Chris Rock, Margaret Cho, Dana Carvey—the nation's best comics have all been on stage here at some point in their career. It's the largest comedy club in the city, where top national and local talent are featured Tuesday through Saturday. Showcase night is Sunday, when 15 to 20 rising stars take the mic. There's usually an all-star showcase or a special event on Monday as well. One of my favorite regulars is Bobby Slayton, a hilariously abusive potty-mouth who tears into anyone dumb enough to sit in the front row (particularly blondes). Tickets are $8 to $15, and there's a two-drink minimum nightly.

Take me out to the ballgame... The Bay Area baseball scene is definitely a tale of two cities: The Oakland A's, with four world championships and a once-terrific ballpark that has been turned into a monstrosity by the return of the Raiders, and San Francisco, with no world titles and a world-class stadium. The **San Francisco Giants** opened the millennium by playing their first regular-season game at the $300 million **SBC Park** against their archrivals, the Los Angeles Dodgers. Nearly 30,000 of SBC's 40,800 seats were sold out to season-ticket holders before the stadium was even finished, making this downtown baseball-only park the hottest ticket in town. Fans are thrilled to get out of windy, cavernous Candlestick Park (officially renamed **Monster Park**) with its infield minitornadoes and freezing-cold night games. The weather at SBC is typically sunny and bright, and the crowd lets out a cheer every time a Barry Bonds home run sails out of the park and into the inlet of the bay now known as McCovey Cove (in honor of the team's legendary slugger, Willie McCovey).

    If you can't even get bleacher seats, you can always join the "knothole gang" at the Portwalk (located behind right field) to catch a free glimpse of the game through cutout portholes into the ballpark. In the spirit of sharing, Portwalk peekers are encouraged to take in only an inning or two before giving way to fellow fans. One guaranteed way to get into the ballpark is to take a tour of SBC Park and go behind the scenes where you'll see the Press Box, the Dugout, the Visitor's Clubhouse, a Luxury Suite, and more. All tours run daily every hour starting at 10:30am with the last tour leaving at 2:30pm. Call for current ticket prices. There are no tours on game days, and limited tours on the day of night games. For tickets, call or log on to their website (Tel 415/972-2400; www.sfgiants.com, click on "SBC Park" and "Ballpark Tours" from the drop-down list).

Meanwhile, over at the **McAfee Coliseum,** the red-hot **Oakland A's** are as much MTV as MLB. Players like pitching ace Barry Zito, who dyed his hair blue and moonlights as a guest host on a local radio talk show, have brought fans back to what used to be a small, sunny ballpark with wide-open wooden bleachers. The Raiders blitzed the bleachers and put in a huge, high-rise wall of 10,000 luxury seats—not used for regular-season baseball—and an enclosed "club" where people can sit inside, drink cocktails, and watch the game on TV (what's the point?). The only thing left from the good old days is the beloved, old-fashioned manual scoreboard—a faint reminder that there was baseball before television.

Come the end of summer, football teams start filling the stadiums: the **San Francisco 49ers,** who play on Sundays at Monster Park August through December, and the **Oakland Raiders** *(Boo! Hiss!)*. Bay Area football fans are often characterized as falling into two distinct molds: the wine-and-brie set at Monster Park and the Bud-and-burgers bunch at the McAfee Coliseum. Either way, tickets can be hard to come by, but you can usually snag one from a ticket broker.

Hockey and basketball start in October and November. The **San Jose Sharks**—whose logo of a shark devouring a hockey stick made their licensed hats and clothing into best sellers before the team played its first game—skate at the **San Jose Arena,** about an hour south of San Francisco. **The Golden State Warriors** play at **Oakland Arena.** The season runs November through April, and most games start at 7:30pm. Finally, if you like to play the ponies, you have a couple of choices for a sunny day at the races: **Bay Meadows** in San Mateo or **Golden Gate Fields** near Berkeley. Bay Meadows seems to be preferred by San Franciscans, who are loathe to cross the Bay Bridge for any reason, but Golden Gate Fields is a real salt-of-the-earth racetrack.

The Index

Alcazar Theater (p. 207) UNION SQUARE A variety of top-quality, if not exactly new, plays are produced here.... *Tel 415/441-4042, 415/441-6655. 650 Geary St. MUNI bus 19 or 38.*

See Map 12 on p. 202.

American Conservatory Theater (ACT) (p. 207) UNION SQUARE The Geary Theater is home to the renowned repertory company.... *Tel 415/749-2ACT. www.act-sf.org. Geary Theater, 415 Geary St. MUNI bus 5.*

See Map 12 on p. 202.

Bay Meadows (p. 213) SAN MATEO This is a beautiful place for thoroughbred horse racing, with picnic facilities and a playground for children.... *Tel 650/574-7223. www.baymeadows.com. 2600 S. Delaware St. Take CalTrain directly to Bay Meadows. To drive: Take Hwy. 101 South to the Hillsborough exit, head west, and follow signs to track. Seasons run Jan 21–March 29 and Sept 4–Nov 14. Post time 12:45, 7:15 on Fri.*

Beach Blanket Babylon (p. 204) NORTH BEACH It wouldn't be San Francisco without this totally wacky musical revue—and the gigantic, ridiculous headdresses that made it famous—at Club Fugazi, a cozy cabaret in North Beach. Reserve or buy well in advance.... *Tel 415/421-4222. www.beachblanketbabylon.com. Club Fugazi, 678 Green St. MUNI buses 15, 30, or 45. Shows Wed–Thurs 8pm, Fri–Sat 7 and 10pm, Sun 1 and 4pm.*

See Map 12 on p. 202.

Curran Theater (p. 207) UNION SQUARE The Curran presents both warmed-over Broadway hits and Broadway-bound musicals.... *Tel 415/551-2000. www.bestofbroadway-sf.com. 445 Geary St. MUNI buses 19 or 38.*

See Map 12 on p. 202.

Dance House (p. 204) MISSION DISTRICT This Mission District dance studio showcases local choreographers and ethnic traditions.... *Tel 415/970-0222. 1275 Connecticut St., at Army St. MUNI bus 19 (cab recommended).*

See Map 12 on p. 202.

Dancers Group Studio Theater (p. 210) MISSION DISTRICT Dance buffs are excited about this small Mission District studio.... *Tel 415/920-9181. www.dancersgroup.org. Studio B, 3252A 19th St. 24th St. BART station.*

See Map 12 on p. 202.

Exit Theater (p. 208) CIVIC CENTER Closer to the mainstream than many neighborhood theaters, this small theater-district house is gaining a national reputation for avant-garde "classics".... *Tel 415/931-1094. www.sffringe.org. 156 Eddy St. Civic Center BART/MUNI Metro station; MUNI buses 19 or 31.*

See Map 12 on p. 202.

Golden Gate Fields (p. 213) ALBANY Across the bay in Albany (next to Berkeley), Golden Gate Fields offers thoroughbred horse racing and a view of the bay—but not at the same time: The track faces Interstate 80.... *Tel 510/559-7300. www.golden gatefields.com. Take shuttle or cab from N. Berkeley BART station. AC Transit (Tel 800/559-4636) runs buses direct from Transbay Terminal. To drive: cross Oakland–San Francisco Bay Bridge and take Interstate 80 east to Gilman St. exit; turn left to get to track. Seasons run Nov–Jan and April–June.*

Golden Gate Theater (p. 207) UNION SQUARE This grand old theater offers Broadway touring shows and revivals.... *Tel 415/551-2000. www.bestofbroadway-sf.com. 1 Taylor St., (near Sixth and Market sts. Powell St. BART/MUNI Metro station; MUNI buses 6, 7, 8, 9, 21, or 66.*

See Map 12 on p. 202.

Golden State Warriors (p. 213) OAKLAND See the McAfee Coliseum and Oakland Arena below.

Intersection for the Arts (p. 208) MISSION DISTRICT The oldest experimental arts center in the city features plays, visual arts, jazz, and readings.... *Tel 415/626-3311. www.theintersection. org. 446 Valencia St. 16th St. BART/MUNI Metro station; MUNI bus 26.*

See Map 12 on p. 202.

Lorraine Hansberry Theater (p. 204) UNION SQUARE Some of the most prominent black playwrights and performers are featured at this downtown theater, which focuses on new approaches or pieces with social significance.... *Tel 415/474-8800. www.lhtsf.org. 620 Sutter St. Powell–Mason cable car; MUNI buses 2, 3, 4, or 76.*

See Map 12 on p. 202.

Magic Theater (p. 208) FORT MASON New plays by American playwrights are the main attraction at this Fort Mason theater.... *Tel 415/441-8822. www.magictheatre.org. Building D, Fort Mason, Marina Blvd., at Buchanan St. MUNI bus 28.*

See Map 12 on p. 202.

THE INDEX

ENTERTAINMENT

Marines Memorial Theater (p. 207) UNION SQUARE Theater district home to serious drama.... *Tel 415/771-6900. www.marines memorialtheatre.com. 609 Sutter St. MUNI buses 2, 3, 4, or 76.*

See Map 12 on p. 202.

The Marsh (p. 204) MISSION DISTRICT The place to see the latest avant-garde productions, it's hip, it's fun, it's good, and it's reasonable.... *Tel 415/826-5750 (800/838-3006 for ticket hotline). www.themarsh.org. 1062 Valencia St. 24th St. BART/MUNI Metro station; MUNI bus 26.*

See Map 12 on p. 202.

McAfee Coliseum and Oakland Arena (p. 213) OAKLAND Some marketing genius decided to gentrify the image of the Oakland Coliseum Arena—presumably to make higher ticket prices for Warriors games more palatable by changing its name to "The Arena in Oakland," but that didn't work, so they went for the money and now it's the McAfee Coliseum and Oakland Arena. Locals still call it the Coliseum and fans haven't exactly been flocking to see the Warriors lately. Though it looks like a really cool spaceship hangar from the outside, it's just another generic NBA arena on the inside. The Coliseum, home to the A's and the Raiders, is right next door.... *Tel 510/569-2121 for arena information; Tel 510/638-4627 for A's information; Tel 510/864-5000 for Raiders' information. www.coliseum.com. 7000 Coliseum Way, Oakland. Coliseum BART station.*

Mission Cultural Center for Latino Arts (p. 208) MISSION DISTRICT Latino artists from many different cultures are featured at this Mission District showcase.... *Tel 415/821-1155. www.mission culturalcenter.org. 2868 Mission St. 24th St. BART station.*

See Map 12 on p. 202.

Monster Park (p. 212) SOUTH SAN FRANCISCO Home to the 49ers, it's wonderfully balmy throughout the football season.... *For tickets, call Ticketmaster (Tel 415/421-TIXS) or a ticket broker. www.sf49ers.com. Bus service available through MUNI (Tel 415/ 673-MUNI). If you must drive (not recommended), take Hwy. 101 S. to stadium exit.*

Oakland A's (p. 213) OAKLAND See the McAfee Coliseum above.

Oakland Ballet (p. 210) OAKLAND This lively young company is made up of brilliant dancers. Their performance hall, the landmark Art Deco Paramount Theater, is breathtaking.... *Tel 510/ 465-6400. www.oaklandballet.org. 2025 Broadway. 19th St. BART station (three stops from San Francisco's Embarcadero station).*

Oakland Raiders (p. 213) OAKLAND See the McAfee Coliseum above.

Orpheum Theater (p. 207) CIVIC CENTER Fans of big Broadway musicals love this restored Spanish baroque theater in the theater district.... *Tel 415/551-2000. www.bestofbroadway-sf.com. 1192 Market St. Civic Center BART/MUNI Metro station.*

See Map 12 on p. 202.

Phoenix Theater (p. 209) UNION SQUARE A progressive located in the theater district downtown, the Phoenix presents works by local as well as world-famous playwrights.... *Tel 415/989-0023. 414 Mason St. Powell–Mason or Powell–Hyde cable car; 38 MUNI bus.*

See Map 12 on p. 202.

Project Artaud Theatre (p. 204) MISSION DISTRICT Dance, theater, and multimedia productions appear at this well-run Mission District experimental theater.... *Tel 415/626-4370. www.artaud.org. 450 Florida St., between 17th and Mariposa sts. 16th St. BART/ MUNI Metro station; MUNI buses 12 or 33.*

See Map 12 on p. 202.

The Punch Line (p. 212) DOWNTOWN San Francisco's laugh central for more than 25 years. It's where Robin Williams got his start. Shows are Tuesday through Thursday and Sunday at 9pm, Friday and Saturday at 9 and 11pm.... *Tel 415/397-4337 (415/ 397-7573 for recorded information). www.punchlinecomedyclub. com. 444 Battery St., between Washington and Clay sts., plaza level. MUNI buses 12, 15, 41, or 83. Cover varies.*

See Map 12 on p. 202.

San Francisco Ballet (p. 204) CIVIC CENTER The city's premier classical ballet troupe performs at the Opera House. Some balcony seats are available for most performances, even without advance purchase.... *Tel 415/865-2000. www.sfballet.org. 301 Van Ness Ave. Civic Center BART/MUNI Metro station.*

See Map 12 on p. 202.

San Francisco 49ers (p. 213) SOUTH SAN FRANCISCO See Monster Park above.

San Francisco Giants (p. 212) SOMA See SBC Park below.

See Map 12 on p. 202.

San Francisco Opera (p. 204) CIVIC CENTER San Franciscans have had an unconditional love affair with opera since the gold rush. You can go in a tuxedo or in blue jeans—nobody cares. The season runs from September to January and during June. Get tickets far in advance.... *Tel 415/864-3330. www.sfopera. com. War Memorial Opera House, 301 Van Ness Ave. Civic Center BART/MUNI Metro station.*

See Map 12 on p. 202.

San Francisco Symphony (p. 204) CIVIC CENTER Buy tickets before you get to town or give your hotel concierge a generous tip to do it for you as soon as you arrive. If you can't get into a regular performance though, try to get into a dress rehearsal (cheap, casual, and intimate).... *Tel 415/864-6000. www.sf symphony.org. 201 Van Ness Ave. Civic Center BART/MUNI Metro station.*

See Map 12 on p. 202.

San Jose Arena (p. 213) SAN JOSE The Sharks haven't brought home a Stanley Cup yet, but their fans don't care. About an hour south of San Francisco.... *For tickets call Tickets.com (Tel 415/478-BASS, 510/762-BASS, 800/225-BASS outside CA); for other information, call the arena (Tel 408/287-7070 or 800/366-4423). www.sjsharks.com. Take CalTrain from Fourth St. and Townsend St. depot to 65 Cahill station; free shuttle from station to arena. To drive: Take Hwy. 101 S. to Guadalupe Pkwy.; exit at Julian St.; take right. Follow Julian St. to Burns Ave. S., then turn left, and follow signs to stadium. Free shuttle from parking lot.*

San Jose Sharks (p. 213) SAN JOSE See the San Jose Arena above.

SBC Park (p. 212) SOMA Most seats in the Giants' new downtown ballpark have already been sold to season-ticket holders, but general admission on seats is often available, or you can stroll along the Embarcadero and watch through the "peepholes" for free.... *For tickets to Giants games, call Tickets.com (Tel 510/762-2277). www.sfgiants.com. N Judah (Embarcadero) trolley.*

See Map 12 on p. 202.

Theater Rhinoceros (p. 204) MISSION DISTRICT This Mission District company focuses on gay and lesbian issues.... *Tel 415/861-5079. www.therhino.org. 2926 16th St. 16th St. BART/MUNI Metro station.*

See Map 12 on p. 202.

THE INDEX

ENTERTAINMENT

HOTLINES &
OTHER BASICS

Airports... Two major airports serve the city: **San Francisco International Airport (SFO)** (Tel 650/821-8211; www.fly sfo.com) and **Oakland International Airport (OAK)** (Tel 510/563-3300; www.oaklandairport.com). Most travelers use SFO, which is 14 miles south of downtown San Francisco (via Hwy. 101 or 280). Fares to either airport are usually identical, so if a flight to SFO is sold out, there may still be available seats on flights to the lesser-known OAK, which is only a few minutes from the Coliseum BART stop (four stops from San Francisco's Financial District). Keep in mind, however, that public transportation from SFO is less expensive and far more accessible.

Airport transportation to the city... Public transport is available from the San Francisco airport to downtown via **BART (Bay Area Rapid Transit)** (Tel 510/464-6000; www.bart.gov), which runs daily from SFO to downtown San Francisco. This route avoids traffic on the way and costs substantially less—about $6 one-way—than shuttles or taxis. Just jump on a free airport shuttle bus to the International terminal, enter the BART station in the International terminal, and you're on your way. A **taxi** ride to the city center costs about $30 to $35 plus tip and usually takes about 20 to 30 minutes, depending on traffic. They're located on the airport's lower level between terminals (during busy periods a uniformed taxi dispatcher will hail a cab for you). Shuttle vans that carry up to six passengers offer door-to-door service for around $17 to most hotels and take 20 to 30 minutes; they're easy to catch at the airport, but reservations are required for your return trip from the city to the airport. Some of the most popular shuttles are **Bay Shuttle** (Tel 415/564-3400, **Door-to-Door Airport Express** (Tel 415/775-5121), **Lorrie's Airport Shuttle** (Tel 415/334-9000), **Quake City Shuttle** (Tel 415/255-4899), **Super Shuttle** (Tel 415/558-8500; www.super shuttle.com), and **Yellow Airport Shuttle** (Tel 415/282-7433). The **SFO Airporter** (Tel 650/246-8942; www.sfo airporter.com) is an express bus that offers door-to-door service to most major hotels for $15; no reservations are required. The airport offers a toll-free hotline (Tel 415/817-1717) for information on ground transportation. It's available weekdays from 7:30am to 5pm local time. During operating hours, a real person answers the line and gives you a rundown of all your options for getting into the city from the airport. **Bayporter Express** (Tel 877/467-1800 in the Bay Area, or 415/467-1800 elsewhere; www.bayporter. com) is a popular Oakland Airport shuttle service that charges $26 to downtown San Francisco.

All-night pharmacies... Forgot your pills, eh? Not to worry. **Walgreens 24-Hour Prescription Service,** 498 Castro St. (Tel 415/861-3136) or 3201 Divisadero St. (Tel 415/931-6415), will come to the rescue.

Babysitters... First ask the concierge if your hotel offers child-care service. Otherwise, try an agency that is a member of the San Francisco Convention and Visitors Bureau, such as **American Childcare Service** (Tel 415/285-2300; www.americanchildcare.com), which offers private in-room service at your hotel, excursions arranged for children 12 and older, and is fully licensed, bonded, and insured.

BART... Bay Area Rapid Transit (BART) is essentially a commuter railway that links neighboring communities with San Francisco. There are eight stations in the city itself, but they're not terribly useful for getting around the city (take the bus—it's faster). Fares depend on the distance of the ride, but for a special excursion fare, you can ride the entire system as far as you want, in any direction you want, as long as you exit the system at the same station you entered. All tickets are dispensed from machines at the stations. Call or check the website (Tel 510/464-6000; www.bart.gov).

Buses... San Francisco Municipal Railway (MUNI) buses are marked on the front, side, and back with the number of the line and the destination. Fare is $1.50. To find out which bus to take to get where you want to go, call (Tel 415/673-MUNI; www.sfmuni.com). Route maps are usually posted at the bus stop shelters as well. Official MUNI route maps are available throughout the city at newsstands and many other stores for $2.

Cable cars... There are three cable-car routes: The **Powell–Hyde** line begins at Powell and Market streets and ends at Victorian Park near the Maritime Museum and Aquatic Park; the **Powell–Mason** line also begins at Powell and Market streets, but it ends at Bay and Taylor streets near Fisherman's Wharf; and the boring **California Street** line starts at California and Market streets and ends at Van Ness Avenue. Fare is $5 per ride.

Car rentals... Suit yourself—pick up a tiny little bread-box-on-wheels from Enterprise Rent-A-Car at the airport for less than $25 a day, while a zippy convertible like a Mazda Miata will set you back about $85 a day. Here are several rental companies, all of which are available at SFO: **Alamo** (Tel 800/327-9633; www.goalamo.com), **Avis** (Tel 800/331-1212; www.avis.com), **Budget** (Tel 800/527-0700; www.budget.com), **Dollar** (Tel 800/800-4000; www.dollar.com), **Enterprise** (Tel 800/325-8007; www.enterprise.com), **Hertz** (Tel 800/654-3131; www.hertz.com), **National** (Tel 800/227-7368; www.nationalcar.com), and **Thrifty** (Tel 800/367-2277; www.thrifty.com).

Cash... **American Express** has a downtown office with full financial services, including personal-check cashing, at 455 Market St. (Tel 415/536-2600). To find the nearest ATM that will accept your **Cirrus Network** card, call (Tel 800/424-7787); for **PLUS System,** call (Tel 800/843-7587).

Climate... Mark Twain supposedly said the coldest winter he ever spent was summer in San Francisco. It's true that July can be downright chilly, but the truth is that the city is rarely—if ever—what a New England Yankee would call cold or what a Georgia belle would call hot. In fact, the weather is predictably unpredictable. A sunny morning can turn into a chilly afternoon, just as a thick morning fog often gives way to a gorgeous sun-drenched day (or, as I'm fond of saying, "If you don't like the weather, wait five minutes"). The standard pitch is that temperatures don't drop below 40°F (5°C) or rise above 70°F (21°C), but don't believe it. Every year there are many 80°F (27°C) days that are sworn to be the exception; there's no predicting when they might occur. In general, September and October are the warmest months, and May through September are the driest. No matter when you visit, be sure to pack warm clothing and dress in layers.

Concierges... If you're not staying at a hotel that offers the services of a resident concierge and you want personalized travel planning, shopping excursions, entertainment, ticket purchasing, or any other special arrangements, enlist your own private concierge—after you arrive or while you're still planning your vacation. Your best bet is **Ideas Unlimited/ Unlimited Ideas** (Tel 415/668-7089 [800/900-4884]; www.iuui.com).

Dentists... In the event of a dental emergency, see your hotel concierge or contact the **San Francisco Dental Office,** 131 Steuart St. (Tel 415/777-5115), between Mission and Howard streets, which offers emergency service and comprehensive dental care Monday, Tuesday, and Friday from 8am to 4:30pm, Wednesday and Thursday from 10:30am to 6:30pm.

Doctors... If you have a serious emergency, you should dial 911 or go directly to a hospital emergency room. The **Saint Francis Memorial Hospital,** 900 Hyde St., between Bush and Pine streets on Nob Hill (Tel 415/353-6000), provides emergency service 24 hours a day. The hospital also operates a physician-referral service (Tel 800/333-1355 or 415/ 353-6566).

Driving around... You don't need a car to explore downtown San Francisco—in fact, driving a car in the city can be a nightmare. You're likely to end up stuck in traffic with lots of aggressive and frustrated drivers, pay upward of $30 a day to park, and spend a good portion of your vacation looking for a parking space. The city is compact but can be very confusing with all the one-way streets, so if you're going to drive, be sure to get a map. Your driver's license from any other state (and most Western nations) is valid in California for a year, but there are a few things you should know about local safety precautions and laws. Remember, San Francisco is a city of hills (43, to be exact), and since you probably don't want your car to roll down one while you're not in it, there's only one sure bet: **Curb your wheels.** Turn the front tires toward the street when you're parked facing uphill and toward the curb when you're parked facing downhill. This is not just a good idea—it's the law in San Francisco. Know what the **curb colors** mean: Red means no stopping or parking; yellow means all commercial vehicles may stop for up to a half-hour; yellow-and-black means only commercial trucks during business hours; green-yellow-and-black is a taxi zone; blue is for cars with California disabled placards; green means all vehicles may stop for up to 10 minutes; white means all vehicles are limited to a 5-minute stop while the adjacent business is still open. Also keep an eye out for those sneaky **street-cleaning signs.**

Emergencies... Like anywhere else, **call 911,** but don't be surprised if you get put on hold. Other emergency/information numbers: **Ambulance** (Tel 415/931-3900), **Poison Control Center** (Tel 800/876-4766), and **Suicide Prevention** (Tel 415/781-0500).

Festivals & Special Events

From the crowning of Japantown's Cherry Blossom Queen and the Gay Pride Parade of self-styled queens to Chinese New Year and Día de los Muertos (Day of the Dead), San Francisco's extraordinary diversity is celebrated year-round in one festival after another. A complete monthly listing is published in the

Bay City Guide, free at information racks in the airports and at most hotels. Here is a brief sample of some of the major events:

JANUARY: **San Francisco Sports and Boat Show** (Tel 415/404-4111), Cow Palace; 9 days. **Tet Festival** (Tel 415/885-2743), Vietnamese New Year, held at Larkin and O'Farrell streets.

FEBRUARY: **Chinese New Year** (Tel 415/982-3000; www.chinese parade.com) can be in late January or early February, depending on the lunar calendar; it climaxes with a giant parade down Chinatown's Grant Avenue.

MARCH: **St. Patrick's Day Parade** starts at Market and Second streets and goes past City Hall.

APRIL: **SF International Film Festival,** one of the most popular film festivals in America, Kabuki 8 Cinemas, Fillmore and Post streets (Tel 415/561-5000; www.sffs.org). **Cherry Blossom Festival** (Tel 415/563-2313), held in Japantown and Golden Gate Park's Japanese Tea Garden, offering traditional arts, music, theater, and food booths.

MAY: **Bay to Breakers** (Tel 415/359-2800; www.baytobreakers.com), a kooky-costume footrace across town from the Embarcadero (on the bay) to the ocean. **Black and White Ball** (Tel 415/864-6000), a flashy fundraiser held in odd-numbered years to benefit the San Francisco Symphony; the Civic Center is closed off for this all-night party-hop that attracts the city's biggest celebrities and those who are willing to pay $200 apiece to rub shoulders with them. **Carnaval** (Tel 415/920-0125; www.carnavalsf.com), a weeklong fiesta in the Mission District, leading up to a parade that ends up on 14th Street (near Harrison St.) with a huge samba party. **Cinco de Mayo,** 2-day fiesta; parade runs from 24th and Mission streets to Civic Center Plaza.

JUNE: **Lesbian/Gay/Bisexual/Transgender Freedom Day Parade** (Tel 415/864-3733; www.sfpride.org), a celebration of gay pride with floats and groups from the Sisters of Perpetual Indulgence to Dykes on Bikes. **Stern Grove**

Midsummer Music Festival (Tel 415/252-6252; www.sterngrove.org), a series of free 2pm Sunday concerts held at 19th Avenue and Sloat Boulevard, featuring local performers, from the opera and symphony to jazz and ballet.

JULY: **San Francisco Marathon** (Tel 800/698-8699; www.runsfm.com), mid-month. **Fourth of July Celebration and Fireworks,** an event that can be somewhat of a joke—more often than not, fog creeps into the city to join in the festivities. Sometimes it's almost impossible to view the million-dollar pyrotechnics from PIER 39 on the northern waterfront.

SEPTEMBER: **San Francisco Shakespeare Festival** (Tel 415/422-2222), free performances in Golden Gate Park run through October. **San Francisco Blues Festival,** for a schedule, call (Tel 415/979-5588; www.sfblues.com), outdoors at Fort Mason; 2 days. **Opera in the Park** (Tel 415/861-4008), a free opera in Golden Gate Park, kicks off the San Francisco Opera's fall season.

OCTOBER: **Fleet Week** (Tel 415/705-5500; www.fleetweek.com), gather along the Marina Green, Embarcadero, Fisherman's Wharf, and other great vantage points to watch incredible aerial performances by the Blue Angels, flown in tribute of our nation's marines.

NOVEMBER: **Día de los Muertos (Day of the Dead),** a Mexican fiesta and parade in the Mission District designed to honor the dead and entice their spirits to return for the party.

DECEMBER: *The Nutcracker* (Tel 415/865-2000) and **Sing-It-Yourself Messiah** (Tel 415/864-6000) are extremely popular holiday traditions that usually sell out far in advance.

Gay and lesbian resources... The lesbian and gay communities in the Bay Area are very well organized and have countless resources at their disposal. The *Bay Area Reporter* is the best-known gay publication, with complete listings of organizations and events. It's distributed at bars, bookstores, cafes, and stores around the city.

MUNI Metro streetcars... There are six streetcar lines that operate underground, downtown, and on the streets in the outlying neighborhoods. It's mostly used by commuters, however. (I've never been on one.) Fares are the same as for buses—$1.50.

Newspapers... The city's main daily is the *San Francisco Chronicle*, distributed throughout the city and Northern California. The massive Sunday edition includes a "Date-book" section—an excellent preview of the week's upcoming events. The free weekly *San Francisco Bay Guardian* and *San Francisco Weekly*, tabloids of news and listings, are indispensable for nightlife information; they're widely distributed through street-corner kiosks and at city cafes and restaurants.

Parking garages... One of the reasons I urge you not to drive in the city is the maddening dearth of parking spaces, wickedly efficient parking enforcement personnel, and absurdly expensive parking lots. Yes, San Francisco does have relatively inexpensive parking lots, but there are only 10 of them, and unless you know where to go (or get lucky), you won't find them. In **Chinatown,** try the Portsmouth Square Garage, with an entrance on Kearny between Washington and Clay (504 spaces), or the Golden Gateway Garage, with an entrance on both Washington and Clay streets between Battery and Davis (1,095 spaces). In the **Nob Hill/Union Square area,** there's St. Mary's Square Garage, with entrances on Pine, Kearny, and California, bordered by Grant (828 spaces), or the Sutter-Stockton Garage, with entrances on Stockton and Bush, bordered by Grant and Sutter (1,865 spaces). Right in **Union Square,** try the Union Square Garage, with an entrance on Geary Street, bordered by Powell, Post, and Stockton (1,030 spaces), or the Ellis-O'Farrell Garage, with entrances on O'Farrell and Ellis, bordered by Powell and Stockton (925 spaces). If you're hanging out in **SoMa or near the SFMoMA,** I recommend the Fifth & Mission Garage, with entrances on Mission or Minna, bordering Fourth and Fifth streets (2,622 spaces), and the Moscone Center Garage, with an entrance on Third Street, between Howard and Folsom (732 spaces). Finally, two cheap garages near the **Civic Center and Hayes Valley** are the Civic Center Garage, with an entrance on McAllister between Polk and Larkin (840 spaces), and the Performing Arts Garage, with an entrance on Grove between Gough and Franklin (612 spaces).

Phone facts... The area code for San Francisco is 415. As is the case with most big metropolitan areas, though, the number of area codes in San Francisco is expanding with the population and use of the Internet and other digital services. For now, dial 1-510 before numbers in Berkeley, Oakland, Richmond, and most of Alameda County; dial 1-925 for numbers in Walnut Creek, Concord, and most of Contra Costa County; dial 1-650 for numbers on the Peninsula; and dial 1-408 for numbers in San Jose and Santa Cruz. When in doubt, dial the operator. Local calls are free on private phones, 50¢ in a pay phone. For directory assistance, dial 411. TDD users: California Relay Service relays calls between a TDD caller and any other phone in the United States and allows people without TDD to call TDD users. It is a free, 24-hour service, 365 days a year. All calls placed through California Relay are billed at discounted Sprint rates. To use the service, call (Tel 800/735-2929 if you have a TDD [800/735-2922 if you don't have a TDD]).

Safety... San Francisco, like any other large city, has its fair share of crime, but most folks don't have firsthand horror stories. In some areas, you need to exercise extra caution, particularly at night—notably the Tenderloin, the Western Addition (south of Japantown), the Mission District (especially around 16th and Mission sts.), the lower Fillmore area (also south of Japantown), around lower Haight Street, and around the Civic Center. In addition, there are a substantial number of homeless people throughout the city with concentrations in and around Union Square, the Theater District (three blocks west of Union Sq.), the Tenderloin, and Haight Street, so don't be alarmed if you're approached for spare change. Basically, just use common sense. For additional crime-prevention information, call **San Francisco SAFE** (Tel 415/553-1984).

Taxis... It's fairly easy to hail a cab on major thoroughfares, especially in tourist areas, but if you're on a tight schedule, it's best to phone in advance for door-to-door service (the wait is usually 5–15 minutes during the day, occasionally up to a half-hour during rush hour or on busy weekend nights). There are more than 40 taxi companies listed in the Yellow Pages, but the most commonly used are: **Yellow Cab** (Tel 415/626-2345), **De Soto** (Tel 415/970-1300), **Luxor** (Tel 415/282-4141), and **Veteran's** (Tel 415/552-1300). Since the city is no more than 7 miles in any given direction, most cab rides are around $5 to $10 plus tip (15% is customary).

Tipping... Gratuities are not included in restaurant or bar checks. Most guides suggest 15 percent of the total amount as a decent tip, but 20 percent has become more commonly accepted at restaurants. Taxi drivers should be tipped around 15 percent; skycaps and bellpersons should get at least $1 per bag each time they carry it.

Towaway zones... Nobody loves to tow cars more than San Francisco's Finest. It's big money for the city (almost 30% of all parking tickets issued in the state are issued in San Francisco), and the odds are always against you if you park illegally. You'll shell out a minimum of $35 for the most minor parking violation, plus another $100 or more for towing, plus storage fees. If you park in a disabled zone, the violation alone will cost $250 to $275, not to mention the towing fees and hassle of getting the car back.

Visitor information... The **San Francisco Convention and Visitors Bureau,** 900 Market St. (at Powell St.), Hallidie Plaza, Lower Level, San Francisco, CA 94102 (Tel 415/391-2000; www.sfvisitor.org), is the best source for specialized information about the city. Even if you don't have a specific question, you might want to request the free Visitors Planning Guide and San Francisco Visitors kit. It includes a 6-month calendar of events, city history, shopping and dining information, and several good, clear maps, plus lodging information. If you simply need specific information faxed to you, you can call (Tel 800/220-5747); follow the prompts to receive information by fax only. The bureau highlights only members' establishments, so if it doesn't have what you're looking for, that doesn't mean it's nonexistent. You can also get the latest on San Francisco at the following websites:

- The *Bay Guardian,* the city's free weekly page: www.sfbg.com
- The SF Gate, the city's combined *Chronicle* and *Examiner* newspapers: www.sfgate.com
- Channel 7, ABC, and KGO's city guide: www.city search7.com.

GENERAL INDEX

234

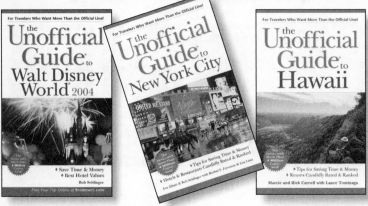
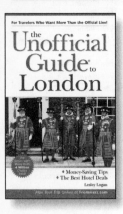
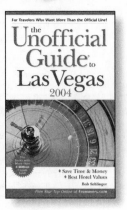
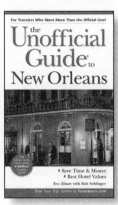

FROMMER'S® COMPLETE TRAVEL GUIDES

FROMMER'S® DOLLAR-A-DAY GUIDES

FROMMER'S® PORTABLE GUIDES

FROMMER'S® CRUISE GUIDES

FROMMER'S® DAY BY DAY GUIDES

Amsterdam	London	Rome
Chicago	New York City	San Francisco
Florence & Tuscany	Paris	Venice

FROMMER'S® NATIONAL PARK GUIDES

Algonquin Provincial Park	National Parks of the American West	Yosemite and Sequoia & Kings
Banff & Jasper	Rocky Mountain	Canyon
Grand Canyon	Yellowstone & Grand Teton	Zion & Bryce Canyon

FROMMER'S® MEMORABLE WALKS

Chicago	New York	Rome
London	Paris	San Francisco

FROMMER'S® WITH KIDS GUIDES

Chicago	National Parks	Toronto
Hawaii	New York City	Walt Disney World® & Orlando
Las Vegas	San Francisco	Washington, D.C.
London		

SUZY GERSHMAN'S BORN TO SHOP GUIDES

Born to Shop: France	Born to Shop: Italy	Born to Shop: New York
Born to Shop: Hong Kong, Shanghai	Born to Shop: London	Born to Shop: Paris
& Beijing		

FROMMER'S® IRREVERENT GUIDES

Amsterdam	Los Angeles	Rome
Boston	Manhattan	San Francisco
Chicago	New Orleans	Walt Disney World®
Las Vegas	Paris	Washington, D.C.
London		

FROMMER'S® BEST-LOVED DRIVING TOURS

Austria	Germany	Northern Italy
Britain	Ireland	Scotland
California	Italy	Spain
France	New England	Tuscany & Umbria

THE UNOFFICIAL GUIDES®

Adventure Travel in Alaska	Hawaii	Paris
Beyond Disney	Ireland	San Francisco
California with Kids	Las Vegas	South Florida including Miami &
Central Italy	London	the Keys
Chicago	Maui	Walt Disney World®
Cruises	Mexico's Best Beach Resorts	Walt Disney World® for
Disneyland®	Mini Las Vegas	Grown-ups
England	Mini Mickey	Walt Disney World® with Kids
Florida	New Orleans	Washington, D.C.
Florida with Kids	New York City	

SPECIAL-INTEREST TITLES

Athens Past & Present	Frommer's Exploring America by RV
Cities Ranked & Rated	Frommer's NYC Free & Dirt Cheap
Frommer's Best Day Trips from London	Frommer's Road Atlas Europe
Frommer's Best RV & Tent Campgrounds	Frommer's Road Atlas Ireland
in the U.S.A.	Retirement Places Rated

FROMMER'S® PHRASEFINDER DICTIONARY GUIDES

French	Italian	Spanish